The Para-State

The Para-State

AN ETHNOGRAPHY OF
COLOMBIA'S DEATH SQUADS

Aldo Civico

UNIVERSITY OF CALIFORNIA PRESS

University of California Press, one of the most distinguished university presses in the United States, enriches lives around the world by advancing scholarship in the humanities, social sciences, and natural sciences. Its activities are supported by the UC Press Foundation and by philanthropic contributions from individuals and institutions. For more information, visit www.ucpress.edu.

University of California Press
Oakland, California

Library of Congress Cataloging-in-Publication Data
Civico, Aldo, author.
  The para-state : an ethnography of Colombia's death squads / Aldo Civico.
    pages   cm
  Includes bibliographical references and index.
  ISBN 978-0-520-28851-5 (cloth : alk. paper)
  ISBN 978-0-520-28852-2 (pbk. : alk. paper)
  ISBN 978-0-520-96340-5 (ebook)
  1. Death squads—Colombia.   2. Paramilitary forces—
Colombia.   I. Title.   II. Title: Ethnography of Colombia's death squads.
  HV6322.3.C7C58 2016
  986.106'35—dc23

                                              2015022453

Manufactured in the United States of America

25 24 23 22 21 20 19 18 17 16
10 9 8 7 6 5 4 3 2 1

In keeping with a commitment to support environmentally responsible and sustainable printing practices, UC Press has printed this book on Natures Natural, a fiber that contains 30% post-consumer waste and meets the minimum requirements of ANSI/NISO Z39.48–1992 (R 1997) *(Permanence of Paper)*.

To my parents, Irmi and Domenico, and to my nieces and nephew, Caterina, Margherita, and Riccardo

CONTENTS

Caribbean Sea

Barranquilla
Cartagena

PANAMA

VENEZUELA

Magdalena River

Tarazá
ANTIOQUIA
Puerto Berrio
Medellin
Puerto Boyacá

Pacific
Ocean

Bogotá

COLOMBIA

Cali

ECUADOR

BRAZIL

PERU

N

0   100 miles
0   100 kilometers

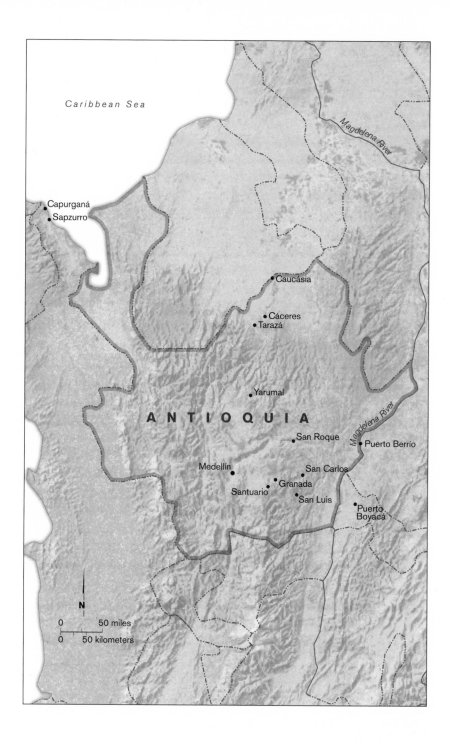

Caribbean Sea

Magdelena River

Capurganá
Sapzurro

Caucásia

Cáceres
Tarazá

Yarumal

A N T I O Q U I A

San Roque
Magdelena River
Puerto Berrío

Medellín
San Carlos
Granada
Santuario
San Luis
Puerto
Boyacá

N

0   50 miles
0   50 kilometers

ACKNOWLEDGMENTS

I would like to express my gratitude to the many people I met in Colombia, and especially in Medellín, who welcomed me into their homes and entrusted me with their stories. I have changed all the names of my interviewees (except in the case of public figures) because, to protect their identities, I cannot name them here.

I thank all the friends in Medellín who gave me logistical and moral support throughout my fieldwork: in particular, Clara Inés Avendaño Rojas, Aurelio Soto Duque, Federico García Olarte, Frank Varelas, and Antonio José Marín Isaza. I give special thanks to Claudia Osorno, who has spent hours transcribing my interviews. I am grateful to the personnel of the Fundación Mundo Mejor, who supported me in the early stages of my research. I am also thankful to Gustavo Villegas and Jorge Gaviria and the personnel of the Peace and Reconciliation Program of Medellín for facilitating access to demobilized members of the paramilitaries. A special thanks also to Pedro Echavarría, Juan David Pascual, and Julio Palomeque, who assisted me in many ways during my fieldwork in Medellín.

My conversations with people who have personal knowledge of Colombia's armed conflict were particularly illuminating for my research. I thank in particular León Valencia, Francisco Galán, Álvaro Jímenez Millán, Antonio José García Fernández, Juan García Fernández, Carlos Valendia, Juan Carlos Cuéllar, Yezid Arteta Dávila, and Moriz Akerman. Furthermore, I am grateful for the insights I received from scholars in Colombia, in particular María Clemencia Ramírez, Martha Nubia Bello, Mauricio Romero, Eduardo Pizzarro, Gustavo Duncan, Alejo Vargas, Elsa Blair, María Victoria Uribe Alarcón, Iván Orozco, Jorge Alberto Giraldo, Gonzalo Sánchez, and Claudia López Hernández. I also appreciate the support I received from writers and journalists. I am especially thankful to Héctor Abad Faciolince, Fidel Cano, Daniel Coronell, Jineth Bedoya Lima, Marta Ruíz, Juanita León, Steve Dudley, Juan Forero, and Alonso Salazar for the multiple and insightful conversations we had.

In the United States, I benefited enormously from the conversations I had with several colleagues. I thank in a special way Carolyn Nordstrom, Kimberly Theidon, Mary Roldán, Allen Feldman, Marc Chernick, Forrest Hylton, Winifred Tate, Jon Carter, and Adam Isacson. During my doctoral work, I had the privilege of being mentored by anthropologists whose work has inspired me and whose advice I have treasured. In a particular way, I thank Michael Taussig, who has followed my fieldwork from the very beginning and who joined me for several days in Medellín. Thank you also to Lambros Comitas, who has guided me with wisdom and great care during my doctoral studies. I am grateful also to Andrea Bartoli, who first suggested and encouraged me to undertake doctoral studies in anthropology. I am particular in debt to Victoria Sanford, who over the years has been a wise mentor and a loyal friend, guiding me through every step of my career.

My research would have not been possible without the financial support I received from Columbia University and Teachers College during my doctoral studies. Furthermore, I thank the Open Society Institute for the grants I received. During the writing of this book, the encouragement of my colleagues at the Department of Sociology and Anthropology at Rutgers University in Newark has been important. Thank you in particular to Clayton Hartjan, Sherri-Ann Butterfield, Brian Ferguson, Genese Sodikoff, Alex Hinton, Jamie Lew, Ira Cohen, Kurt Shock, Isaias Rojas-Perez, and Sean Mitchell.

Over the years, a solid team of friends has in many different ways provided support, friendship, and intellectual engagement: Leoluca Orlando, Sergio Fajardo, Juanes, Catalina Cock, Didier Velasquez, David Ramirez Mejía, Lucia Gonzalez, Saruy Tolosa, Tata Tabón, Hans Burkhard, Rafael Augusto Restrepo, Yerson Gonzalez, Wilmar Andres Valencia, Diego Alejandro Marin, Laura Cisneros, Manuel Mejia, Andrés Cancimance, Edwin Aguirre, Ariel Fernando Avila, Juan Fernando Rojas, Fernan Martinez, Hans Jurt, Flavio Pedroni, Enrico Donzelli, Carlos Bajo, Siegfried Hitzler, Antony Montelibano, Michele Zanzucchi, Maria Luce Ronconi, Lucia Fronza Crepaz, the Gude family, Pat Markey, Julian Ciabattini, Marc Bacuyag, Paolo Caroli, Laura Simms, Ishmael Beah, Josie Lianna Kaye, Alba Taveras, Alex Fisher, Peter Coleman, Beth Fisher-Yoshida, Ana Margarita Almonacid, Emmanuel Marquez, Cindy Buhl, Jim McGovern, Gimena Sanchez, Deborah Harding, George Vickers,

Cindy Arnson, Tim Phillips, Wendy Luers, Ina Breuer, Alejandro Eder, Alba Stella Barreto, Maria Eugenia Garcés Campagna, Juan Esteban Zapata Avendaño, Jeferson Ferreira, Adriana Buitrago, Jennifer Buitrago, Kevin Buitrago, Juan Mesa, and Joan Lopez. In particular, I would like to remember some friends who have inspired me and guided me and who have recently passed away: Chiara Lubich, Roberto Mazzarella, and Terry Gunn.

I have been very lucky to find a great editor, Reed Malcolm, who has shepherded me throughout the entire writing process. A special thanks also to J. K. Fowler for editing my manuscript. I am in debt also to the three reviewers of the manuscript, who helped me a great deal with their encouraging and insightful comments and suggestions.

I also give a special thanks to my partner, Carlos Eduardo Marquez Salazar, who has supported me with great patience, friendship, and care during the writing process, encouraging me in moments of frustration and tiredness.

I express heartfelt and deep gratitude to my parents, Irmi and Domenico, my brother Mattia, as well as to the rest of my family, for the love and unwavering support they have provided me throughout my life.

Everyone I mentioned, and those I have forgotten to mention, have played an important role during my research and writing process. It goes without saying that any error in argument or interpretation I might have made is my responsibility alone.

PROLOGUE

FROM THE FIELD JOURNAL

BOGOTÁ (AUGUST 26, 2003)

Late at night, my cell phone rings. Speaking from an unknown location, the commanding voice of a man who introduces himself as Freddy notifies me that Doble Cero, the leader and head of the Bloque Metro paramilitary group, has consented to meet me on the following Sunday. I am asked to be at the church in the main square of San Roque, northeast of Medellín, at 8:30 A.M. I assure Freddy that I will be there, though I'm not sure where San Roque is and how best to get there. I feel adrenaline rising in my body.

I'm excited about the prospect of this encounter. Over the past two months, I have sat down with and listened to internally displaced people who have relocated to Medellín in the aftermath of violence. Several are victims of Doble Cero's paramilitary group. The previous week, a journalist in Medellín asked me if I wanted to meet a paramilitary leader. Driven by curiosity, I agreed. Yet I had not received any news until now, and I had given up hope. I was to fly back to New York the following Monday.

I look at a map, noting that San Roque is a small town in the Eastern Antioquia region. I call Mónica, the wife of a local friend, Guillermo, because she is from that area. Mónica and Guillermo are friends I met in Medellín. She tells me that the road is in bad shape and that it will take me about four hours by car from Medellín to reach the town. She also tells me to be very prudent, as the area is known to be rife with conflict—since the time that the paramilitaries first established their presence within the region, she has not been able to visit her family's ranch. "Piénsalo bien, antes de ir. . . . Sea prudente y cuidate mucho" (Think twice before you go. . . . Be prudent and take care of yourself), Mónica says in a motherly tone. It is her way of telling me not to go.

MEDELLÍN (AUGUST 31, 2003)

I drive out of Medellín at 4 A.M. in a car that I have borrowed from a friend. Damian, a friend from Uruguay, agrees to accompany me, as I prefer not to take the trip by myself. Medellín is still enveloped in darkness when we leave. In Niquía, a small village just outside Medellín, we pass an army checkpoint and venture toward Puerto Berrío with no trouble, traveling through Matasano, Barbosa, and Cisneros. From here, a steep and unpaved road will take us from the bottom of a narrow valley to the height of a plateau. I am leaving behind the world as I have experienced it until now, penetrating a thick forest fraught with uncertainties and perils. The testimony of one of my interviewees, Doña Alba, who, together with her children, witnessed her husband's killing, plays over and over in my head, heightening my uneasiness. The tales of terror that I have collected from paramilitaries' victims have instilled in me a fear of the groups, and their terror has sunken into and taken hold of me. The abstract is now becoming all too real in the form of fear and anxiety. I wonder if I should have followed Mónica's advice to decline the meeting. The testimonies of victims, their narrations of violence and terror, and the prospect of sitting down with a paramilitary leader have lured me toward this space, and I am now experiencing both repulsion and attraction. Once I step fully into this space, will I be able to come back, or will I lose myself?

After almost two hours of slowly zigzagging along about 9 miles (14.5 kilometers) of impervious road, we reach the plateau. On the horizon, we spot the town of San Roque. One can sense the extent to which a hostile geography has shaped the history of particular regions of Colombia and the imaginary of its people, making it difficult for them to experience their country as a single and undivided nation.

As a way to control my symptoms of fear as we approach San Roque, I try to envision my encounter with Commandant Doble Cero. I don't know much about him, besides the fact that at the end of the 1990s, he established the Bloque Metro, which was part of the Autodefensas Unidas de Colombia (AUC), or United Self-Defense of Colombia, paramilitary umbrella. I also know that his group has sown terror in Medellín and Eastern Antioquia, killing intellectuals, human rights activists, community leaders, and union leaders, and has carried out a massacre and selective killings in the town of Granada, where I went several times last month to collect the testimonies of victims. I've also read in newspapers that Doble Cero is now engaged in a ruthless internal war against the Cacique Nutibara paramilitary group, which at the end of 2001 ousted the Bloque Metro from Medellín and subjugated the city under its domination. Doble Cero is losing both men and territory in this war.

Approaching San Roque, we notice a military checkpoint at the gate of the town. We have not come across any other car on the road to San Roque, and ours is the only one traveling toward the town. I become worried since I do not know how to justify my notebooks, the digital camera, and, ultimately, my presence as a foreigner in a place not tailored for tourists. What should I say? What should I reveal about myself? Should I make up a story? Would it be safer to tell them that I am a journalist? And what am I writing about? One thing seems prudent: I should not reveal that I am about to have a clandestine meeting with Doble Cero, even though his presence here, I am quite sure, is not a true secret but rather a secret made public, particularly with regard to the military. For Michael Taussig, a public secret is knowing what not to know, and I instinctively sense what I should not know and reveal about Doble Cero. In searching nervously for an intelligent way to disguise and preserve this shared public secret, I experience the power that comes with every secret—how my silence and the excuse that I am thinking of making up to mask the truth about my presence here so early on a Sunday morning is revealing not only the presence of Doble Cero, but also my secret and invisible bond to him. Now, through him, the soldiers and I are bound within the same reality.

The military patrol, composed of four or five soldiers, stops our car. "Good morning. Please step out." One soldier looks at my Italian passport and has me lean against the car with my legs and arms spread. Another soldier searches my pockets and frisks my waist and legs. Another inspects the car with meticulous attention, looking under the seats, into every compartment, and inside the trunk. The soldiers see and touch my notebook, my pen, and my camera; however, they do not dare ask any questions about the motives for my trip to San Roque. In fact, there is no need to utter what we all share—that is, the public secret of Commandant Doble Cero's presence in San Roque and my imminent meeting with him. In our reciprocal silence—the military and I do not exchange any words except for initial and final greetings—we reveal our common bond to Doble Cero and the truth of his presence.

My encounter with the military at the checkpoint confirms what I have heard repeatedly about the paramilitary in Colombia: that a smokescreen links paramilitary members with regular armed forces. But at the checkpoint, I also sense that this public secret is part of the paramilitary's power, like a taboo whose power resides in what is not spoken and is instead obscured and negated.

After we greet the soldiers, my friend and I park the car in front of the church, as previously instructed, and wait. The square is busy with a flurry of people at the stands of a local peasant market. A few minutes pass, and then three men surround the car. They greet me and ask me my name. There is a moment of nerve-racking confusion about my last name, and one paramilitary questions if I am really the one they are waiting for. "¿Es ese el gringo?" (Is this the gringo?) one asks. "Ese es" (This is the one), the oldest among them affirms.

Eventually, a paramilitary in his midtwenties gets into the car, and we leave San Roque on a bumpy and narrow road. After a couple of miles, we stop before a humble house where a woman is mopping the porch. Though we park on her property without asking permission, she shows neither impatience nor disappointment. Apparently indifferent to our presence, she continues mopping as if we are not there. Normal abnormality. Men riding horses pass by, throwing furtive and curious looks at us.

The paramilitary traveling with us attempts to communicate our position on a radio, but there is no signal. So we continue to wait. After a while, another young man, riding a motorbike in jeans, a T-shirt, a baseball hat, and dark sunglasses, approaches us. When he lifts his T-shirt, I spot a gun stuck into his jeans. The two paramilitaries exchange some words, and the motorcyclist takes off.

More time elapses, and I begin to chat with the paramilitary. He tells me that he grew up in San Roque. After serving in the military, he asked to join the paramilitaries. Initially, he had hoped to get a different kind of job. Not finding one, he decided to turn to Doble Cero. "I'm paid 400,000 pesos [about US$200] a month. It's not much, right? I should've stayed on with the army," he says. The young man has now been a member of the Bloque Metro for four years. He shows me his left arm, which has a long scar and is shorter than his right arm. "I stepped on a land mine," he says. A splinter penetrated one of his lungs. "I couldn't breathe," he says while bringing his right hand to his chest. "I could have died," he adds, with no particular emphasis.

"How is the situation now?" I ask him.

"It's better now. This area is now clean," he says with a smirk of pride.

"What do you mean by *clean?*" I insist.

"Before, the guerrillas made their presence felt even in the town. They killed police officers right where we met in the square before the church. Now there are about twenty of us present in the town, and everyone knows us very well," he says with a tone of satisfaction.

About half an hour passes. Commandant Doble Cero arrives in a four-wheel-drive Land Rover escorted by two men and two dogs, Pippo and Chicharrón. The commander and his men are in military uniforms; Doble Cero, unshaven, wears a cap with the inscription *comando* and polarized mirrored sunglasses, which make it impossible to measure his gaze. They are all heavily armed, each carrying an assault rifle with a telescope as well as a handgun hanging from his belt. Doble Cero invites my friend and me to step into the Land Rover. I sit in the front next to Doble Cero, who is driving. He puts his rifle between my legs. The cold metal presses against my left thigh. "How many times have you been to Colombia?" he asks me.

"This is the fourth time. I almost feel Colombian at this point," I say jokingly. The commander bursts into spontaneous and open laughter. We drive for the next few minutes in silence. I look at the beautiful landscape, the glowing green and the gentle curves of the hills, and I think that the perceived harmony of the land surrounding me contrasts nicely with the violence, the blood, and the terror that inhabit this space. I wonder if I have made the right decision in meeting Doble Cero. He seems courteous, but what if something goes wrong? What if he plans to tell me things and then, at the end of the day, kill me? Or kidnap me? As we drive on, fear sneaks deeper into my mind. "Maybe this time I've gone too far," I wonder.

After about twenty minutes, we arrive at the top of a hill and park before an abandoned cottage overlooking a wide green valley. Doble Cero, Freddy (his second in command, the man who had called me a few days ago), my friend, and I sit under a gazebo around a bulky, round wooden table, guarded by two heavily armed paramilitaries. A gentle breeze caresses my face. Doble Cero finally takes off his sunglasses, revealing a look that is anything but cruel, cold, or malignant—it is not what I have expected. Observing his round, dark eyes, I am puzzled. "It's the gaze of a caring father," I think to myself.

I begin the conversation, explaining to Doble Cero and Freddy why I am interested in meeting with them. I tell them that I have traveled to Granada and listened to the testimonies of several victims, and that I want to understand why that massacre occurred. I then tell them that I will protect their identities in my notes and in my writing. "We are in a permanent situation of danger,"

Doble Cero says. "You can write the truth—also about where we met." I pat the dog sitting at my feet to disguise and control my nervousness. Then Doble Cero takes out a ballpoint pen and a sheet of paper and sketches the shape of Colombia. "Let's draw some lines here," he says and begins to lecture me about the history of his country. "The guerrilla is the army of the left, while the paramilitaries are the armies of the right," he says. "And the drug cartels are the meeting point between the two."

Freddy remains silent all the while that Doble Cero talks. At times, Freddy smiles or nods in agreement with his commander. When a child, who seems to be mentally impaired, approaches us with curiosity and a large smile that suggests, "I know who you are," Freddy tells him to leave us alone. To be more persuasive, he raises the assault rifle that is resting on his lap. The child walks away.

We interrupt the conversation only twice. The first time is because of a call from a *New York Times* journalist to Doble Cero's cell phone. Once the call has ended, Doble Cero jokes that we are in the countryside of Colombia while the journalist is sitting in an office overlooking Times Square. One can tell how much Doble Cero, a charming man, likes to engage in public relations. The second time, we pause to have lunch. One of Doble Cero's subordinates serves us mess tins containing *sancocho,* the typical soup of Antioquia made of chicken, potato, and carrots. Over lunch, Doble Cero tells me that he was once an army official but was expelled from the army.

The sun is already sinking behind the hills when we end our conversation. We get into the Land Rover and drive back to the place where we have parked the car. As we approach, Doble Cero's manner turns less charming and more brusque. He puts on his polarized mirrored sunglasses again. Is this a way to assert his authority? When I take leave of him, I ask if he has ever thought of writing a book about his experience. "The time has not yet come. I still need to survive the last chapter," he says with irony. We get into the car, and the paramilitary who escorted us here in the morning takes us back to San Roque. The driver gets out at the point where, upon our arrival, we had run into the army checkpoint. "My day is not over. I need to go to a nearby town," Doble Cero says, departing with a smile.

NEW YORK (SEPTEMBER 23, 2003)

Today the Colombian newspaper *El Tiempo* reports that for the past ten days there has been intense fighting between the Bloque Metro and other paramilitary groups, such as the Central Bolívar, the Cacique Nutibara, and the Bloque Calima. As a result, over six hundred peasants have been forcibly displaced. "The AUC and the Bloque Central Bolívar launched a desperate offensive against my men," Doble Cero declares to a reporter. At the core of the paramilitaries' internal war is Doble Cero's refusal to join the AUC in the disarmament and demobilization process with the government of President Álvaro Uribe. In an interview a few months ago, the president explained that he would not sit down with drug kingpins disguised as paramilitary leaders.

The report highlights the fact that Doble Cero is surrounded, and it is doubtful that he has the manpower to rebut the offensive. These are probably the last weeks or even days of the Bloque Metro. Are these also the last days of Doble Cero?

NEW YORK (MARCH 5, 2004)

Today I receive an email from Doble Cero. Over the last few months, the newspapers have reported that the Bloque Metro has been annihilated but that Doble Cero has been able to escape and find refuge. I had written him an email a few days ago, suggesting that he write me his life history. His transcribed response follows:

> I'm very glad to hear from you again. We received your communication, and for security reasons we are responding to you from a different account. For us as well, it'd be important to exchange ideas with you. . . . If you are interested in meeting with us, it must be under absolute conditions of secrecy and confidentiality. You would have to travel to a city of the Caribbean coast, such as Cartagená, Barranquilla, or Santa Marta. I tell you this so you can organize yourself. You also need to have a cell phone here in Colombia in order to define details, such as the hotel where you will stay, the meeting place, time, and so on. If you are interested, we can be in initial contact through this medium.
>
> A series of events occurred after which our military structure practically disappeared; this is something very interesting from a political point of view, since for us it is now clear that in order to rebut a joined aggression of both the armies of drug traffickers and of the national government, one would need to rely on drug trafficking to get funds and fight; but this goes against our ideological convictions about the [root causes of the] crisis in Colombian society, and [our] role is to be part of the solution and not the perpetuation [of the problem].

NEW YORK (MARCH 6, 2004)

I think about Doble Cero's offer, and I am tempted to go and meet him, but I consider it too risky and decide to tell him that I cannot travel to Colombia at this time. Doble Cero responds, saying that we can work by corresponding over email and that he will start telling me about his life and respond to my questions. From his emails, I get the impression that he senses that his life is in danger: "I look forward to your communication so that we can start working over email to buy time, which is not a renewable resource in this king of situations."

NEW YORK (APRIL 12, 2004)

I've been emailing back and forth with Doble Cero, who has started to share details about his life prior to joining the paramilitaries. Today I receive a unique message from him in which he seems to hint that telling me his own history is having a sort of cathartic effect: "What do you think about all of this? What's [your] interest in this work? I'd like to know more about your work. For me, up to now, to talk with you has been useful and a form of self-analysis."

ROME (MAY 31, 2004)

Today is a sad day. This morning, news reaches me that Doble Cero has been killed. I am in an Internet café at the bottom of Via Veneto when my friend and colleague, Victoria Sanford, sends me an email with a link to a *New York Times* article. "I believe that this is the guy you were talking to," she writes. Doble Cero was killed on Friday, May 28, 2004. Here is what correspondent Juan Forero writes:

> Assassins in Colombia have killed a dissident leader of a right-wing paramilitary force who had harshly criticized his colleagues for trafficking in drugs as the organization embarked on American-backed disarmament negotiations with President Álvaro Uribe, Colombian officials said.
> The leader, Carlos Mauricio García, 39, who went by the name Rodrigo Franco [or Doble Cero], was shot in the head as he walked along a trendy beachfront stretch on Friday night in the Colombian coastal city of Santa Marta.

Reading the news, I feel overwhelmed with sadness. I leave the Internet café and begin aimlessly wandering through the streets of Rome. I call a friend to share the news, and a knot forms in my throat. Why am I feeling grief for the killing of a paramilitary leader? Who did Doble Cero represent to me? Who did he become to me over the past three months of our intense email exchange? Did he turn into someone more than just an informant? Perhaps even a friend? And who was I to him? Was I just an anthropologist interested in his experience and view of the Colombian armed conflict, or had I become something more, maybe a trusted friend? What does this experience suggest about the intersubjectivity between the ethnographer and the other? Is this intersubjectivity at all possible (and opportune) when the other is responsible for gross human rights violations?

The challenge and beauty of the anthropological endeavor are found when analysis and understanding stem from a deeply human encounter. It is this encounter, with all its contradictions and challenges, that suggests further issues to explore, lays the ground to think about political violence, and asks us to reconsider traditional definitions of the state.

Introduction

What are the circumstances that encouraged thousands of young men over the past three decades to join paramilitary groups in Colombia? How did they make sense of their experience? What does their lived experience suggest about the larger forces that shaped both the history and the practice of violence in Colombia, especially in a country that, since its first constitution in 1886, has enjoyed stable, longstanding democratic institutions? And, in turn, what does the longstanding experience of violence since Colombia's independence suggest about notions of modernity, state, and democracy? What meanings do perpetrators of gross human rights violations attach to these notions?

These were the leading questions that emerged from my fieldwork conducted between 2003 and 2008 among victims and victimizers of paramilitary violence in Colombia. Paramilitary groups have been a permanent feature throughout the history of Colombia since its independence in the nineteenth century. Throughout the decades, such groups have appeared in different shapes and with different names, and they have operated by means of kidnapping, disappearance, torture, selective killings, and massacres, fueling the desires and fantasies of a variety of interests: the desire for power by individuals and groups, the greed of businessmen, the aspirations of politicians and their political parties, the ambitions of the army's military campaigns, and, for the past thirty years, the ever-spreading influence of drug cartels. Since the beginning of the 1980s, supported by a justificatory counterinsurgency discourse, paramilitary groups, employing a terror tactic of shock and awe, penetrated and eventually dominated entire regions, as well as neighborhoods, towns, and rural villages, beginning in areas where the influence of guerrillas has historically been most significant. In fact, the narrative of a weak and inefficient state, incapable of providing security and of defending private property from the menace of guerrillas, has often justified the need for the establishment of paramilitary groups.

The staggering statistics of the long-standing armed conflict in Colombia gives a sense of the pervasiveness of the country's violence, to which paramilitaries contributed in a significant way. In its report *¡Basta ya! Colombia: Memorias de guerra y dignidad* (Enough Already! Memories of War and Dignity), the Grupo de Memoria Histórica (2013) calculated that between 1958 and 2012, the conflict produced a total of 220,000 deaths, 81.5 percent of which were civilians and only 18.5 percent of which were combatants. There were a total recorded number of 25,000 disappeared, 1,754 victims of sexual violence, 6,421 forcibly recruited minors, 4,744,046 internally displaced people, and 27,023 kidnappings. In other words, according to the report, between 1958 and 2012, twenty-six people were displaced in Colombia every hour. Since 1996, one person was kidnapped every eight hours, and one person was a victim of land mines every day. Colombia is second only to Afghanistan as the country with the highest number of land-mine victims.

The report also highlighted that paramilitary death squads were the main perpetrators of these crimes as compared to other armed actors, such as the guerrillas and law enforcement agencies. In fact, paramilitaries were responsible for 1,166 of the 1,982 massacres carried out in Colombia between 1980 and 2012—about 60 percent of the total number of massacres. Furthermore, paramilitaries selectively killed 8,903 people; that is, 38.4 percent of the total 23,161 victims. They were responsible for 42.1 percent of the disappearances. As the report highlighted, "For the armed groups, the civil population has been a source of political, economic, moral, and logistical support, which contributed to the end result of the conflict. For the victimizers, it matters little if this support is consensual or forced" (ibid., 37).

Though the numbers are astonishing, it is the stories of the people who suffered and witnessed the violence that mediate, in a more comprehensive way, the overwhelming experiences of violence and brutality, including their ambiguities and complexity. As Carolyn Nordstrom (1997) observed in her seminal book on the Mozambican war, it is by lending an ear to the stories of violence that violence ceases to be a mere tactic or a means to an end, putting forward a reality that rationality struggles to grasp and one that defies attempts for a coherent and causal explanation. Anthropology can insert itself into the gap between events and what is often labeled as absurd, irrational, illogical, and unfathomable because it escapes human comprehension. Anthropology can attempt to bridge this gap in favor of comprehension and interpretation of meanings that may contribute to transcending violence and finding alternative strategies to prevent it.

In my own experience, the paramilitaries ceased to be a distant and sterile notion to which none of my life experiences helped me to relate to when I came across stories such as the one about Camilo and his family. It was while learning about his experience that I confronted both the emotional and intellectual challenge as an anthropologist to face the inhuman and unfathomable nature of our shared human condition.

In 2006, I met Camilo at a shelter for internally displaced people in downtown Medellín. At the time, Camilo, twelve years old, had just arrived in town, displaced by violence, together with his mother and three siblings, including his older sister and two younger brothers. From the balcony of the shelter overlooking an intersection, Camilo was observing the changing colors of a traffic light, attempting to figure out its function. In response to his inquiry, I told him that red was for stop and green was for go. I was astounded that this was the first time that Camilo had ever seen a traffic light. "This way, cars don't crash into one another," I said. Camilo repeated my explanation, memorizing and making sense of something that he had just learned. Countryside and urban areas in Colombia are often worlds far apart, and violence had just forced Camilo and his family to land on an unknown planet.

Only a few days prior to our meeting at the shelter, Camilo had witnessed the killing of his father at the hands of a paramilitary squad. His family lived and worked on a farm owned by Camilo's father's parents. They raised cattle and grew produce, such as yucca. They shared part of the land they owned with poor peasants and allowed them to grow their own crops. Camilo once described his father as generous with the poor, but also admitted that at home he was at times violent. "He did not always treat me or my mother well," he shared. Though Camilo was, as noted, twelve years old at the time of our encounter, he had attended only two years of primary school. To go to class, he had to ride a horse for two hours across the fields, and his father had Camilo join him in his own work, something for which even today Camilo prizes his father.

One afternoon, when Camilo came home from school, he saw that paramilitaries had surrounded their farm. Some were arguing with his father, who had refused to comply with their order to sell and permanently abandon the land that his family had owned for a few generations. Camilo then heard a few shots and saw his father fall to the ground. He rushed forward to embrace his father but was stopped and hit in the head with a rifle butt by one of the paramilitaries. Camilo's father met his resistance against the paramilitaries with his own death. Today, Camilo told me, the butchers who killed his father are growing coca on his family's land. For years to come, in nightmares, Camilo has relived the scene of the killing of his own father. The history of Camilo echoes the tragedy that Latin American people have endured throughout the centuries.

The night of the killing, Camilo and his family collected their loved one, put him on an improvised stretcher, and walked in the darkness for hours to reach the closest village for a quick burial. Then, with no money and a few belongings wrapped in plastic bags, they took a bus to Medellín, disoriented and powerless, hungry and thirsty. For a few days, they stationed themselves at the city bus terminal, sleeping on the floor as if frozen and unable to take the next step in their lives. Eventually, a police officer noticed them, asked about their condition, gave them some food, and directed them to the shelter where I met Camilo on the day that he had arrived, as he was wondering about the workings of the traffic light.

At first, I met the paramilitaries only at second hand, through the tales of terror from their victims. Indeed, the original plan of my fieldwork was to collect the testimonies of internally displaced people and to observe how they had reinvented their lives in an urban area. My interest was in the resilience of victims living in the midst of violence and conflict. This is a theme that still interests me today, since the stories of survivors provide humbling insights into the possibilities of human nature. The tales of survivors are not only tales of horror, but also tales of hope. Only later, while I was learning about the paramilitaries through their victims, did I have my encounter with the paramilitary leader Doble Cero.

It was therefore the tales of terror shared by victims, such as Camilo's testimony, that provided me with my initial questions about the Colombian paramilitaries. Over the years, as my fieldwork deepened and my encounters and readings multiplied, I came to see the paramilitaries as a larger phenomenon far more complex and articulated than their overt violence, which is the most visible and repulsive manifestation of their reality.[1] In fact, multinational corporations, national companies, local businesses, influential politicians, and high-ranking military officials have been providing staunch support to paramilitary groups and have both invoked their existence and armed them through the years. Moreover, support has also come from common people, who are often thankful for the kind of order that they provide or, at a minimum, have seen them as a minor and necessary evil to exterminate the brutes—the guerrillas, but also the *desechables,* literally the disposable people, the scum of the earth, such as drug addicts, petty thieves, and homosexuals. The paramilitaries have functioned like a sanitation department, disposing of the waste. "In my town, the paramilitaries prohibited men from wearing long hair. They distributed fliers with the list of people who had to abandon the town or else they'd be killed. They imposed a curfew under which by ten o'clock at night we had to be in our homes," a young man from a town in northeastern Colombia once told me. Yet the killings, disappearances, and torture committed by the paramilitaries are only a clue, one hinting at a larger and deeper involvement of a society that has been sanctioning their existence and their violent deeds.

Three fieldwork encounters in particular provided me with the opportunity to gain a better grasp of the complexity and articulation of the paramilitaries as a social phenomenon. I spent most of my time in Colombia at the margins of cities and towns, recording observations in my notebook and collecting testimonies of paramilitary combatants and their victims—although these three encounters took place at the home of the political counselor of the U.S. embassy in Bogotá, at an apartment in a middle-class neighborhood of Medellín, and in a Colombian Army aircraft flying into a former stronghold of the Fuerzas Armadas Revolucionarias de Colombia (Revolutionary Armed Forces of Colombia; the FARC) guerrillas, respectively.[2] These three encounters provided a larger framework in which to interpret the stories that I was hearing at the margins. The individuals whom I met and the stories that they shared were spatially and socially far removed from the spaces where violence occurred and yet intimately connected to them.

My first encounter was with the owner of a mining company operating in Urabá, a subregion in northern Colombia marked by decades of violence and where paramilitaries have annihilated social and peasant movements for the past three decades. A senior official of the U.S. embassy in Bogotá, with whom I had become acquainted and who was aware of my research, offered me a meeting with the prominent business leader to listen to his arguments. We met in the large, posh living room of the diplomat's apartment. The wall-to-wall window provided a startling view of Bogotá, observed from above as a shiny center of modernity where business, commerce, and sophisticated gastronomy coexisted. The peripheral and marginalized area of Ciudad Bolívar could barely be spotted on the horizon. We were sipping full-bodied red wine, our ties loose, and the conversation flowed casually. The entrepreneur, who was originally from Medellín, had words of admiration for the Colombian president at the time, Álvaro Uribe Vélez[3]—the leader with an iron fist. "Finally there is someone occupying the presidential palace who is working for the country," said the business owner, a short, obese man in his midfifties with small, chubby hands. "After the fall of the Soviet Union," he continued, "the guerrillas are no longer guided by ideology but by the pragmatism of the cocaine market. They are experiencing the end of history." He conceded that Colombia had suffered a deficit in democracy primarily because of the intertwining of drug cartels and political leaders. The businessman then made reference to the paramilitaries in Urabá.[4] Of course, he clarified, he was in disagreement with the brutality of their methods—the torture, the disappearances, the massacres, and the selective killings the paramilitaries carried out so efficiently, especially in Urabá, where they operated in cahoots with the military—but in the absence of the state, he asserted, the presence of self-defense groups was necessary to do business and, by extension, they served the common good of the region. Without the intervention of the self-defense groups, my interlocutor insisted, there would be no more banana companies in Urabá today. He sipped more wine and then concluded, "What we need to do in Colombia is to forget. We don't need memory, but forgetting. This is the necessary condition for reconciliation."

With these words, it seemed to me that the businessman was advocating for the cleansing the memories of the complicities, the silence, and the indifference that, over decades, had allowed for the paramilitaries' widespread social cleansing of peasants, social movements, union and human rights leaders, intrusive journalists, and inconvenient politicians. It sounded as if this cleansing of memory represented the summit of a larger project within which the disagreeable (yet deemed necessary) deeds of the paramilitaries were only the most visible steps. In fact, once a whole society has forgotten, there is nothing left to reconcile, since reconciliation presupposes the recognition of, and the identification with the enemy—that is, with the radical Other—as well as his or her inclusion and appreciation. Lacan (1977) argued that mediation is a conversation that links two subjects, thus allowing for the emergence of a truth. Forgetting is the negation of this mediation and the repression of truth. I put down my glass of wine.

The second encounter happened in an apartment in a middle-class neighborhood in Medellín, only a few blocks away from where the legendary drug kingpin Pablo Escobar was killed. It was the apartment where I was staying during my fieldwork in Medellín, and some friends had organized an evening in which I would share some of my field experiences with interested acquaintances. My friends had been wondering for a while what it was like spending time in marginal areas of Medellín and the countryside, where they themselves did not dare set foot. When I sat down in the living room before an audience of about thirty people, I noticed a distinguished individual sitting in the front row whom I had never seen before. I did not worry, and I continued candidly sharing some of the salient moments from my fieldwork among members of the paramilitaries. In particular, I dwelled on the figure of Commandant Doble Cero.

At one point, the distinguished man sitting in front of me raised his right arm halfway, asking to speak. "Go ahead," I said, offering a courteous smile.

"I want to congratulate you and express my admiration for having met a true patriot," the anonymous guest stated in reference to Doble Cero, with some excitement in his voice. He explained that he was a lawyer, and that his brother was a prominent member of the Congress of Colombia. He had had a chance to meet and appreciate Doble Cero as a paramilitary. The lawyer described him as someone who had dedicated his life to fight the curse of the guerrilla and was a true patriot, unlike the drug lords, he added, who had tainted the paramilitaries' self-defense project. He then went on, providing his opinion on current events. At the time, in 2006, the scandal of so-called para-politics had broken out. Prosecutors had looked into the connections between regional politicians and the paramilitaries, and dozens of Colombian congressional members were under investigation. Several were already behind bars. "I know several of those politicians," the anonymous guest continued with a tone that betrayed his outrage and disbelief.

The distinguished lawyer, as a member of the conservative elite of Medellín, had just delivered, before an audience of people mostly unknown to him, an open apology for the paramilitary project—for its necessity, for its noble and patriotic cause as well as that of politicians who had received the support of the paramilitaries and guaranteed and strengthened their legitimacy. There was no prudence, and even less embarrassment or shame, in his words and attitude. To the contrary, he prided himself on his friendship with Doble Cero. To me, this was a moment of shock due to the frankness and openness of such a public confession. It was a moment in which support for the paramilitaries by middle- and upper-class members of Medellín became tangible; it was a moment of illumination about the depth and breadth of the paramilitaries and their articulations.

The third encounter happened aboard a military aircraft flying into the region of La Macarena, a former stronghold of the FARC guerrillas. The top generals of the Colombian army, as well as military and civilian personnel of the U.S. government, were on the plane. The area, which lies behind the Western Cordillera surrounding the capital of Bogotá, was one of the main strategic counterinsurgency theaters of the Colombian government during the Álvaro Uribe Vélez administration. For decades, the Colombian deputy defense minister had explained, not only the institutions of the state, but also the very notion of the state, had been absent from this region. In a territory that FARC guerrillas had dominated for more than four decades, the population, the deputy minister told me, perceived the state as hostile and foreign. During the flight, I was sitting next to a civilian official, an economist, whose task was to coordinate the so-called consolidation process; that is, the blending of military intervention and socioeconomic development in a unified counterinsurgency effort. I asked the civilian official why governance functions were delegated to the military. The economist admitted that it was a problem that even the army's generals recognized, but he highlighted that La Macarena was an innovative experiment in which security and development went hand in hand. "We have to think and we have to act like a colonizing state," the economist observed. "We are penetrating an untouched and unexplored territory that we had to first conquer by battling against a hostile population, since every reality, even within civil society organizations, was previously penetrated and controlled by the FARC guerrillas."

It was an insightful conversation. What struck me was the mention of the FARC as the only threatening presence, since the civilian official's description of the local reality obliterated the role of paramilitary groups and influential drug cartels in the same area. The classification of the landscape and its people as being organically part of the FARC was a reification of reality turned into a place like that in Conrad's novel *Heart of Darkness,* one to be conquered and enlightened. La Macarena was imagined and described as a dark area, existing outside of the perimeter of civilization, and as a space inhabited by barbarism and wild men. Because of the longstanding domination of the FARC, La Macarena was spoken of as a space still existing in a state of nature, devoid of history and civilization. Such being the perceived reality of La Macarena, it had to be captured, interiorized, and transformed, with the help of what Walter Benjamin called "the predatory violence of the military," into a space of enlightenment, modernity, and civilization (Benjamin 1986, 283). Wasn't this a variation of the same justificatory discourse that I had heard from the business owner and lawyer when they explained the necessity of the existence of paramilitary groups?

Which commonalities, then, do these three different encounters share? And how are they linked to the violence perpetuated by paramilitaries across Colombia? What links the necessity of the paramilitaries' presence in Urabá with the glorification of the counterinsurgency as embodied by Doble Cero and the state's efforts to colonize areas historically dominated by the guerrillas? Is the perception and production of an exteriority conceived of as an untamed space—a thick and impenetrable forest like the one inhabited by savages in *Heart of Darkness*—a space that had to be ordered and enlightened? In other words, I suggest that it is the reification of individuals, landscapes, and history that glue together the three previously mentioned encounters. This objectification is immanent to paramilitaries' existence and to the production of violence, and it invites inquiry not only into the nature of paramilitaries in Colombia, but also into the conventional definitions of the state.

This book is about the violence committed by paramilitaries in Colombia. I draw on the narratives of paramilitary combatants in order to provide a cultural interpretation of Colombia's history of violence and the larger forces at play in that history. What has motivated large numbers of men to join paramilitary groups and disseminate terror and death? What meanings do these men attribute to their practice of violence?

The experience of the paramilitaries whom I met is the starting point of my inquiry; it is what hooked me. However, I am also interested in exploring the larger historical, social, and cultural repository underpinning their practice of violence and their justificatory discourse. In fact, as Begoña Aretxaga and Joseba Zulaika emphasized while analyzing political violence in Northern Ireland, subjectivity is grounded in history (Aretxaga and Zulaika 2005, 59). As part of this exploration, I am interested in analyzing the articulation that exists between paramilitary groups and the state, not only in order to inquire about the nature of paramilitaries' violence, but also to wonder about the immanence of this violence to the state.

Over the past three decades, several anthropologists have undertaken pioneering research on political violence. Though late into the debate, these anthropologists have pushed the boundaries of this analysis beyond conventional and established frameworks, which had previously emphasized the instrumentality of violence, the cause-effect continuum, rational choice theory, or an understanding of violence as an anomaly or a reality pertaining to the premodern state. Instead, this new anthropological analysis has focused on understanding what lies beyond that which is taken for granted and has attributed relevance to history, structural violence, predispositions, and the technologies and mechanisms that produce violent realities. The understanding and analysis of cultural forms of violence is anthropology's unique contribution to coming to terms with violence through the field's discourses and practices. Having positioned themselves at the margins of societies where violence and its effects are recorded, anthropologists have made relevant contributions to an interpretation of its discursive formations.[5]

Whether focusing on victims or victimizers, anthropologists have attempted to show that violence, rather than an irrational force that needs to be tamed, represents a force inherent to the modern experience and to both authoritarian regimes and neoliberal democracies (Aretxaga 1999; Paley 2001). In other words, they underlined that violence does not just belong to the reality of a premodern state, but also has an intimate connection to reason (Taussig 1991). That is to say, violence is not external to modernity and does not represent an anomaly of social order, but is a part of the modern state, even in democratic regimes.

The dangers and risks involved in doing fieldwork on violence and the hazards of entering the field are a possible reason (and a plausible one, indeed) that research on perpetrators is still sparse. Yet there might be an additional explanation, which lies in the fact that the intensity and brutality of such violence make it difficult, disturbing, ethically questionable, and, at times, psychologically overwhelming to meet the gaze of, and cross paths with, the victimizers. The brutality and spectacular nature of their violence consign the perpetrator to the embodiment of the inhuman, radical Other, one whom it is almost unbearable to conceive of as another person, since this would require a certain degree of identification and recognition of a shared humanity and a shared capacity for the inhuman.

And yet, as Slavoj Žižek wrote, this inhuman Other is characterized "by a terrifying excess which, although it negates what we understand as humanity, is inherent to being human" (2008, 47). In a cultural interpretation of Colombia's sectarian violence during the 1950s, the so-called La Violencia, María Victoria Uribe (2004) titled her study *Antropología de la inhumanidad,* an anthropology of the inhuman, which referred not only to the spectacular nature of the terror during La Violencia, but primarily to the unbearable truth about our own humanity: the human capacity for the inhuman, monstrous, irrational, unfathomable, and traumatic. Therefore, can anthropology afford to avoid the direct encounter with the inhuman as expressed by victimizers, and approach the study of violence while mainly prioritizing the narrative of victims or by showing sympathy or tolerance for freedom fighters? In retreating from contact with perpetrators, doesn't anthropology turn its back on the possibility of grasping and reflecting in an even more comprehensive way the inhuman, which is part of the human experience? Doesn't anthropology deny itself another opportunity to direct our gaze into the abyss of our humanity? In avoiding the direct encounter with the perpetrator, doesn't anthropology risk mimicking the very one it abhors, the one who through violence dehumanizes and objectifies the victim as the enemy? Isn't the avoidance of the encounter with the perpetrator a form of the inhuman as well?

To be sure, the experience of intersubjectivity with members of paramilitary death squads was not an easy endeavor. It was often uncomfortable and puzzling to somehow connect with these killing men. There were moments when I had my fill of listening to their experience, and there were times when I wanted to leave the room in which I was meeting with them in disgust. This particular ethnographic work forced me to push my own psychological and intellectual boundaries and bring within my own horizon an undesirable Other as I stepped into an unknown and unexplored world. Granted, for me it was not as challenging as it would have been for a victim of paramilitary violence, since neither I nor any member of my family has ever been kidnapped, tortured, or killed by these or other armed groups. On the other hand, a certain empathy with the paramilitaries whom I met—while in no way a justification of their crimes or sympathy for their cause—is a necessary disposition for the understanding and interpretation of violence's cultural forms in Colombia. Without an authentic and deep experience of intersubjectivity, it is not possible to explore the worlds of individuals who embrace a violent life (Bourgois 1995, 13). It was, for example, the profound and equally uneasy experience of intersubjectivity and infatuation, of empathy, and of closeness that allowed Truman Capote ([1966] 1994) to access the life of killer Perry Smith and narrate the contours of his massacre of the Clutter family Kansas, narrated in Capote's nonfiction "novel" *In Cold Blood*.

In addition to the testimonies of the victims, the narratives of violent perpetrators are an important contribution to the understanding not only of the complex biographies of individuals, but also of the contours within which these biographies arise and violence is performed. The encounter not only with victims, but also with perpetrators, opens a valuable opportunity to create an alternative to violence, to write against terror, which, in my interpretation of Taussig, is about pointing the finger against the powerful and the violent as well as about the possibility, through recognition and reflexivity, to transcend and overcome the inhuman aspects of our own human condition. Writing against terror means holding up a mirror to the rawness of our own humanity. This calls for us to embrace the risk of an encounter with the violent Other, to sit down with the perpetrator of gross human rights violations, to accept the probability of humanizing the Other, to discover what is human in the violent Other, and ultimately to face the uneasiness of seeing oneself in the abyss of the inhuman. By accepting the possibility of recognizing an alterity with the one perceived as the radical Other, anthropology can offer its own particular contribution to an experience beyond enmity and violence and create an alternative that fends off and transcends violence.

This book is based on data that I collected over multiple travels to Colombia between June 2003 and August 2008. Sometimes my trips spanned one or two weeks, while at other times, I remained in the country for a few months. The bulk of the data used in this book were collected between April and August 2006 during the fieldwork that I did for my dissertation.

The first time that I traveled to Colombia also coincided with the first time that I had the opportunity to set foot in a village whose residents, a few months before my arrival, had been victims of a paramilitary massacre. In an area strategically located near the border between Colombia and Panama, the village that I visited had, for a long time, been a safe haven of the FARC guerrillas until the paramilitary forces irrupted, sowing terror and death. At the time, I was a graduate student at Columbia University and a researcher affiliated with the Center for International Conflict Resolution. A friend and a colleague who, at the time, was working at Antioquia University in Medellín invited me to collaborate on a project on sustainable development that he and his colleagues were promoting on the northern coast of Colombia in an area bordering Panama. I was asked to design and facilitate a conflict resolution workshop for about forty community leaders in the village that we visited.

For several years, Colombia had been present in my own imagination, and I had been keen to visit the country. In fact, during the 1980s, as I was growing up in Italy—my country of origin—news reports often labeled Italy's southern regions, where the Mafia had established its stronghold, as Europe's Colombia. Like many of my fellow Italians, I knew about drug kingpin Pablo Escobar, and I still remember the day I saw the news on TV of his assassination by the Colombian police. There was much talk about the Medellín and Cali cartels and their links to the Italian Mafia. Colombia was spoken of as a country ridden with organized crime, corruption, and violence—dynamics that, in our collective imagination, we associated with the actions of the Mafia in Southern Italy.

In my early twenties, I had joined a social movement against kidnapping, a phenomenon that at the time was a plague in Italy. The Mafia used to kidnap members of wealthy families from Northern Italy and hide them in Calabria, one of Italy's southern regions. Because of my activism, I had the opportunity to meet kidnapping victims and their families, who shared the stories of their ordeals with me. Some of them were young men like me, and their testimonies of how they had survived living for more than two years in the thick and impervious mountains, sequestered in caves under inhuman conditions, made a deep impression on me.

At the beginning of the 1990s, I decided to move from the quiet town in Northern Italy where I grew up to Palermo in Sicily, where a large social urban movement against the Mafia was increasingly vocalizing, and publicly manifesting, their resistance against the Mafia, breaking the longstanding law of silence known in Mafia jargon as *omertà*. I wanted to be part of that movement and have a front seat in making history within the anti-Mafia movement.

The years that I spent in Palermo coincided with a very difficult time for the city. This was the time when car bombs planted by the Cosa Nostra exploded, killing the prosecutors Giovanni Falcone and Paolo Borsellino,[6] whose investigations had brought down the top leadership of the Sicilian Mafia and revealed for the first time the inner workings of the Cosa Nostra. The killings of the two prosecutors and the outrage of Palermo's citizens, who took their anger to the street, made a profound impact on me and certainly shaped the personal and professional choices that I have made since. With my decision to move to Palermo and work for the anti-Mafia leader Leoluca Orlando, I had unconsciously wanted to follow in the footsteps of my Austrian grandfather—my mother's father. He was an engine driver, a union leader, a Social Democrat, and a Catholic who, when he became aware during World War II of what Nazism represented to freedom and democracy, armed a partisan group of a few young men and eventually liberated a large valley in Austria from Hitler's occupation. In any case, the exciting as well as difficult years that I spent in Palermo were important for me to initially grasp the Mafia phenomenon, including how it operates in the underworld of crime and how it expands and consolidates its domination by extending its tentacles into politics, finance, and business while also shaping people's predispositions and practices. Those years certainly prepared me for my encounter with Colombia and shaped my understanding of paramilitaries and their violence.

In April 2001, together with my colleagues from the Antioquia University, I boarded a small aircraft in Medellín. After about one hour, we landed on a narrow strip of asphalt ending in a soccer field within a fishing village. The air was hot, and the view of the sun sinking into the ocean was stunning. The beauty of nature was in stark contrast to the stories I had heard about the violence that this village had endured. The same night that we arrived, we were informed that we should not present our workshop as one focused on conflict resolution. Nor should we talk about peace, because such words were charged with meanings that could endanger us as well as the participants and might be interpreted as us siding with the leftist ideology of guerrillas. I was surprised and, being naive and ignorant of the dynamics of Colombia's armed conflict, I considered it somehow perverse that speaking of peace was banned in a space saturated with violence. As I talked with community leaders, I sensed that the presence and violence of paramilitaries had frozen time in that village, suspending it in a violent present that seemed to be permanent and pervasive and negated the possibility of any alternative future. Among residents, trust waned and cooperation had become sparse. Violence had suddenly turned one's neighbor into an unknown and a possible threat. Suspicion and terror, rather than solidarity, had become the norm for this community, turning it into a place of fear. This was the first time that I was faced with the aftermath of terror, and that three-day stay in that fishing village convinced me to pursue fieldwork in Colombia for my dissertation.

I chose Medellín as the site for my ethnography because I had a seminal network of friends there and because the city—the capital of the Antioquia region—had been an epicenter of Colombia's political violence. Historically, Medellín had been Colombia's capital of business and commerce, but it was also the city where Pablo Escobar established his powerful drug cartel at the end of the 1970s, opening drug routes to the United States. When I first traveled to Medellín, in April 2001, the city was experiencing one of highest murder rates in its history. Guerrilla militias were still present in some marginal areas of the city, while paramilitaries had aggressively begun the takeover of the city. On my first day in Medellín, I was mugged in the morning and witnessed a shooting in the afternoon. There was a sense of constant peril, chaos, and disorder. People were frustrated; they had lost confidence in President Andrés Pastrana's attempts to negotiate a peace agreement with the FARC guerrillas, and several whom I spoke to—mostly professionals living in Medellín's middle-class neighborhoods—called for a U.S. military intervention while paramilitaries spread their presence and influence across the country.

When I started my fieldwork, in June 2003, my original idea was to look at how internally displaced people were reinventing their lives in the aftermath of violence and adjusting to an urban setting; Medellín was one of the primary repositories of displaced people. I began my research in Moravia, one of the most densely populated marginal areas of the city, listening to the testimonies of paramilitaries' victims. These were mostly peasants, who, under the threat of paramilitaries or after witnessing the assassination of their loved ones—as was the case of Camilo and his family—had decided to collect a few belongings and come to Medellín in search of safety. I spent a few days sitting down with them, listening to their tales of horror, taking notes on the dynamics of violence, learning about the guerrillas and the paramilitaries, and starting to get a feeling of how different and distant the experience of violence and war is from the theoretical notions that we often encounter in books. I began tracing back the stories that I was listening to, and I ended up in Colombian rural towns where my interlocutors had lived under the domination of guerrillas and paramilitaries and from where they had eventually been uprooted and evicted.

It was by traveling to these towns and visiting them for a few days that I first felt in my own flesh the intimidating and menacing presence of the paramilitaries. At first, it was a ghostly presence, felt through a sense of constant surveillance and measured by the care of the words people uttered and the comfort they took in remaining silent. As I talked to more individuals, gaining their trust and traveling to more of these towns, I eventually learned how to recognize members of the paramilitaries, walking in civilian clothes among the regular people, sitting at cafés, or standing at street corners. Eventually, it was a local journalist who offered me the opportunity to arrange a clandestine meeting with Doble Cero, the founder and leader of the influential paramilitary group Bloque Metro, as I detailed in the prologue. That encounter with Doble Cero opened the door into the world of perpetrators, together with the announcement, at the time that I started my fieldwork, of the disarmament and demobilization of the Autodefensas Unidas de Colombia (United Self-Defense of Colombia; AUC)—the paramilitary umbrella organization led by Carlos Castaño—which redirected the focus of my research to the men who had joined the paramilitaries and committed gross human rights violations. I became interested and engaged in a kind of fieldwork that I had not anticipated.

I met some of the paramilitaries whom I interviewed through the disarmament, demobilization, and reintegration (DDR) program of the city of Medellín. The director, Gustavo Villegas, and his staff were instrumental in giving me access to demobilized members of the paramilitaries, to the workshops that they attended as part of their reintegration process in marginal areas of the city, and to some of the paramilitary commanders. The members of the paramilitaries whom I met through the DDR program were part of the collective demobilization process, of which Medellín was the first site. To better control the over eight hundred former combatants who had been disarmed and demobilized, the DDR program had preserved the previous paramilitary groups' chain of command. I soon found that this made it more challenging for me to collect long narratives and life histories, as the former paramilitaries I approached felt observed, which made them more reticent. I was able to circumvent this difficulty by approaching and meeting members of the paramilitaries who had not been part of the collective demobilization but had instead demobilized individually. The demobilization of individual combatants was an additional national DDR program that the government of Colombia had conceived of, providing a series of benefits, such as housing, vocational training, and schooling, to guerrillas and paramilitary members alike who had made the decision to desert their ranks in exchange for providing valuable intelligence. For their own safety, several of these former combatants had come to Medellín, since they had had to leave the areas of Colombia where they had been active paramilitary members. It was possible for me to meet these former combatants thanks to friends and acquaintances who worked as social workers or psychologists and had some of these individuals among their clients. They told them about me as well as my research, and several expressed an interest in meeting with me. Because they were disjoined from their organization and not under a chain of command, I found them eager to spend time with me, share their stories, walk around Medellín, and take me to other areas of the country. It is primarily through them that I also had the opportunity to meet with paramilitary members and groups that had not demobilized and were still active, subjugating several areas of Medellín, as well as towns across Colombia, to their rules. While both the national and local governments were publicly pronouncing the success of their DDR program, I was spending some of my afternoons in Medellín with paramilitaries who had never put down their weapons and who continued to control neighborhoods and rural towns, attending to drug trafficking and other illicit market business. Some of them moved on to become the pillars of new criminal groups in recent years, such as the Paisas or the Urabeños, which continue the practice of violence and terror previously carried out by the paramilitary groups affiliated with the AUC.

The paramilitaries whom I initially interviewed introduced me to their companions, thus becoming collaborators in my research. I spent days and weeks with some of them, in a few cases having the opportunity to visit their homes, meet their families, wives, and children, and follow them on trips across the country. I saw them crying, laughing, happy, and depressed. Seeing them as human beings, and not as the embodiment of perverse evil, made the endeavor all the more challenging and difficult. Seeing them as bloodthirsty and irreducible assassins probably would have eased my endeavor. But it is precisely the fact that the totality of their existence and humanity is not exhausted by the qualifiers of "killer" or "torturer"—and that their stories are much more complex than reducing the totality of their identity to their violent actions—that makes it even more relevant to attempt an anthropology of experience that can shed some light on the contours of their existence and violent practices.

During my fieldwork, I became familiar with their stories, feelings, and dreams, while they familiarized themselves with this strange gringo who had come from New York and displayed interest in their stories and was ready to listen. In fact, it was their stories, the turns that their lives had taken, and my desire to try to understand why someone is willing to join an armed group and commit atrocious acts of violence, rather than their violent deeds and their paramilitary membership itself, that interested and motivated me. At the same time, to meet someone genuinely curious about their lives and narratives has been for several of them a unique experience, as it was for me to know stories that were so far away from the comparatively safe, comfortable, and peaceful place in Italy where I grew up under the care of loving parents.

Being a foreigner and an outsider, with no stake in their lives, helped me gain access to them and facilitated my task of recording their narratives.

Rather than the ethnography of a defined and circumscribed space, my fieldwork had a nomadic character. I followed victims and perpetrators who had welcomed my interest in their stories around in their often itinerant and uncertain lives. I followed them through the streets of downtown Medellín and hiked up hills through the city's marginal areas with them. I traveled with them to remote towns and villages, becoming familiar with the landscape of violence that constitutes Colombia. I sat down with paramilitaries in the small and humble apartments that they shared with their family or in the bodegas that are often the only legal commercial activity existing within the peripheries of poor cities and towns. I collected detailed and lengthy life histories and conducted long semistructured interviews, recording and later transcribing them. Several times, I gained the most interesting insights while engaging in informal conversations or observing the interaction of paramilitaries among themselves as well as with the residents of a neighborhood or town. In regions that were the cradle of the paramilitary movement in Colombia, I visited farms and met some of the ranchers who had established and supported paramilitary groups and drug cartels. I visited paramilitary leaders in high-security prisons in both Colombia and the United States, and I met young criminals in juvenile prisons. I spent days in shelters where displaced people, often victims of paramilitaries, waited for some aid from government programs, and I then traced their lives as they moved from neighborhood to neighborhood in search of affordable housing or a way to make some money. Often I met the children of displaced people at street intersections where they sold candies to drivers and passersby to make a living. The spaces of death where I dwelled were also often spaces of marginalization and misery, and I realized how narrow the possibilities and choices in life become when these spaces circumscribe one's existence.

From listening to the stories of the paramilitaries whom I met, I learned a lot about their upbringings, their country, and their internal armed conflict, but also about myself—a white male who grew up in Europe and now lives in New York. Though listening to the graphic descriptions of the crimes that my interlocutors had committed was often uncomfortable, difficult, and even repugnant, at one point I had to recognize that the potential for evil and the ability to harm others equally resided within me. It was in this moment of honesty and realization, which happened while I was recording the life history of a paramilitary member in a humid and humble room in downtown

Medellín, that I learned to mirror myself in the narrating Other, to suspend moral judgment, and to stop looking down from a higher moral pedestal on the life of perpetrators. This was the moment when my interlocutors turned from objectified paramilitary combatants into fully human individuals, endowed with complex personal histories in which the often reified and made-up distinction between victim and victimizer is often blurred. Such times were moments of empathy, though not of sympathy, for their lives and their violent deeds. These encounters and conversations did not represent for me a cultural shock, but rather, as Carolyn Nordstrom and Antonius C. G. M. Robben have emphasized, an existential shock (1995, 13; cf. Mahmood 1996, 14–25).

The potential for resorting to violence when confronting danger and being hijacked by fear became vivid to me, even in just those instants when I felt that my safety was in peril. These were moments in which I had to confront not the violence suffered or committed by others, but the possibility for violence that lingers within myself. Later in my fieldwork, a rumor went around that one of the demobilized paramilitaries whom I had interviewed, believing that I, coming from the United States, must be a wealthy man, had plotted with others to kidnap me for ransom. When I learned about that rumor, I felt both angry and very fearful, and for a split second I wished someone could kill this particular paramilitary in order to get rid of the threat. It was the angry thought of an instant, but I was later shocked and puzzled that such a strong emotion and horrendous idea could rise from deep within me and present itself so clearly in my mind. In that moment, I experienced what fear can do to you, and how the environment in which I had been immersed for some time had allowed for that instinctive thought to be produced. I thought of Kurtz and how he lost himself among the savages, fascinated by abomination. It doesn't take much, I thought, to mirror and be ready to mimic the violent Other. How much I could now see myself in that Other; how bonded, rather than separate, I was. The thought of eliminating the Other, reified now as a dangerous threat, was not so much engendered by the experience of fear in itself, but rather by the environment circumscribed by violence, in which (at that point) I had been dwelling for some time and in which, little by little, inadvertently and subtly, I was taking the risk of losing myself, blending in with the surrounding reality. I was now mirroring myself in the desire to have someone killed because I had perceived him as a serious threat. It did not occur to me to question if the rumor was at all true, nor did it occur to me to go to the police, having learned all too well that it would have been inefficient in stopping the threat. In a moment, my instinct was to take the rumor as a certain fact, and I felt rushed to do what I considered to be the most effective for my own safety within the environment that I had somehow become a part of.

For some time, I wondered about the appropriateness of sharing this particular experience. Would readers who have not had the opportunity to wander in a space marked by terror and death—to come into close contact with its shadows, to look into its abyss and gaze at its fantasies, to feel the fascination of abomination—be able and open to understanding such an experience, or would they reject and dismiss it? I resolved that it was important to share it, because it is foolish to think that the endeavor of an ethnographer is an aseptic one, within which one remains untouched by the people, the stories, and places one encounters. Instead, fieldwork is a deep, existential encounter, and ethnographic seduction, as Antonius Robben (2005) highlighted, is part of the fieldwork experience and one of its risks. Not only might we be seduced by our interlocutors, but we might seduce them as well. Within this experience rests the risk of losing oneself in the field under the illusion of blending oneself with the surroundings. In becoming aware of this dynamic, one has an opportunity for insight and interpretation. As the episode that I related above shows, the ethnographic encounter does not let one be indifferent, and the experience might be even more intense when one carries out fieldwork in a context of conflict and violence. Cynthia Keppley Mahmood, for example, in presenting her fieldwork among Sikh militants, highlighted that to write about them "as if I had not become personally, existentially entangled with them and their quest would be an inexcusable hypocrisy" (1996, 1). Fieldwork can be an existential shock that leads you into the depths of human nature, but gazing into them is an opportunity to think about alternatives to violence.

The more I listened to the stories of young men whose personal stories were entangled in the maze of the paramilitaries, the less I came to see them as merely biographies of separate individuals. Rather, their narratives brought into evidence the background from which these life stories emerged, much like sculptures in low relief. Increasingly, I saw their subjectivity as rooted in history, which in turn caused me to wonder about the larger forces that allowed for those life histories to come about.

The ethnographic evidence that I was collecting in the field pointed to an interlacement among the paramilitary death squads and other agents that represented the state, such as law enforcement officers and military person-nel, but also local and national politicians and business owners. What did the reality of this interlacement imply about the nature of the paramilitaries? In fact, as I suggest in this book, the ability of these illegal and violent groups to connect with agents and institutions of the state is a fundamental character-istics of the paramilitaries in Colombia. At the same time, these interconnec-tions presupposed a reciprocity on behalf of the state without which that linkage was not possible. A more intriguing inquiry, then, became to inter-pret which light the reality of the paramilitaries shed on the nature of the state. If the relation of the paramilitaries to the state was an immanent qual-ity of their nature, was the state's relation to the paramilitaries also an imma-nent quality of its nature, and in particular that of the liberal state?

This question was also suggested to me by my previous experience as an observer of the Italian Mafia. As I will detail more specifically in chapter 5, scholars, prosecutors, and journalists coined the expression *intreccio* in order to capture the intertwinement of the multiple forms and levels of alliance among the Mafia and the state and to define the convergence of interests that the *intreccio* expresses. This intertwinement is the immanent quality of the Italian Mafia without which the Mafia would not exist. It is this intertwine-ment that allows for the Mafia's existence and perpetuation and converts it into a system of impunity. And while the emphasis is mostly on the *intreccio* as a key feature of the Mafia as a criminal phenomenon, I suggest that atten-tion needs to be paid equally to what the *intreccio,* as an immanent quality of the state, reveals about the nature of the state itself.

Anthropologists have questioned the state's fixity as category of analysis for some time now and, based on the observation of everyday encounters with the state, have preferred to interpret the state as a phenomenological reality produced through discourses and practices of power (Aretxaga 2003; Gupta 1995; Mitchell 1999; Nagengast 1994). Accordingly, the state was pre-sented as a mask (Abrams 1988), as magical (Coronil 1997; Taussig 1997), and as a fantasy (Navaro-Yashin 2002), all echoing Radcliff-Brown's assertion that the state "is a fiction of the philosophers" (1940 [1970], xxiii).

And yet encounters with the state, as a hierarchical mode of organizing power, are real and concrete to citizens who are its subjects, especially when they are confronted with repression and arbitrary violence. Such are, for example, the encounters with the state at its margins, where, as Das and Poole have highlighted, "the state is imagined as an always incomplete project" (2004, 7) and where threats to security are constantly engendered

(Goldstein 2010, 2012). This notion of margins, which, more than geographical spaces, are epistemological ones, refers to a liminal threshold in which order and disorder, lawful and unlawful, norm and exception, outside and inside conflate. It is in these spaces that arbitrary violence is practiced as legitimate and necessary, and where the reality of intertwinement takes shape. It is within these spaces, as Aretxaga highlighted, that "anything can happen" (2003, 405), since the "inside" comes into contact with an outside that is conceived as wild and unruly, and where the state, in order to extend its sovereignty, does not hesitate to intertwine with agents, such as the paramilitary death squads in Colombia or the Mafia in Italy. If, therefore, it is at the margins that the effects of power can be observed, it is also at the margins that the *intreccio* as an immanent quality of the state's nature and of its strategy can be recorded. This notion of the state at the margins refers to the definition of state suggested by Deleuze and Guattari, who defined the state as an apparatus of capture that presupposes an exteriority on which the state asserts a right to capture: "The State itself has always been in relation to an outside and is inconceivable independent of that relationship. . . . The State is sovereignty. But sovereignty only reigns over what it is capable of internalizing, of appropriating locally" (1987, 360).

When analyzing the effects of neoliberal processes, some anthropologists have pointed to the eroding effect that flows of money, commodities, weapons, and ideologies have on states' power, contributing to the deterritorialization of an increasingly diasporic and transnational world (Appadurai 1996; Ferguson 2006). In a post 9/11 world, Jean Comaroff, for example, stressed that when the state outsources certain functions, it weakens itself (2011, 70). And yet, as Carolyn Nordstrom highlighted, the "shadow networks" that today mark a transnational reality, though they are not composed by states themselves, "neither are they entirely distinct from, or opposite to, states—they work both through and around formal state representatives and institutions" (2000, 36). In other words, being at the same time inside and outside the state, they are an extension of the state's power. To this respect, in more recent times, anthropologists have been writing about the hybrid state as an analytical category to capture the intertwining of multiple actors exercising forms of political authority, including crime cartels. Analyzing the role of criminal "dons" in inner-city neighborhoods in Kingston, Jamaica, and their relation to the state, Rivke Jaffe defined the hybrid state as that system of governance that emerges from the entanglement between organized crime and the state, both intertwined in a relationship of collusion while sharing control over urban areas and populations as part of a displacement of functions (Jaffe 2013, 735; see also Civico 2012; Goldstein 2012; Kosmatopoulos 2011; and Trouillot 2001).

Rather than an erosion, absence, or even failure of the state, the intertwinement between illegal actors and the state is an extension of the state's sovereignty into spaces that are produced as an exteriority that still lives in a natural condition and is in need of colonization—as the Colombian senior official expressed to me as we were flying into an area once dominated by the guerrillas. In other words, it represents an extension of the state's power, not its diminution, "generating patterns of 'variegated' or 'graduated' sovereignty" (Jaffe 2013, 735).

In his cultural interpretation of young combatants in Sierra Leone and Liberia, Danny Hoffman (2011) used Deleuze and Guattari's notion of "War Machines" to analyze the relation, processes, and practices of neoliberal rationalities and economies of scales. Intrinsically, War Machines stand in opposition to the state apparatus, and the two terms are in and of themselves mutually exclusive. While the state is an apparatus of capture, the war machine is a line of flight, like the movement of nomads generating constant deterritorialization. Deleuze and Guattari wrote that the war machine "is of nomadic origin and is directed against the state apparatus" (1987, 230). But war machines are destined not to be eternal and are eventually captured by the state. In this process, the war machine changes in nature and in function, since it is now "directed against the nomad and all state destroyers" (ibid., 418).

Paramilitary death squads in Colombia, then, can be interpreted as the war machine acquired by the state to produce violence and extend its sovereignty over spaces seen as external, wild, and unruly. Rather than seeing paramilitaries as weakening the power of the state, their intertwinement with the state should be interpreted as the modus operandi of the state at the margins. The notion of state and war machine suggested by Deleuze and Guattari should serve not for descriptive purposes, but rather as an epistemological strategy to highlight the *intreccio* as an immanent quality of the state and one that is expressed in the fluidity of processes, practices, and mechanisms by which the state reinforces and perpetuates its power—including collusion with criminal organizations, such as paramilitaries and death squads.

Chapter 1 provides an account of a meeting that I had at a ranch in the Middle Magdalena region with a man everyone called El Doctor ("the doctor"), a former drug lord and supporter of the paramilitaries. The events in the Doctor's life intermingle with the history of paramilitaries' rise in the 1980s in Colombia. The Middle Magdalena region, in fact, was the cradle of the paramilitaries, a project that rapidly extended to other regions across the country. The ranch, where important meetings in the history of paramilitaries in Colombia took place, therefore also became a metaphor for the country and the entanglements that have shaped much of its recent history.

Chapter 2 presents the abridged life history of several members of the paramilitaries whom I have met and interviewed during my fieldwork over the years. Beyond an account of events that led several young to men enroll in the paramilitaries, these stories highlight the context in which such biographies have developed. The lived experiences of paramilitaries allows us to look at the linkages that exist between the personal stories of individuals and the larger forces and social worlds that are at play in the production of those webs of significance that, as Clifford Geertz suggested, we ourselves spin. The lived experience of these young men are the stories of individuals who have been living at the margins, recruited to be the mediators of terror on that threshold that Taussig (1987) has defined as the "space of death."

Chapter 3 provides an analysis of paramilitaries' spectacular violence, focusing on the notion of *limpieza* ("cleansing") used by paramilitaries to justify their massacres, selective killings, and disappearances. Analyzing the history of the paramilitaries' penetration of a subregion of the Antioquia department and the ethnographic data that I collected in a town where paramilitaries committed a major massacre, the chapter not only presents the modes of conquest and domination applied by the paramilitaries, but also interprets the spectacularity of their deeds as the expenditure of their force, which in turn consolidated their power as well as their legitimacy.

Chapter 4 is an ethnography of cocaine in a rural area of Colombia. It presents an account of my visit to rural areas of the country run by a drug lord and his private army of paramilitaries. In this chapter, I present a description of the life of the town, the work of peasants in a coca field, and the policing done by paramilitaries. The observations and interviews recorded during my stay highlight how cocaine has become a commodity that regulates the economic, political, and social dynamics of societies living in rural areas. Cocaine is a commodity that allows for both desire and terror to flourish, engendering the contradictory and complex reality that marks what I call despo-capitalist spaces, in which paramilitaries and drug lords dominate with the direct or indirect assent of the state.

Chapter 5 provides an interpretation of the nature of the Italian Mafia and the intertwinement between states and organized crime. To this end, I suggest a comparison between the origins of the Mafia in Sicily and that of the paramilitaries in Colombia, underlining how the relationship with the state is what characterizes the Mafia. Beyond the complicity that often exists between paramilitary groups and the military, this chapter also takes into consideration the ties that the paramilitaries have developed in the fields of politics and business. Thus, the paramilitaries appear as a war machine that the state has acquired. The chapter questions traditional definitions of the state as being the entity that holds the monopoly on the use of force and analyzes how its articulation with illegal groups, such as paramilitaries, does not suggest that the state is either absent or weak in the spaces where paramilitaries are dominant, but rather suggests that the state's intertwinement with the paramilitaries is one of the modes of capture in which the state engages to express its function in areas that it produces as an externality.

The final chapter is an account and interpretation of the disarmament, demobilization, and reintegration process of paramilitaries in Medellín, which began in 2003. It is a process that emerged from a negotiation between the paramilitaries and the Colombian government and that saw leaders of the paramilitaries lobbying before Congress, which resulted in lenient punishment for the authors of massacres and the massive displacement of people. Based on my historical overview of the process, coupled with my own observations, I suggest that it was a transformation of the relation that allowed the state to reaffirm its own legitimacy rather than sever its ties with the paramilitaries.

1

"Everything I Did
in the Name of Peace"

It was pitch-dark, hot, and humid when I arrived at the ranch of the man everyone calls El Doctor, the Doctor, in 2010. The lights of the cab that had driven me here from Bogotá flashed upon a locked gate; it seemed nobody was waiting for me. I wondered if I had come to the correct place. I was only a few miles away from Puerto Boyacá, the town in the Middle Magdalena region that served as the cradle of the paramilitaries and was an epicenter of the armed conflict in Colombia. The man for whom I was looking had been a pioneer of the paramilitary movement and drug trafficking.

A few minutes had passed before a short man with a round face and short black hair came to the gate and, mistrustful, inquired who I was and whom I was looking for. "I'm here to see El Doctor," I announced. He made a few calls and finally invited me to get into his car. We proceeded at a snail's pace on an unpaved and rocky road, with the headlights fending off the moonless night. While penetrating into the heart of the estate, I spotted the dark shapes of cattle lying restfully on the grass. After several minutes, and after crossing three gates all locked with thick chains, we reached a one-story compound.

El Doctor was waiting there, surrounded by a few men in sleeveless shirts and blue jeans. In the back, there was the noise of a power generator. El Doctor greeted me in a friendly manner and introduced me to his workers, agronomists, and veterinarians, some of whom had been working for him for ten years. "These are my workers and not my bodyguards," El Doctor said, sensing my impression. "The estate does not need security, and neither do I." A sign of his self-confidence? A mark of his power and control over the territory? He repeated a similar assessment time and again. "The gates impede cattle thieves." But would anyone dare to steal the cattle of El Doctor?

We walked by a small swimming pool and entered his home. "This is not a recreational farm. Here we work the entire day," he stated. Once inside the spacious salon that served as both a living and dining room, we sat on rocking chairs for a small chat before going to rest. A large, disk-shaped wooden table, which a dozen people could comfortably sit around, dominated the space. The maid served freshly squeezed orange juice.

El Doctor explained that only recently had he returned to the estate. In fact, he had been released a few months earlier, in January 2010, after serving a six-year conviction for drug trafficking in a U.S. federal prison in Texas and negotiating a reduced sentence. Once back in Colombia, he had primarily dedicated himself to his wife and two daughters, who were denied visits to him while he was behind bars in the Texas prison. Now he was determined to take his cattle business back into his own hands.

On the day of my arrival, El Doctor had gone to a bank in Puerto Boyacá to pay the salary of his workers and buy seeds and chemicals on the black market (all smuggled in from Venezuela, I later learned) for the farming of his livestock. This was the first time since his release that he had gone to the town, and he'd been pleased by the people's warm welcome. "They recognized me and came up to say hello. Many are calling me because they would like to meet. They no longer do it to ask me favors, as in the past. They well know that I don't have those ties anymore, but they want to see me and pay their respects. But here at the ranch, I don't receive people anymore—only occasionally, and only special people." He relished the recognition and deference shown by locals in spite of his extradition and the years that he had been away. There was a mixture of nostalgia and relief in his voice. I sipped more orange juice.

"How big is your ranch?" I asked.

El Doctor lifted his gaze, now glittering with pride, and announced that he had been a pioneer in cattle genetics when he had imported the first specimens of tropical livestock from India to Colombia in the 1980s. "Today I own 4,000 head of cattle and 2,000 hectares [4,942 acres] of land, and a total of 160 people work for me," he responded. Then he paused and, with the sadness of a victim, added: "Before my arrest, I almost had 500 workers. Many lost their jobs because of my disgrace, and now I am in no condition to hire them back. Before they had a good life; now they are living in poverty." When he was arrested and extradited, the state did not confiscate all of his land, he explained without animosity. Some of that land now belongs to his daughter, while additional land is still under the names of the previous owners. "They still might confiscate some of my property. It will be a major loss, but in any case, I will give it to the state without any resentment." We turned the light off and went to bed.

The following morning, after a comfortable sleep, I met El Doctor's wife, who served me breakfast with a choice of tropical fruit, cereal, *arepa*—the traditional Colombian cornbread—sausage, eggs, and a fresh, tender cheese produced at the farm. The previous night, El Doctor had spoken very highly of his wife, praising her for standing behind the business while he was in prison. "More often than not, when the husband is away, women let the business fall apart. Women end up listening to people who trick them. But this is not the case with my wife. She had no knowledge of farming, but she learned and got good at it."

The wife, once a bank executive, was a firm woman of average height, her long, thick hair collected behind her neck with a rubber band, and she had a vigorous gaze like that of a captain who is used to steering his vessel through storms and knows no hesitation. She wore a large white shirt, and at her neck was a wide, elegantly embroidered collar. She spoke in small sentences as if emitting verdicts, pronouncing every syllable with sharpness. "In this farm, we work very hard," she said, initiating her conversation with me by highlighting the work ethic of the house. "This is a humble estate and is not pretentious at all," she continued and provided a social analysis of the different kinds of farmhouses. Pretentious farms, she said, belong to drug barons, the so-called *traquetos,* the people engaged in cocaine trafficking who make a show of their wealth, with thick gold chains around their necks, large-cylinder-capacity cars, and stunning young women. "Those people are of a different class. I have to say 'those people' because I do not consider myself a part of them. They believe that belonging to a class is a matter of money, when instead it's a genetic thing," she added with a touch of disdain and irony. "Class is something a mother passes on with breast-feeding. Cali, the city I am from, has a widespread *traqueto* culture. They are ostentatious and pompous. They are the so-called emerging class, rooted in a culture of illegality. Colombia is shaped by such a culture and lives off it."

The veterinarian showed up, interrupting our conversation, to submit a shopping list to El Doctor's wife for review. In the meantime, El Doctor had joined us and sat down at the table for breakfast. In full light, I got a better sense of his features, his dyed-brown hair, a slightly inflated belly, the golden frame of his glasses, the watery eyes that bestowed upon him a melancholic and somehow tired mien. I observed his ability to listen, never interrupting, always calm, absent any animosity, and at the same time always ready to engage in captivating and gripping conversation. These qualities certainly contributed to his gaining the trust and respect of powerful drug lords and paramilitary leaders, as well as the fondness of the people of the Middle Magdalena region. El Doctor was a man of charm and grace, a man of council, the *consigliere* to whom to turn for decisions, a role that he seemed to enjoy. Like a sun, he stood at the center of a universe held together by symbolic acts of loyalty, which, in turn, were reinforced and validated by a practice of gift exchange. El Doctor proved his own magnanimity, providing jobs, food, security, intercessions, and favors. Because there is no free gift, in exchange El Doctor received respect, labor, information, protection, and, most of all, unwavering loyalty. In fact, as Marcell Mauss observed, the gift exchange's reciprocity is characterized not only by economic transition, but also by a variety of acts of politeness, from banquets to rituals to military service (1990, 5). El Doctor's power emanated naturally not only from his possessions, but also from the fact that, like a god, he held the power of life and death, of condemnation and pardon, over the people who depended on him. As Mauss remarked, what is at stake in a system of reciprocity is honor, which explains, for example, why the Mafia boss in Italy is named "a man of honor." Standing at the center of the reciprocity system, honor is not dependent on wealth, but is maintained by the obligation to give: "To refuse to give, to fail to invite, just as to refuse to accept, is tantamount to declaring war; it is to reject the bond of alliance and commonality" (ibid., 13).

I thus realized that it was the politics of honor engendered by gift exchange that conferred status on El Doctor. When his wife brought before him a chicken, struggling in a potato sack to be slaughtered, in a display of mercy he instructed her to put the sacrificial offering back into the pen for a few more days before it would be killed. A thought spontaneously sprang into my mind: How many times did El Doctor pardon an enemy sentenced to death by paramilitaries? I saw in that chicken a possible metaphor for a guerrilla sympathizer tied up and brought in front of a paramilitary leader for the final judgment. El Doctor's show of magnanimity, the capacity to grant temporary pardon, was an attribute of power that conferred upon him the mythic quality of a god.

For El Doctor, it all began in the mid-1970s. Colombia had only then discovered cocaine as a source of quick wealth. No vast coca fields yet existed in the country, or laboratories that could convert coca leaves into cocaine base, or chemists who knew the sophisticated formula to transmute cocaine paste into the white powder filling the nostrils of millions in the United States and around the world. Nor had a mythical figure such as Pablo Escobar yet appeared on the horizon. President Nixon had just announced the crackdown on drugs, but the United States was still years away from its declaration of an all-out war on drugs. El Doctor did not belong to any cartel, since there was no such thing back then. Only smugglers and cocaine freelancers such as himself existed, importing cocaine base from Bolivia and Peru.

When he started out, El Doctor was not a major player in the drug business; he was no Carlos Lehder, Pablo Escobar, Benjamín Herrera, or Gilberto Rodríguez-Orejuela—whom historian Paul Gootenberg labeled the "Schumpeterian heroes" of the wholesale cocaine trade (2008, 4). Rather, he was one of the many Colombians who in the early 1970s would travel with cash to Bolivia and Peru, buy cheap cocaine paste, and resell it in Colombia.[1] "I did so between 1975 and the beginning of the 1980s," El Doctor confessed. Born into a Conservative family in a small mountain town of the department of Antioquia,[2] he witnessed the sectarian violence between Conservatives and Liberals during the 1950s,[3] while he was still a child: "For the past twenty years, my hometown has witnessed cruel violence, and I consider myself a person displaced by violence." While attending law school in Bogotá, he shared with other students a small apartment in an alley of the Chapinero neighborhood, which is today booming with clothing stores, small restaurants, and gay clubs. After graduation, El Doctor moved to a town in the southern department of Nariño, at the Ecuadorian border, where he opened a money exchange office. His clients considered him as a trustworthy and loyal man, and that's why they started calling him El Doctor: "It was during this time that I got to know all those implicated in drug trafficking and who later became the bosses of the cartels." Though he did not volunteer any details, it is during that period that he opened his own cocaine business, accumulating the wealth that he later invested in mining, property, and estates, such as the one where I was sitting, listening to his stories and meeting his wife, workers, clients, and friends:

> I had gone to work at the border with Ecuador, where I owned three bureaus of exchange. Everyone trusted me and gave me their cash, and I was making money from the exchange. I was a currency exchanger. But that's also where I got involved with the issue, because I also got to know those who sold [the cocaine base]. So I got involved little by little. I was a kid, on my own, and filled with ambition. Therefore, instead of continuing to make money with the exchange, I also made money on the side [with the cocaine base] until

I stopped in 1982. But I continued to be linked to everyone because they knew me, and I was doing them favors. They became my clients in the livestock business—very special clients indeed. They liked me because I had served them. For being a fool, I became stuck with them. One commits much bullshit, and, as my father always said, we don't stop being a bratty child and fool in life. But that's history for me now. I already paid [my penalty] to the United States. When one pays to the United States, one pays to the entire world. Neither Italy nor Colombia nor Spain nor the U.K. comes after you. [The United States] are the world police, aren't they?

Successful with the money exchange bureau at the border, El Doctor branched off to Cali, where he eventually fell in love and married the woman who would become his second and current wife. In 1985, he acquired 17 percent of the airline Intercontinental de Aviación, which, according to Colombian and U.S. authorities, was created to camouflage drug shipments and launder money, a fact that El Doctor contested. According to the U.S. Drug Enforcement Agency (DEA), El Doctor had turned into one of the major leaders of the powerful North Valley Cartel. The indictment papers called him the *consigliere* responsible for mediating the cartel's internal conflicts and the interests of members and associates of other cartels. According to the DEA, he conspired in the "illegal trafficking of cocaine, money laundry, extortion of state agents and Colombian politicians, kidnapping, torture and killing of enemies of the cartel" (quoted in López López 2008, 217). In a U.S. State Department report, El Doctor is mentioned as an attorney and counselor to the North Valley Cartel, someone "viewed as an elder statesman and highly respected intermediary," and as "a major investor in cocaine shipments . . . and was involved in the laundering of millions of dollars of drug proceeds between Colombia, Ecuador, Mexico, Vanuatu, and the USA." [4]

"My mistake," El Doctor explained, "was that I was not able to keep a distance from those people, and I let myself get involved in their dealings." While he was perceived as a powerful and wealthy man by the people turning to him, El Doctor perceived himself also as a cog, almost trapped in a system that he himself, and in no minor way, had contributed to bring about and strengthen. He described himself as being increasingly drawn in, almost as if falling into a state of trance, and eventually possessed by the ambitions and desires awakened by cocaine and its trades. In marginal areas of Colombia, as I will explore in chapter 4, cocaine has become a key material symbol, which has turned individuals such as El Doctor into a part of a larger social system that, together with wealth and its own apparatus of repression, has accumulated social power.

It was humid in this valley near the Magdalena River, the air sticking to the skin and soaking one's shirt. The water of the swimming pool was still. Surrounding the property, Indian neem trees, which emanate an odor resembling that of onions, kept the nasty mosquitos at bay. In the afternoons, the natural repellant was bolstered by the spraying of powerful chemicals. Mosquitos were not the only hazard. Snakes, insidiously crawling through the grass, have attacked workers at the ranch several times. One man had to have his fingers amputated after being bitten. In a conflict deeply rooted in the peasant reality of the country, the snake has become a metaphor for the enemy, who hides and kills in surprise attacks. Hanging around this ranch in the heart of Colombia, one could appreciate the great effort that it took to tame and domesticate wild nature. Wasn't this what paramilitaries, like contemporary Mr. Kurtzes living in the heart of darkness, had supposedly set out to do for their country with a patriotic spirit—to advance modernity by subduing the savage guerrilla?

Before he got into trouble with justice, El Doctor was a recognized leader in the region. Several people in the region as well as in Bogotá, described El Doctor as someone to turn to for sound advice, to mediate a conflict, or to get help. People relied on him, requested him, and revered him. Many showed up at the ranch to pay their respect. "This here was the heart of the life in the entire area," said Octavio, a visitor and a long-time associate of El Doctor, with a deep sense of nostalgia for times he remembered as glorious. All around were the traces of a life now gone and of a dream abruptly interrupted by the arrest and the extradition of El Doctor in 2004. "Up to forty people would show up," El Doctor told me, standing in front of the barbecue grill at the border of the swimming pool, which had not been used for years. "I always had some meat ready, and we cooked it together with fried plantains. Everyone was happy, and no one left my ranch on an empty stomach." Satisfying the needs of the surrounding community, feeding everyone, and welcoming everyone as a guest—these are metaphors for the influence of the powerful. Anthropological studies of chiefdom have shown that not mere possession, but its sharing, is a mark of the powerful. The generous expenditure of wealth, rather than its accumulation, confers prestige and authority upon a chief. Studying primitive economy in the Trobriand Islands, for example, Bronisław Malinowski observed that the social code required that the one who possessed had to share, and that the higher the rank, the greater the obligation. Thus, generosity was a trait of chiefs and the "essence of goodness" ([1922] 1984, 97). While I was listening to El Doctor, who, like a paternalistic feudal lord, both dominated and cared for his subjects by showing his generosity, I could not help but think about the initial scenes of Francis Ford Coppola's *The Godfather,* when the Italian American Mafia boss entertains his guests and talks business and orders killings while hosting a lavish party on his estate for the wedding of his daughter.

To find refuge from the heat, El Doctor and I sat down in the pavilion next to the swimming pool, overlooking a green pasture where a horse was grazing. A maid and her teenage daughter first dusted the space. There were two pool tables covered with cloths, mattresses piled on one. At one end of the pavilion was a large, S-shaped bar with several stools, and on a shelf rested empty bottles of vodka, rum, and whisky. At the opposite end, leather rocking chairs encircled a small and short wooden table. Light generously filtered through a mosquito net extending along the four glass walls while electric fans hanging from the ceiling provided a light breeze. The silence and emptiness of the place today invited one to imagine the fullness of the life that once existed within the space. Here, in this pavilion, the silence was not a quality of peace. Rather, it was noise interrupted—life turned off.

El Doctor explained that in the very spot where we'd sat down an important summit among competing wings of the North Valley Cartel had taken place.[5] The heads of the cartel had arrived one day in August 2003, escorted by their army of security guards, after they had signed a pact of nonaggression mediated by El Doctor and guaranteed by the leader of the paramilitaries of the Middle Magdalena region. Boss Diego Montoya, who was hiding in that region, arrived last on a helicopter. It was a tense and heated meeting, and El Doctor failed in his mediation attempt. Since then, the war between the different factions of the North Valley Cartel continued and intensified:

> It was here that I tried to negotiate the peace between two factions of the North Valley Cartel, between the boss Diego Montoya, now under arrest, and [Wilber] Varela, who was recently killed by one of his own men in Venezuela. I had warned them that unless they were able to reach an agreement, they would end up killing each other. And that's exactly what happened. See? I got into all of these problems only for one reason: because I have always been interested in peace. And I made mistakes, which I have now paid for.

His self-proclaimed interest in "peace" turned El Doctor into one of the main strategists of the paramilitaries in Colombia, since the Middle Magdalena was the region where cattle ranchers first united to fight against the leftist insurgency. He had been a victim of the guerrillas, kidnapped twice by the FARC and forced to pay ransom, and in 1990, they had bombed one of his farms. Later, El Doctor became part of a group called the Twelve Apostles, which was in cahoots with the state-hunted drug kingpin Pablo Escobar. In 1993, he helped to mediate a conflict between a wing of the Ejército de Liberación Nacional (National Liberation Army; ELN) guerrillas, who had decided to demobilize, and drug traffickers from Southern Colombia. According to witnesses, El Doctor was instrumental in saving the lives of several men and women (Rondero 2006). "I was always of the conviction," he commented, "that it is better to commit mistakes and even to die in the midst of a conflict, rather than doing nothing and being nobody."

My stay at the ranch was a time of enlightenment. For some years before that point, I had listened to the testimony of victims and victimizers. I had walked through the neighborhoods at the margins of major urban centers, traveled to small towns and villages and visited coca fields, and sat down with ministers, ambassadors, and artists, as well as numerous members of paramilitaries, guerrillas, and urban gangs. Each conversation, each encounter, each observation had provided an important fragment of a larger, complex puzzle that I still struggled to see from a distance and grasp in its entirety. It was as if every encounter, every story I heard, would draw me into the substance of the fragment, preventing me from seeing the whole. Many times I got frustrated, since the painstaking description and understanding of a detail always risked leaving out an important trait of the country. It was like coming across an image, beginning to observe it, being drawn into it, and eventually falling into it, discovering yet another image and drifting into it deeper and deeper. The more I focused on the dynamics of causality, the more I was missing the point. Only when I sat in front of El Doctor, listening to his erudite narrative at the heart of his hacienda surrounded by workers to whom he related with heartfelt paternalism and tropical trees repelling mosquitos, and imagining snakes hiding under leaves and crawling through grass, did I truly sense how Colombia was a phantasmagoria of images past and present and of fantasies about the future; how its reality was suspended between magic and modernity; and how much magic was present in Colombia's project of modernity. Colombia, both so premodern and so modern in its longing for progress, its shameless use of violence, and its exclusion of peasants, the poor, the African Colombian population, the indigenous, and the different. Colombia, with its 1991 Constitution, institutions, and laws, was still so elitist, feudal, and, I dare say, almost genocidal in its disregard for all peripheral realities and the repression of social movements advancing demands for rights.

I had ended up in the right place. I experienced the hacienda and El Doctor, whom some of his workers called *el patrón,* as servants would refer to their feudal lord—an allegory, which, as in Walter Benjamin's interpretation, is rich in signs, experience, and intuition, with the power to take one beyond the mere observable: "Tout pour moi deviént Allégorie" (Baudelaire, quoted in Benjamin 1968, 156). The Middle Magdalena Valley. The ranch. The pavilion. The rocky chairs. The empty bottles of whisky. The humid embrace of the hot air. El Doctor: his pose, and the unspoken revealing more than the uttered. The cattle ranchers and the drug kingpins. The snakes and the pardoned chicken. The paramilitary and the guerrillas. The resentment and the pride. These were all fragments unmasking the depths of Colombia, disclosing the social being of proclaimed truths. I then realized that I was sitting at the intersection of past and present, in the eye of the storm of Colombia's cultural practice of violence; the place where myth and modernity, dream and reality, came together and gave form to what Lacan called the Real.

What is the origin of the paramilitaries in Colombia? Why were they established, and by whom? What did the accounts of El Doctor and others whom I met in my fieldwork suggest about the beliefs, ambitions, and fantasies of my interlocutors? Paramilitary groups have been a constant feature in Colombia's history of violence, the private army of local strongmen, landowners, cattle ranchers, political bosses, and, increasingly, drug barons. Over time, they established political and military control over the territories they ruled, imposing their law, policing villages and towns, administering justice, and carrying out political cleansing with the ultimate purpose of protecting the interests of their leaders and supporters. Compared to other local actors, the paramilitaries became a superior source of power, as Gustavo Duncan (2006, 47) wrote.

Historians often have conventionally distinguished three generations of paramilitary groups in the recent history of Colombia. The first generation corresponds to the era of so-called La Violencia, the sectarian violence between the elites of the Liberal and Conservative parties in the 1950s. With the mission to fight the FARC guerrillas, the second generation of paramilitary groups was established at the beginning of the 1980s in the Middle Magdalena region, which provided a model for the paramilitary groups later assembled in the Autodefensas Unidas de Colombia (United Self-Defense of Colombia; AUC) umbrella established at the end the 1990s. These latter paramilitary groups demobilized between 2003 and 2006 during the administration of President Álvaro Uribe Vélez, and in more recent years, new paramilitary units, known by the acronym Bacrim (for "Bandas Criminales"), which protect the business of drug lords, have been operating in the same areas once dominated by the AUC. These new groups are referred to as the third generation of paramilitaries in Colombia.

The original sectarian violence between the Conservative and Liberal elites broke out after the killing in Bogotá of the populist Liberal leader Jorge Eliécer Gaitán on April 9, 1948. At the time, Gaitán was the most popular political figure in the country and had successfully galvanized and excited the imagination of the masses. His killing occurred during the Inter-American Conference in Bogotá and sparked days of disorder. Churches, trams, and public buildings were destroyed. From the capital, the violence spread like wildfire to the periphery of the country, deepening the sectarian attitude among political elites and the violent competition for political and economic domination and regional hegemony (Palacios 2006; Pécaut 2001; Roldán 2002).

In the departments of Caldas and Valle de Cauca, local Conservative political chiefs recruited hitmen, called *pájaros* (birds), to eliminate political opponents and consolidate their strongholds. The *pájaros* operated in a fashion similar to that of more recent forms of paramilitary groups in Colombia: they assembled people in the squares and separated the men from the women and children, who were then sent home while the bloodshed occurred. In certain towns, as historian Mary Roldán highlighted, paramilitary organizations "emerged as the primary form of official public political order maintenance" (2002, 109).

In a seminal study of La Violencia, the sociologists Germán Guzmán Campos, Fals Borda, and Umaña Luna provided a psychological and sociological portrait of the *pájaro*, the political killer:

> He is part of a fraternity, of a mafia with a baffling lethal effectiveness. He is
> unpredictable, gassy, ambiguous, and in the beginning, he was essentially a

town man. At the outset, he operates by himself, with incredible speed, without leaving fingerprints behind. His group has at its disposal automobiles and a car fleet involved in pillaging, with drivers as partners in crime and in the sharing of the divestment. The designated victim falls infallibly. (1980, 184)

At the time, one of the best-known political hitman was León María Lozano, whose nom de guerre was El Cóndor, the scavenger bird that eats dead animals—a name for a professional killer, which in itself causes fear and terror. In 1959, during La Violencia, the medical doctor Julio Alberto Hoyos sent a note to the president of the Senate in which he described, in detail, the work and alliances of El Cóndor:

> Several men from Tuluá,[6] who are Liberals but also Conservatives, fearing for their lives because they were accused of sympathizing with the Liberals, told me, some in a whisper and others outright like Don Joaquín Sierra, that El Cóndor was the mastermind and at times the perpetrator of the spreading violence. For having opened his mouth, the night of the day on which he issued a statement, [Sierra] was assaulted in his home; but he was able to escape and ended up on the Atlantic Coast. From my research in Tuluá, I was able to confirm that El Cóndor was working in cahoots with the police and investigators, and he managed to have the members of these institutions take part in his squad [or *pajería*], and this happened not only in Tuluá, but also in several other parts of Colombia; in fact, where there was a police station a group of malefactors also existed, made up of police officers and private citizens, who, in the shadow of political sectarianism, killed, set [homes] on fire, and robbed.[7]

La Violencia was a time of bloodshed, which further fueled cycles of vengeance, with massacres, rapes, and the burning of houses. Political interests, fantasies, and passions ignited the violence along with economic interests and greed, and hacienda foremen turned to their own benefit the institutional disorder and took control of strategic areas and resources of the regional economy through murder or the threat of it (Palacios 2006, 165).

In 1959, the factions laid down their weapons and signed an agreement, which established the Frente Nacional (National Front), thus marking the official end of La Violencia. This political arrangement established that the Conservative and Liberal parties would take turns in governing the country and controlling the public administration. While ending the civil war and reducing widespread violence, the agreement—characterized by strong centralization—left out important actors, such as the Communist Party, from participation in the political process and frustrated the democratic aspirations of social organizations in the rural regions. The Frente Nacional was an imperfect political arrangement that ultimately consolidated the traditional elite's domination of Colombia. Peace came with a cost, since the ensuing grievances fueled further resentment, resistance, and ultimately rebellion. The decade of the 1960s saw the emergence of guerrilla groups, most notably the Revolutionary Armed Forces of Colombia (FARC) and the ELN,[8] and the 1970s saw their expansion in several areas across Colombia.

The second generation of the paramilitaries began in the early 1980s when, in the Middle Magdalena region (as I describe more in detail below), the local elite established armed self-defense groups. With the intention of protecting private property from the attacks of the guerrillas, these self-defense groups soon became expressions of a larger hegemonic project whose principles were rooted in the counterinsurgency doctrine of the Cold War. The Middle Magdalena region represented an experiment, which was later exported across Colombia.

A case in point was the establishment of a paramilitary organization in Córdoba and Urabá, two regions in Northern Colombia characterized by an important banana and meat industry, as well as a long history of peasant and worker movements and the presence of guerrillas. In fact, at the beginning of the 1990s, the Castaño brothers, Fidel and Carlos, established the Autodefensas Campesinas de Córdoba y Urabá (Peasant Self-Defense Forces of Córdoba and Urabá; ACCU), dedicated to repressing social movements, selectively killing union and community leaders, and eliminating guerrilla forces. Their political cleansing happened just after Colombia, in 1988, had adopted the popular election of mayors, who up until then were appointed by the president; in 1991, as a result of the peace process with the M-19 urban guerrillas, Colombia had adopted a more inclusive constitution with an emphasis on democratic participation. In a study about paramilitary forces in Córdoba and Urabá, Mauricio Romero wrote that the ACCU had managed "to form an imagined political community and compete for popular, middle class, and elite loyalties with both the national state and the leftist insurgents" (2000, 52).

Doble Cero, the paramilitary commander whom I had clandestinely met in the mountains of Eastern Antioquia, had been the right-hand man of Fidel Castaño, and, as a former officer of the army, he had engineered and implemented the military strategy and led the social cleansing in Córdoba and Urabá. During our conversation under a gazebo at our meeting, he had narrated the beginnings of the ACCU:

Fidel was a friend of the people of the Middle Magdalena because of his ties with the military and the self-defense of the Middle Magdalena. At that time, the self-defense groups were legal, but when he realized the intertwinement with the drug lords and that Pablo Escobar and the Mexicanos were using these people, the man, who had a bit of a vision, understood that this was going to become a problem and would be the end of [the self-defense groups]. Thus Fidel decided to leave. He went to Córdoba and bought a farm and land at a low cost.... There he established his own paramilitary group and waged war against the guerrillas of the EPL [Ejército Popular de Liberación, or Popular Liberation Army]....

In August 1991, Fidel Castaño called me to Las Tangas, his farm.[9] Since I was working at the time in Urabá [for a banana company], it was not difficult for me to travel from there to the south of Córdoba. I went there ... and he asked me if I was going to work with him. He told me that he was working on agrarian reform with local communities and social projects with peasants. All of this sounded very good and meaningful to me. During the days that I was there, he showed me all of his projects, and thus I decided to give up my work at the banana company and work with Fidel for the rebuilding of the social fabric in the department of Córdoba.

Similar to the Middle Magdalena region, as we will see, the ACCU experiment, deemed successful, expanded into other areas of Colombia at a time when the national government was entering peace talks with the guerrillas of the FARC and ELN. In fact, in 1997, while the government of President Andrés Pastrana was engaged in negotiations with the insurgency in Southern Colombia, where the guerrilla forces had their rearguard and dominated a third of the country, Carlos Castaño established an umbrella organization in the north with the purpose of regrouping the different and diverse paramilitary groups dispersed throughout the country under one roof. What the ACCU had accomplished—in the mind of Carlos Castaño, a man often described as overambitious, megalomaniac, and short-tempered—in Córdoba and Urabá, such as the high degree of domination, the political cleansing, the annihilation of social movements and the guerrillas, had to now be exported to the rest of the country. Thus, with financing from influential companies and powerful drug cartels, the AUC was established. Once again, the intention of the paramilitaries was not only to protect the economic interests of local elites, but also to oppose the national government's policies, which to the sponsors of the paramilitaries looked faint-hearted with regard to the guerrillas; indeed, sometimes the government was considered the guerrillas' accomplice when it chose to engage with them in peace talks. This perception of the central government has marked the polarization between the center and the periphery, between the traditional Colombian oligarchy and the regional emerging elites, and it has been a steady feature of Colombia's history and at the core of much of its political violence.

The AUC expanded its domination over much of Colombia, eventually becoming a strategic component of the country's counterinsurgency efforts, and achieved significant popular support, primarily among the middle and upper classes. Through widespread terror, massacres, selective killings, disappearances, and torture, the paramilitaries of Carlos Castaño—often in cahoots with the army and with local police—spread their domination over the villages, towns, and neighborhoods of Colombia's main cities. In a report denouncing their abuses, Human Rights Watch (2001) portrayed the paramilitaries as the sixth division of the Colombian army. They were at the center of a complex intertwinement, weaving into a single political and military project combatants, political leaders, drug traffickers, and business owners, the legal and the illegal. In Colombia, the paramilitaries achieved what the Marxist insurgency had always been accused of pursuing, *la combinación de todas las formas de lucha* (the combination of all forms of struggle). From the periphery of the country, the paramilitaries expanded not only geographically throughout Colombia, from north to south and east to west, but also determined the outcome of elections and imposed mayors, governors, and even representatives of the national congress on the population; high-ranking officials of the military and of the state's security agency were associated with the paramilitaries and worked in tandem with them. The paramilitaries became a war machine of the apparatus of capture in the despo-capitalist spaces of Colombia.

At the end of 2001, a few months after President Álvaro Uribe Vélez had won a landslide in the presidential election with the promise to use an iron fist against the insurgency, Carlos Castaño announced a unilateral demobilization of the AUC. Between 2003 and 2006, over thirty-two thousand members of the paramilitaries disarmed and entered a demobilization and reintegration process. Congress passed the controversial Justice and Peace Law in 2005, guaranteeing lenient sentences in exchange for full collaboration and reparation for victims. The government engaged in ambiguous talks with the leaders of the AUC, and what at the beginning the government had presented as a negotiation process ultimately turned into the prosecution of the AUC leaders, who were locked up in a high-security prison. In May 2008, when the paramilitaries began to unpack the truth regarding their alliances with political parties, business owners, and the army, the AUC leaders were extradited to the United States on drug-trafficking charges. In the meantime, newly armed groups formed, led mainly by former middle-rank commanders of the paramilitaries, and today these groups are identified as the third generation of paramilitaries.

The history of paramilitaries in Colombia—of its so-called second generation— is a complex and cruel one, which began at the outset of the 1980s in the Middle Magdalena region. El Doctor was a main character in that history, an influent instigator of the armed self-defense groups.

The Middle Magdalena region is a geostrategic area of Colombia. It is the belly of the country, sitting at the intersection of four important regions: Antioquia, Cundinamarca, Santander, and Northern Santander. Already in the early times of the Spaniard colonization, its large and navigable river connected the northern coast with the center of the country for the export of coal and bananas. As El Doctor explained, the Middle Magdalena region now exports the meat and milk used throughout the entire country. In addition, Middle Magdalena is today a strategic gateway for the trafficking of drugs and is at the same time home to a large military base, which also hosts U.S. military advisors.

The region has been an area of economic exploitation and modernization, and violence has not been a mere byproduct of the process of modernization but its engine during the development of oil drilling, the establishment of haciendas, and the restructuring of the local economy. As elsewhere in Latin America (Green 1999, 10), political violence here has been the manifestation of a historical structural violence of injustice and inequality. In the most detailed study of the region's history, Carlos Medina Gallego noted that over the years, residents have become accustomed to "the practice of violence as a mechanism of power, of subsistence, and of pressure" (1990, 101).

The first dynamic that caused the increase of violence was exploitation of oil reserves in the region by an American corporation, which began in the 1930s. In fact, like other regions of Colombia, Middle Magdalena was initially a land of settlers who arrived in waves because of the oil drilling pioneered by the Texas Petroleum Company, which at the time had its headquarters in Newark (ibid., 39–40). The company had arrived in Colombia in 1926 to carry out geophysical exploration, and in 1949, it began perforation in the Middle Magdalena region, where workers from across Colombia flocked. Roads and urban centers, such as Puerto Boyacá, were built. At the time, the Texas Petroleum Company was the only game in town, but its expansion in Colombia since the mid-1920s, which was perceived by workers as a mark of American capitalist imperialism, soon created a conflict between the owners and the workers, who organized to demand better living conditions and the freedom to organize in unions. Their protest and resistance was met with repression (ibid., 56–88).

The concentration of land by cattle ranchers, landowners, businessmen, and retired military was a second dynamic that encouraged violence. Vulnerable and defenseless settlers were either forced to sell their land at low cost, were displaced, had to work as employees or day laborers under new landowners, or seek employment with the oil company. In the 1950s and 1960s, settlers and peasants who resisted land concentration and occupied such areas were killed, disappeared, or incarcerated. Often their property was burned. As Medina Gallego noted, the development of political violence and the establishment of guerrilla groups occurred an environment ripe with opposition and resentment (ibid., 117).

In the years of La Violencia, the Middle Magdalena region nonetheless became a safe haven for members affiliated with the Liberal party, who had been forcibly displaced from surrounding regions by the repressive apparatus of the Conservative party. This favored the formation in the region of the Liberal guerrillas, supported by settlers resentful of landowners and tired of military repression. The Liberal guerrillas and their weapons thus became the tools that settlers used to reoccupy previously lost land. At the same time, the Communist Party had extended its influence (ibid.). Present in the region since the days of La Violencia, the guerrillas were in many cases perceived as the self-defense groups of the oppressed.

In fact, during the 1970s, the FARC guerrillas, established in 1964 by former members of the Liberal guerrillas, penetrated the Middle Magdalena region and expanded their influence. The FARC concentrated its initial efforts on the political organization of peasants and served to defend them (ibid., 134). Toward the end of the 1970s, when the guerrilla command in the region changed hands, the FARC increased its military operations through selective killings, kidnappings, and imposing protection money. It was during this period that the FARC kidnapped El Doctor.

At the beginning of the 1980s, the FARC's increased harassment provided the justification for the establishment of right-wing self-defense groups. In his interview with me, El Doctor described the climate and perception at the time among cattle ranchers. He explained that it was impossible for residents of the region to travel safely to major urban centers such as Bogotá or Medellín. Expressing the ranchers' grievance at the time, he said:

We felt caged. We couldn't go to Bogotá by car because [the guerrillas] would catch us on the same road we came from the night before. The guerrillas would show up there every day. And if one wanted to go to Medellín, twenty minutes from here, the guerrillas would catch one as well. The same was true on the road to Bucaramanga. Cucho, who sold me this ranch, told me that in order to come here when he was living in La Dorada in the mid-1970s, he would call the caretaker and ask him to take the livestock to the border of the property to see it because he was frightened to live here. He was not able to enter his own house to sleep, get a drink, or talk with the caretaker because the guerrillas would kidnap him. If a fisherman had two buckets, one was for the guerrillas. If the harvester had two bundles of lemons, one was for the guerrillas. This is how it was here until we freed the area.

Octavio, a local and close associate of El Doctor, told me that he avoided using his van in those years out of fear the guerrillas would stop him and confiscate it:

A person who owned land like this, which was valued at five or ten billion pesos, had to sell it for one billion or a billion and a half, or for whatever he got, because [that person] could not access it. My brother sold his farm, which was a very beautiful farm, at a very low cost because he could not go there. He traveled to La Dorada to meet with a young guy, gave him the money to pay the workers, and my brother, who was a humble guy with no money whatsoever, could only get to La Dorada to give the money to the guy. And thus my brother, who was afraid to come here, said, "Why do I own a farm if I cannot go there? If the one who wants to enjoy it can't [do so]?" And so the moment came when, if something was not done, it would have worsened.

Such stories are traded among the residents of the region, depicting the guerrilla as a powerful, cruel, and savage enemy against whom the state is powerless and weak. The exchanged narratives strengthened residents' perception of the need for an armed self-defense group. Octavio continued:

It was a very difficult situation. I have a friend here who was very supportive of the self-defense groups, and one day I asked him, "So tell me, what's the matter? Why do you work and support the self-defense groups?"
    And he told me, "Octavio, they killed my father, they kidnapped my mother, and she never showed up again. They kidnapped my brother's wife,

and she never came back. My father had finished eating at his farm and went to rest on a hammock. There they caught him. The guerrillas arrived, they surrounded the workers, and they tied up my father in the hammock with a rope. They inserted a large stick under the rope and took him away, and after a few moments, they shot him and left him hanging from a tree branch and left."

This, of course, generated very challenging feelings for the people.

Self-defense groups were therefore established in 1982 at a meeting attended by representatives of the Texas Petroleum Company, members of the Committee of Ranchers, political leaders, army officials, and business owners. Hacienda owners contributed with protection money. "In the '70s," El Doctor remembered, "we paid the self-defense groups five thousand pesos for each hectare. Later, it became ten thousand and went up to twenty thousand. When someone sold a hacienda, he had to give a percentage to the self-defense groups in exchange for security. And everyone accepted this as a lesser evil. It was like a tax." It was also the beginning of the paramilitaries' domination through fear and terror. "We had to be very hard-hitting," El Doctor explained.

Initially, the newly formed paramilitary and the army aimed at dismantling the political organization of the Communist Party and the FARC. Civic, political, union, and peasant leaders were selectively killed. The paramilitary forces intervened as exterminators to "fumigate and purify" the area. In a column titled "The Truce," published by a local newspaper, the insurgency was compared to a terminal disease: "The insurrection is like a cancer. It has to be eradicated at its root and not by applying innocuous ointments to a malevolent tumor or else its spread is inevitable. The truce is a cancer treatment that is always lethal" (quoted in Medina Gallego 1990, 193).

The cancer metaphor, which calls up images of a severely sick body and the necessity of a resolute intervention, a surgery, to extirpate the malignancy, represented by the radical Other. Thus paramilitaries mimicked the terror of the guerrillas, and went one better, too: in a vernacular interpretation of the overall Cold War discourse, the Communist Party and the insurgency had served as the signifiers of evil for a long time, which empowered a justificatory discourse for the eradication of social movements and protest and the systematic and selective killing of political and union leaders. Locked in a dialectic narrative and a mutually empowering synergism, the regional elites and guerrillas have been perpetuating the myths and tales of the savage and the white man that had animated the search for the Golden King, El Dorado, since Spaniards first penetrated the wild forests of Colombia.

The discourse justifying the need for armed self-defense groups did not rest solely on the menacing guerrilla, but also on a narrative that emphasized the weakness of the state and its inability to establish order. It was the state's very inefficiency that sustained the state's reason to acquire a war machine of its own in the form of paramilitaries in untamed regions of Colombia. The production of a discourse about the weakness of the state has thus been central to the production of violence in Colombia. El Doctor's associate Octavio provided me with an example when he shared a story about how the police themselves had once suggested turning to a paramilitary leader to get effective help. In his account, he voiced his frustration and perception of the state's inability to provide security and protection. People such as El Doctor and Octavio saw the establishment of private armed groups dedicated to self-defense as the only effective alternative. Octavio told me:

> People here knew that self-defense was their only protection. Let me tell you a story. About eight years ago, the FARC sent letters to a few merchants of La Dorada with instructions to deliver a bag with twenty million pesos to a granary. With a couple of other merchants, we went to meet with the police commandant. We told him, "Look at the kind of letters we are receiving."
>
> He read the letters, and the first thing that he said was "My friend, we don't have any gasoline, we don't have cars, we don't have this, and we don't have that."
>
> "This is not the point," we told him. "What we are saying is that [the merchants must] bring a bag full of money to the granary! Put two officers in civilian clothes, who will bring the damn bag, and tell them to wait and see who is coming to get it." Nothing.
>
> Do you want me to tell you what he really told us? "You are a friend of Ramón Isaza, the paramilitary leader. Why don't you talk to him? He will help you."

Confronted with the state's inability or unwillingness to debilitate the FARC, El Doctor spoke of the obligation of the local population to organize and form self-defense groups. The need to purge the area of the presence of the insurgency was elevated to the primary and only urgency to be confronted and resolved. Never during our conversation would El Doctor mention workers' labor conditions and rights:

The self-defense groups here were able to operate for such a long time because the population was aware that the groups were here to protect them. Rubén, a friend of mine, told me a story that he had been trying to save money to buy a power generator for his farm. He was selling livestock and had been saving money for three, four years, until he said, "On my next trip when I sell livestock, I will get the rest of the money that I need to buy the power generator."

When he sold the livestock, the guerrillas came to him and told him, "Sir, you need to go to the commander of the front because he needs to talk to you." They took him to talk to the guy, and the guy told him that they needed a certain amount of money—the same amount that Rubén needed to buy the power generator.

Rubén refused and told them he didn't have the money, but they threatened him, and eventually he gave them the money. When he was left without the power generator, which he had desired for about four or five years, he started thinking, "How is it possible that we let ourselves be harassed like this for our entire lives?"

And he went to see a neighbor because he saw that when [the neighbor] was out with the livestock, people went to talk to him. But he had never asked his neighbor who these people were, because in those days one didn't know with whom you could talk. So, he went to see the guy and told him "Are the guerrillas asking you for money?" and the guy denied it. And Rubén told him, "Come on, I know they are asking you for money."

At that point, the guy told him, "Well, I have been giving them money for some time." So four, five, ten of [the ranchers] started to assemble. They contracted someone who knew about security, who knew how to deal with the problem, and they started organizing and seeing what needed to be done. They say that this was the moment they started putting together a fund.

The intertwined discourse of the guerrillas' terror and the state's weakness ultimately produced what El Doctor came to call the cruel yet necessary war:

This has been a cruel war. There were deaths on both sides until the guerrillas had to leave. The country didn't have another area that was worse than this one in the 1970s and 1980s. In no other area of the country had the war against the guerrillas been so cruel. This is why all of the residents in this area are proud for having sent away the guerrillas. This pride is something that is stigmatized by the majority in the rest of the country. They believe that this is evil. Instead, we said that the guerrillas needed to be sent away. If the government was not capable of doing it, there was no other choice. We have been without a guerrilla presence for thirty years.

The same double-terror talk about the guerrillas and the state underpinned the militarization of the region. In fact, in Puerto Berrío, in

Antioquia, the army established a military base that housed the Fourth Brigade. Here, at the end of the 1980s, Doble Cero served as a military officer. During those years, the declared objective of the army was to restore democracy in Colombia. Those were the years of the Turbay Ayala administration, which was characterized by zero tolerance and a repressive policy against the insurgency—including its social and political constituency—and was determined to reduce the influence of the Communist Party. A report written by the Agrarian National Council at the time highlighted that the "military had imposed a climate of terror and the negation of civic rights" (Medina Gallego 1990, 153). Paraphrasing Taussig, one can observe that in responding to terror, the state itself became an agent of terror because, based on its own discourse, it has no other option (2002).

It so happened that under the leadership of General Farouk Yanine Díaz, a School of the Americas graduate, the army at the outset of the 1980s started to establish collaborative relations with civic organizations, arguing for the necessity of unifying efforts to defeat the guerrillas and the Communist Party both militarily and politically (ibid.; Hylton 2006, 72). The population had to collaborate actively, and civilians were recruited as part of the intelligence strategy. El Doctor explained:

> Here we always had a very efficient intelligence because of the lemon harvesters. This area always produced lots of wild lemons. The lemon harvesters roam through all of the farms, and they have the implicit permission to enter and collect the lemons. We ranchers even help them when we see them carrying heavy loads, and we give them a ride to the main road. The lemon harvesters own a cooperative and sell lemons to the big cities. And since they are across the entire territory and in each of its corners, they patrol to see if there is something unusual going on. There is another very efficient intelligence service, which are the peasants who live on the islands of the Magdalena River. We help them with water or groceries, and when there is a inundation, we get them out of there temporarily. We help them economically, and they patrol to see if strangers are coming. They are terrific guardians, and they alert us.

Referring to the recruitment campaign among the population, El Doctor spoke about the choice offered to locals who had a relationship with the FARC: a choice between forcibly being displaced or killed and full collaboration. El Doctor framed it as a black-and-white decision between good and evil:

> The people who united to fight against the guerrillas went to those who, out of fear or for any other reason, were associated with the guerrillas. "If you

want to continue staying with the guerrilla, you have to leave. If you remain, you have to work with us. Choose, or you will be dead." And that's how it happened. The majority accepted and turned as soon as they saw [the existence] of a united front. They turned toward the forces of good.

The region was presented as a successful anti-Communist bastion, and a powerful right-wing movement arose that silenced popular demands. The region was now known as an area free of Communists and Communist ideas. Some mottos of the time included "As long as there is an army, there is a homeland" and "Communists assassins. Out of Middle Magdalena" (Medina Gallego 1990, 161). Under the principles of the National Security Doctrine, designed by the United States during the Cold War to fight Communism, civil society became a terrain of capture: workers, peasants, teachers, and political and union leaders became the targets of a military campaign. The enemy was everywhere, and counterinsurgency became a total war, a dirty war, as in other parts of Latin America at the time. María Victoria Uribe highlighted how the substance of this terror was "its indistinctiveness, ambiguity, and confusion" and how rural inhabitants were killed "because they were perceived as [having] direct or indirect support for the opposition" (2004, 91). Rather than ambiguity, though, self-defense groups in the Middle Magdalena region operated with straightforwardness and on a principle of certainty. It was within this political climate that right-wing self-defense groups, the forerunners of modern paramilitaries in Colombia, were formed in Middle Magdalena to fight alongside the military against the insurgency. This was a cruel war, as El Doctor had admitted, and Octavio provided an illustration:

> At the time, [the self-defense groups] gave an order to kill everyone carrying a message on behalf of the guerrillas. . . . What happened is that the guerrillas would come to you and ask you to give a message to your neighbor [saying] that they wanted to see him. Thus [the self-defense groups] ordered people to kill everyone carrying a message on behalf of the guerrillas. And that was the end of it. The guerrillas changed their methods. They sent guys on motorbikes who would approach you and tell you, "We are so and so, and we need you to go to that place." Therefore [the self-defense groups] ordered the killing of everyone riding a motorbike. And, of course, it is implied that they killed a lot of innocent people, too.

The establishment of self-defense groups in the Middle Magdalena region coincided with the 1982 election of President Belisario Betancur, a Conservative who represented a change in the country's counterinsurgency strategy. The newly elected president proposed an agenda for peace, and, under his direction, Congress approved an amnesty law and established the Peace Commission. Betancur defined his rule as the time for a "new political opening" (Hylton 2006, 70). This represented a shift in rhetoric as compared with the authoritarian years of President Turbay Ayala.[10]

The FARC, as well as other guerrilla groups, such as the Ejército Popular de Liberación (EPL) and the M-19, the urban guerrilla force, entered into a cease-fire with the government and started what at the time was referred to as a "national dialogue." The armed forces, though, did not see Betancur's peace efforts in a friendly light. The military perceived the president as someone aiding the Communist Party and undermining democracy in Colombia. Paramilitary leader Doble Cero, who at the time served as a cadet in the military academy, told me about the army's discomfort with Betancur's policies in an email:

> When Belisario Betancur, a member of the Conservative party, was elected president, his government program of reaching a peace agreement with the guerrillas and giving them political and military benefits generated a great discomfort among the ranks. All of this was mirrored in the instructions that our superiors gave us and even more so when the candidates for officers were indoctrinated with the idea that the army was the fundamental pillar of both a democratic system and individual freedoms, and that all of this was threatened by external, as well as internal, enemies of the democratic system. (Quoted in Civico 2009, 117–18)

Across Colombia, death squads, in alliance with the army, launched a campaign of extermination against the leaders of the Unión Patriótica (Patriotic Union; UP), a leftist political party. Founded with the support of the FARC guerrillas, the party stood for peace and social change. Two years after its foundation, over five hundred leaders of the UP were assassinated, including its presidential candidate, Jaime Pardo Leal. Today in Colombia, it is not uncommon to hear social and political activists talk about the "genocide of the UP" (Hylton 2006, 72–73). At a time marked by the logics of the Cold War, the Middle Magdalena represented for the local elites and the army a laboratory in which to experiment with counterinsurgency tactics as well as retaliation against the peace-oriented policies of President Betancur.

For a better grasp of how individuals such as El Doctor interpreted their committed support for self-defense groups, it is interesting to read an excerpt from the transcript of the dialogue between El Doctor and his associate Octavio at our meeting. El Doctor spoke of his interview with the national newspaper *El Tiempo* and how he had admitted, to the journalist who was interviewing him, the role that he had played in providing support to self-defense groups. Killings and massacres were what El Doctor referred to as the cruel part of the war, but he considered them an unavoidable and necessary evil to guarantee peace in the region. In the dialogue with Octavio, he hinted at how his truth-telling, rather than an act of transparency and honesty, was driven by his need to maintain his good reputation in the region and guarantee his own safety. The conversation is revelatory not only due to the extent of the ideological and material support provided by both El Doctor and Octavio to self-defense groups, but also because of how deep-rooted and dominating the hegemonic power relations developed around the paramilitaries remain today:

> EL DOCTOR: When I returned [from the United States], I had a small problem, and, irritated, I had to go to *El Tiempo* to deny what they were saying about me. They were saying that in the country, many were worried by my return. They wrote it in a small news report. Octavio—you who have been my friend and know it all—did you ever meet someone who was uncomfortable because I returned?

> OCTAVIO: No. That's what I mean . . .

> ED: Son of a bitch! Someone lied, and thus I had to go and be upset. But during the interview, they asked me about this area and about the self-defense groups of Puerto Boyacá. And I, who am always transparent, said that I did collaborate with the self-defense groups in Puerto Boyacá and that I do not regret having collaborated because thanks to it, we have been living in peace for thirty years. None of us regret it, do we? And why should I declare the contrary if it was us who brought peace to this land? Ha! Son of a bitch! W Radio [the national radio channel] attacked me as well as [the journalist] María Jiménez because [the paramilitaries] had killed her sister in Cimitarra. Of course, how am I going to prove that they killed her? Never. I am not the sort of criminal to be in agreement with such a [killing]. Nor am I in agreement with the massacre of La Rochela.[11] These are the excesses that armed groups commit, and I am never going to be fine with that. And if it was in my power to avoid it, I would have done it, even at the cost of my own life. But I was not going to publicly deny [my role] in order to avoid problems with journalists who were asking me questions or look like certain state officials who have double morals and talk in an evasive way about how the [the paramilitaries] were an evil thing. Why am I going to say that and then have all of Puerto Boyacá against me? That'd be so gay, since I live here! I vote here. I will get my breakfast, lunch, and dinner here for the rest of my life! Why should I get myself into trouble?

o: And by the way, one knows how things were around here.

ED: I have the impression that self-defense groups here were the lesser evil as compared to the rest of the country.

In the words of El Doctor and Octavio, both pride and nostalgia existed for the times when the Middle Magdalena region was a counterinsurgency bastion and the guerrillas had been expelled, the influence of the Communist Party annihilated, and order established. But in recent times, cracks in that security bastion have threatened this authoritarian peace. New faces and new armed groups have appeared, petty crimes have been committed, "foreigners"—that is, individuals from outside the region—have been buying land, and, most worrisome, fear and silence have returned to the Middle Magdalena region while the state's unwillingness or inefficiencies remain a perpetual narrative. Maybe, the two men reasoned, there was a need to reorganize self-defense groups, this time not against the guerrillas, but against the private armies of drug barons.

The demobilization and reintegration process of more than thirty thousand former members of the paramilitaries has turned into a failure. Several middle-rank commanders never gave up their weapons since, with their former leaders behind bars or extradited to the United States, it was now their turn to take the drug business into their own hands. Meanwhile, a decent percentage of demobilized paramilitaries, as often happens in post-conflict times, have tasted the uncertainties of their future and opted for the certainties of life as cocaine mercenaries and thus took up weapons again. New groups with exotic names appeared: the Águilas Negras (Black Eagles), the Rastrojos, the Urabeños, the Paisas, the Gaitanistas, and the Ejército Revolucionario Popular Anticomunista de Colombia (Anti-Communist Popular Revolutionary Army of Colombia). They have been operating in the same areas previously dominated by demobilized paramilitary groups, mimicking their methods, sowing terror, delivering threats and fliers, imposing curfews, killing petty criminals and prostitutes to gain support and legitimacy through social cleansing, and controlling strategic routes for drug trafficking. In one aspect, they differ from the previous paramilitary generation: instead of fighting against guerrillas, they now opportunistically ally with them, especially when it's good for the cocaine business. At first, when these new groups appeared, the government was in denial of the phenomenon, refusing to acknowledge the continuity with the paramilitaries and the overlapping of names and territories. The government was eager to maintain the fiction of a successful demobilization and reintegration process, which had enjoyed great endorsement from the upper class and foreign countries, most notably the United States. While the government defined them as a novel and a distinct phenomenon, labeling the Águilas Negras and the other groups as "new emerging criminal bands" and coining the acronym Bacrim, people living in their territories and under their domination instead acknowledged the continuity between these groups and the paramilitaries, recognizing their commanders and persisting in calling the newly reorganized groups paramilitaries.

The Middle Magdalena region was not immune to the new phenomenon, and El Doctor and Octavio were worried that a group of men coming from Medellín and introducing themselves as members of the Águilas Negras had begun to invade their space, which locals felt was almost sacred, and were polluting what had been previously cleansed and upsetting order and tranquility. The presence of these unknown faces, their suspicious acquisition of land, and some robberies were bad omens. El Doctor and his associate complained about the inefficiency of the state and the corruption of police officers. People were once again closed off in silence; the fear to speak up and denounce was back, and so was uncertainty. Maybe, the two men in the rocking chairs reasoned, sitting in the same spot where much of the war against the insurgency had been planned and where rivalry among heads of drug cartels had been mediated, it would be necessary to revive self-defense groups to protect property and lives, to preserve the integrity of the region, to prevent the settling of malicious foreigners, and to repel the invasion of the *pájaros*.

EL DOCTOR (GRIMACING): Things are bad. A few days ago, a woman with her son and daughter-in-law stopped by to say hello. I asked her about what's happening these days, and she did not respond. She said, "I don't know about this, like someone telling you, don't ask me about this." (ED sounds disappointed and disrespected.) How do we not talk about it if there is trust among us?

OCTAVIO (ADDING PASSION AND FORCE TO HIS VOICE): Doctor, we have to create opinion. We cannot go back to the times when we all kept silent.

ED: Yes, because we kept silent, the guerrilla established himself. (The two men share a moment of silence.) What are the authorities saying about what is happening?

O: I tell you, Doctor, everyone is tight-lipped.

ED: I didn't like how they answered me. How they are not gonna tell me, knowing who I am and that I have fought and I know the situation? Things are getting bad. People are content because they killed a few sneak thieves, but that's how it starts. We'll end up in the hands of the Oficina de Envigado,[12] and that saddens me.

One day I spoke to one of the commanders, and he told me that they are not asking for money from anyone because they are well financed. The boss sends us money from Medellín, he told me.

O: So what are they up to?

ED: Why are the police not able to vanquish them?

O: I tell you, everyone is keeping quiet. [During a meeting I and others had with the police,] I asked the police commander, "Why are we not forming an association, a self-defense group?" And the guy told me, "It's not allowed." "How come it's not possible? Why can't we go around with cell phones and call when we see something?"

ED: Son of a bitch!

O: Well, [one of us] stood up during the meeting and said to the officer, "But then we call you and you don't show up." Twenty days ago, I called the police in the evening because a van had entered a farm. It took them forever to come. I didn't see the van coming back. The police arrived on a motorbike, entered, and then came out saying that they didn't see any-thing and left.

ED (STATING THE OBVIOUS): They gave [the police] money.

O: Exactly. And the police commander didn't know what to say. "That's why we preferred the self-defense groups," I told him. (Silence between the two men: they were worried about the present, and were reminiscing about the past.)

O: It would be sad if we end up like in the past, with everyone holding their tongue.

That morning, at the farm of El Doctor, he and his associate had recalled the past, wrapped in memories they described as glorious and heroic but sani-tized of their brutality, their oppression, their massacres, disappearances, and tortures. They were proud for having cleansed a territory once infested by Communists and armed insurgents, pleased that they had been a counterin-surgency bastion, mindful of the results achieved, and forgetful of the excesses of history. Likewise, they worried about the present, about a con-tinuing cycle of suffering, pain, and violence, about the enduring unwilling-ness and ineffectiveness of the state, and about those first black birds that foretold a regression into the nightmarish past. Past and present weaved together in their accounts, shaped by selective memories of what had worked for them yesterday and by the desire to revive old patterns to fight new worries. And yet, in this eternal recurrence were planted the seeds of an imagined utopian future, which awakened the wish and will to make it real, to perpetuate rather than interrupt discourses of violence and terror.

Fragments from the
Shadows of War

Who are the members of the paramilitaries? Who are these men—and some women—who joined the death squads and did the torturing and the killing? Long before I had the opportunity to sit down with some of them, to look them in the eyes and listen to their stories, I had encountered them in the narrations of their victims. Each narration strengthened the image of the paramilitaries as endowed with monstrosity, inhumanity, and savagery— werewolves who dismembered bodies and eviscerated women's wombs. These were people who had often turned against their own communities.

Like poisonous snakes hidden in the grass, Colombian paramilitaries have dwelled among the inhabitants of towns and neighborhoods, establishing a perverse intimacy with their prey and yet cut off from their own communi- ties, which they terrorized while getting in return submission, respect, and a twisted form of envy. The tales shared by paramilitaries' victims were about men in military fatigues, their faces covered by cloaks, embracing dreadful machine guns. "They are happy when they see blood," one displaced woman told me. "I was told (I never saw him personally) that there was a huge and muscular black guy, with a big scar running down his left cheek—another woman told me [about him]. The paramilitaries had displaced him from a town in Eastern Antioquia inhabited on the whole by white people—and he was happy to watch people dying. These were the kind of men who did the killing." There are larger historical and material forces investing the bodies of the members of paramilitary death squads, who, often for survival or for a taste of privilege and power, have become the conductors of absolute fear and the mediators of widespread terror.

In this chapter, I present abridged versions of three life histories that I recorded in Colombia between 2003 and 2005. These are the stories of three men who joined the paramilitaries at different times and who performed different functions and responsibilities within their organizations. What they share, though, is that they all devised death and torture, and yet their lives arose from the disorder that was encircling, unwinding, and unhinging them. From their at times contradictory testimonies, beyond their justification and rationalization of lives spent as violent workers, also emerged pleasures, fantasies, and excitement about a violence that has become an end in itself.

JORGE ANDRÉS

I met Jorge Andrés by chance on a late afternoon in March 2004, in the office of the Peace and Reconciliation Program of the city of Medellín.[1] I had just asked the director of the demobilization and reintegration program to assist me in approaching former members of the Cacique Nutibara paramilitary bloc.[2] Walking out of his office, we ran into a young man in his midtwenties waiting for his turn to be attended by a social worker. Like other paramilitaries I had observed around the office, he had a military haircut and was wearing sneakers, blue jeans, and a short-sleeved white T-shirt. He looked pale, hollow, and excessively thin, and he had a dead smile. His arms hung along his body like tired lianas. In his right hand he held a softly swollen black trash bag. He explained to the director that in the shelter where he was hosted, there were demobilized members of both the ELN and the FARC guerrillas, and he could not remain there. "I'd be just killed," he complained. The director looked at him with compassion.

Jorge Andrés nodded in agreement but without enthusiasm when I asked him for an interview. In order for us to have a quiet conversation, the director offered his office. I took out my notebook and recorder, and he closed the door behind him as he left. We were now alone. Mute and with a lost look, Jorge Andrés was waiting for my questions like a criminal still numbed by his sudden arrest and awaiting a police officer's interrogation.

I started the interview with a seemingly innocuous question, asking Jorge Andrés to tell me something about his family. He did not look up, and his shoulders began to shake. He broke down in sobs, his eyes reddened, and tears left long, dark marks along his cheeks. I was not ready to see a paramilitary weeping and overwhelmed by anguish. "I'm missing my mom," he sobbed at one point, the words coming in broken syllables. At a loss, I did not know how to react. Slowly I left my seat, walked out of the director's office, and asked the first employee I ran into for a glass of water and napkins.

I presumed Jorge Andrés had been a member of the Cacique Nutibara paramilitary group, but I did not know what that experience had been like for him. I had no insight into the role he had played, the orders he had carried out, or where and for how long he had been a combatant for the paramilitary group. Recalling the horrifying deeds that I had heard about from paramilitary victims, I wondered if Jorge Andrés had carried out massacres, if he had tortured and disappeared people, and if he had ever crossed paths with the victims I had met. At that time, looking at him sobbing, a man without consolation, it seemed unbelievable he was an assassin. In him, I could detect no monstrous trait. Every part of him was so human.

As if unpacking his misery, Jorge Andrés opened the trash bag and listed its humble items. A couple of T-shirts, some underwear, and a toothbrush were all of his possessions. Still sobbing, he said he was left with nothing in life—few belongings and no love. For some, I considered, the demobilization from an armed group imposed by their commanders was a hard awakening and a sinking into nightmare. While their victims' trauma was the product of an encounter with the paramilitary, for combatants such as Jorge Andrés, the upheaval was having to leave behind a previous life. It was an experience of dispossession, the stripping away of identity, and a blow to their self-image and their conception of their place in this world. Like a wanderer who lost his way, they were now disoriented, plunged into darkness. Their life as paramilitaries had given them a sense of belonging and a purpose; now they were standing naked in the cold. Holding his forehead in the palms of his hands, Jorge Andrés found no end to his tears.

I closed my notebook and put away the recorder. There was no point in trying to elicit from him any answers to my questions, whose number and intensity after that scene could only grow. How did Jorge Andrés get to this point? How does someone become a paramilitary? And under what circumstances? Was it his decision, or was he somehow forced into the organization? What did being a paramilitary mean to him? And what brought his leaders to decide to demobilize, especially considering that the paramilitary did so at the peak of their dominance in vast regions of Colombia? How did Jorge Andrés see his future in a country where the armed conflict was still going on? But one question was prodding at me with increasing insistence: How similar or dissimilar was Jorge Andrés's biography from those of paramilitary victims? Somehow, his disheartened cry questioned the clear boundary separating victims and victimizers, and for me on that afternoon, the line became thinner and thinner, and—to my unease—almost blurred.

I invited Jorge Andrés to come to the friends' apartment where I was staying in Medellín. This time he nodded in agreement with more confidence, as if someone had thrown him a lifeline. Outside, as we crossed the large square in front of the city hall building, I noticed that Jorge Andrés was keeping slightly behind me, almost in a servile attitude, like a dog follows the steps of his owner, bound by fidelity and a leash. It felt uncomfortable, as it exposed a power relationship between the two of us. If it was not necessarily friendship and love that glued paramilitary members to their commanders, it was probably a sense of belonging, and even more their need for it. I perceived an ancestral habitus that marks the dependency between foreigners and natives, conquerors and the conquered, Spaniards and the colonized, centers of power and peripheries. This was not exclusively a top-down relation, but also one of strategic circularity and reciprocity, since through his attitude the subjugated, aware of his condition, could obtain some services and, at times, negotiate access to small benefits.

At my friends' apartment, Jorge Andrés was smiling. After taking a shower, he ate rice and steak with gusto. It had been three days, he revealed, since he had last had a meal. Unaware that a particle of the Colombian armed conflict and its drama had entered their home, my friends were giving me interrogatory looks, wondering who the young man was. I would not tell them until later, and we gave shelter to Jorge Andrés for a few days. In the meantime, I observed—and enjoyed—the smile that for quick instants appeared on Jorge Andrés's face. There was something of the child in that smile, which made him look all too human.

At night, we sat down in the room that my friends had prepared for him. From my bag, I took out my notebook and recorder. Jorge Andrés started to share his life experience with me, interrupted at times by sobs, glasses of water, and handkerchiefs.

When I was still in the womb of my mother, I lost my father. We were four little sisters and brothers. My mother was in too much pain because my father hadn't left anything for us. We had nothing. We lived as everyone else. My mom was a helper, doing laundry and cleaning so that we could have some food on the table. My brothers and I went to school with empty stomachs. When we came back home, we found a little bit of rice. Sometimes we had to wait for our mom [to come home with some money], who then sent us for some milk or something to eat.

While we were growing up, my oldest brother met a man who gave the impression of being a very good person. But the guy abused my older brother, who was still a teenager at the time, and the man told stuff to my brother so that he'd stay with him. I wasn't aware of what was going on, but from this moment on my brother started bringing money home. My mom had some relief when one of our uncles, who was a carpenter, said he wanted to help us. I didn't know so many things were going on, but when I began to use reason, I realized that my uncle mistreated my mom and seduced her until she became pregnant with my sister. My uncle humiliated my mom a lot because when she would get a job, he would ask her for the money to buy things for himself. He punished us as if he were the father.

Later, we grew up and my mother preferred to forget him. That's when my mother received a visit from one of my aunts. [My aunt] told her that [where she lived] there was a man, her brother-in-law, who wanted to meet my mom to see if they could get married. *Mi mamá le comió todo el cuento* [my mom believed the whole story], and she went there with us. When we got there, we realized what was going on, that we were going to live with a man on a farm. My brothers preferred to go back to Medellín, so my brother went back there while we remained in Fenicia, in the municipality of Riofrío.[3]

Whenever he felt like it, the man had fights with my mother and [eventually] abandoned her. I had to work. I was making like 800 pesos [US$0.50] a day. That is basically nothing. At the time that I was a child, I was nothing. But that [money] helped us. [He pauses, choking and trying not to cry.] And so we ate.

The years passed by. My brothers were growing up. One of them, very talented, learned to butcher and helped this guy [I told you about before]. So he took the other two brothers with him. [My brothers] learned how to butcher, and they began to collaborate there. But I didn't know that this man was going to abuse my brothers.

Years passed by. In 1990, I moved from Fenicia to Medellín, and I was very happy [he sighs] . . . because my brother was working in a butcher shop. So when I went [back] to Fenicia, I asked my mother, "Why don't we . . . [His voice cracks.] . . . Why didn't we go to Medellín?"

She said, "Okay, let's go there, but let's go to the village where I was born." That's the village of Támesis, which is very close by [to Medellín] [now sobbing]. And the day after we unloaded the few things we brought with us, the news reached us that they had killed one of my brothers and almost killed the other. This was very difficult. In 1990, they killed one of my brothers, and in 1994, they killed the other brother, the butcher.

The fact is that the popular militias had arrived in the sector where we lived, in the San Javier barrio of the Comuna 13[4] in Medellín. This was about in 1988 or 1989. They arrived with their own ideology. The militias don't like the bourgeoisie. The bourgeoisie for them are those who have more money to live. For them, everyone in the world has to be the same. They also say that this country has to be free, and that we shouldn't live as slaves to the gringos; that the only thing we own is the land, we need to be free, and that for this reason we have to fight.

A man [from the militia] who arrived [in our neighborhood] was a good man, and he asked my brothers to work for him. My brothers, seeing that he was a good man, went with him. They told me there was a club where he often invited them where there were women doing striptease, and that this man offered [the women] to them so they could have fun. That's how they recruited all the people in the barrios. This man managed the entire city. All of Medellín feared him.

I had a friend called Norberto. He managed some bodegas. He was a good friend of our family. He was killed because he didn't pay the *vacuna* [protection money]. Because we were very young, we lived in hiding from these people because they were recruiting. I saw that the nephew of this man had invited several of my friends. My friends said they were invited to parties. That was so that people would stay on his side, and it's how he bought all the people. The militias there were called to meetings. Since my brothers at some point didn't show up anymore, because they didn't want to collaborate with the cause, the militias decided to kill them. My brothers never liked the militias because they didn't have any ideology. Instead they preferred to focus on their future, children, mother, and siblings. But all of this vanished. We remained without anything, no help, nothing. We had to beg to pay for my brother's funeral [sobbing].

They killed many I knew. They killed almost two generations of people I knew. Almost all of them are dead. Of all the friends I had, only the memories are left. Now that these people [the paramilitaries] are there, there are not many enemies around. What pains me most is that we never could do anything about it. No one denounced these people. Nobody said anything. It was enough that they said they were militias, and that was it. This is how my own vendetta against the guerrillas grew in me, and that's why I went with the self-defense groups.

They hadn't killed my third brother yet when I went with the army. That was July 1995. Of all my brothers, I am the only one who went. I went with great motivation, as they say; I saw that I could get the discharge document. So I tried to behave well, like any of the soldiers there. In the army they taught us how to fight against the guerrillas. We were trained in the use of explosives and in counterguerrilla tactics, which were about how to detain and destroy the enemy. I remember one day when we took the Bogotá-Medellín freeway. At the time, we were guarding a bridge near Puerto Berrío. One day, we saw a suspect car. When we went to see the car, we realized it was full of explosives. They started to shoot at us. The guerrillas were fighting us from a hill. They screamed at us, they insulted us, and they ran away. Our commanders deactivated the bomb and we avoided the worst. Another time, there was shooting at our base. It was the base of Bocas del Cará in the Middle Magdalena. We were there one night when our commander was inspecting us, and we realized the guerrillas were surrounding us, coming from the river. They started shooting at us, screaming, insulting: "Son of bitches, *patiamarrados,* sold out...!"

Many [soldiers] became crazy. One becomes crazy because of all the problems. Many remained in psychiatric care; others wanted to commit suicide. I ended military service when [guerrillas] killed my brother. I received an honorable discharge, but I entered a different world because I didn't have any family anymore.

I went back to Medellín, where I had a girlfriend, who in those days was the only one who would comfort me. My mom loved me very much, but she was with my sister and the husband who kept abusing her. I began to work with a man from Venezuela. I learned to work for the set-ups at the Exhibition Palace. I trusted this man because he was an unconditional friend who had just appeared on my horizon. But he never paid me. At home, they asked because I had been working for so long without getting any money. Sometimes I got money, but it was for the bus, or he was giving me a few thousand pesos. But he told me he didn't have to pay me because he had helped me a lot. I had a very hard time.

I left him without telling him anything because at that time, I had the support of my girl. But [her parents] were not happy with this because they wanted me to contribute like everyone else. They said I was spending the money with another woman, but I didn't have anyone else—I was only with my woman, and I was working. I found another job, as an assistant to a painter. The painter fell ill and I had to paint until an accident happened, and they didn't call me back. I started looking for another job, and I was handing out flyers in order to help my wife [although they had not yet married]. Since this was only a temporary job, it ended.

I went to a village to work as a peasant. When they sent me away from one farm, I went to a different one. I worked collecting coffee, and then I came back to Medellín. Here I didn't have a job. I looked for an uncle who worked as a carpenter, and he told me he thought that I had gone with the guerrillas or with the *paras* and asked why didn't I think of joining them. I thanked him, and I never called him back, nor did I see him for years. But what he had suggested had entered my head, and so I started making friends.

It was a woman who told me that there was a man who was recruiting for the self-defense groups. I asked her to help me. She helped me with this man from the self-defense group. A guy on a motorbike appeared and told me that later he would come and get me. But they caught this man, and so I didn't have anyone with whom to work. One more time I had to ask for hospitality while I was waiting to start working with the self-defense groups.

The day I joined the self-defense groups, I went with a man who introduced me to [the paramilitaries of] the Bloque Cárdenas.[5] I arrived with the recommendation of someone very influential there. That's the only way one can get there with some peace of mind. They asked me what I was doing, and I told them that I was not doing anything and that I was a reservist. One man told me, "Okay, here we are going to work. Here you follow orders like in the army. That's why I like soldiers. If you follow the orders, there will be no problems. Here, if you smoke marijuana or you like to steal, we'll kill you. Now you know how things are here. If you like you can stay, or if you prefer you can leave."

But I knew that once you got there you could not turn back, plus I needed the job because I didn't have a place to sleep or anything to eat. I received the weaponry of a paramilitary whom they had killed in those days. They gave me a rifle, a machine gun, a vest, a backpack with food, six magazines, eight hundred projectiles, a hammock, and a mosquito net. In addition, they gave us meals for fifteen days, which we had to carry in the backpack. The ordinary pay was 400,000 pesos [about US$200 a month]. I don't think there is anyone in the self-defense groups who has lots of money. They are all there to do a job, to free the country so that people can work. My dad died when I was a baby, and he didn't leave anything. We never had anything. So the only option I had in life was to go where they accepted me as I am, just with the clothes I wore and nothing else, without a cent. I was there, available to do whatever they asked me to do. They welcomed me, and while I was there, I was fine. So I took up the weapon and I started to work.

The drill is almost a military one. One has to march, do push-ups, jumps, and shooting training. If you don't know how to handle a rifle, they teach you to load it and unload it. They also teach you why we are fighting, which is our cause, that we want a country with no violence, without anyone humiliating the entire country. The guerrillas took it upon themselves to humiliate and abuse everyone, and that's why the guerrillas have so little support now. Those who still support them do so because they were born with them. Many have already realized that it is not convenient to be with the guerrillas because we cannot all be the same. If there are no more business owners, who will provide jobs? If you leave business owners alone, they will provide jobs to us. They will employ the father, the mother, and so on.

Months passed by. When the army went in one direction, we had to leave. When the guerrillas were in a certain area, we had to fight them, and so one is always apprehensive, waiting to be attacked or waiting to attack. Many times, my companions got scared because they heard noises that they were not accustomed to. We caught many guerrillas who had infiltrated the cities. There were many guerrillas there, and so we had to go after them: the *muchachos* [self-defense members]. . . . The guys interrogated them, and many volunteered to kill them.

One time, they surrounded us, and they killed half of our counterguerrilla squad because of our commander's ill-designed operation. They caught him alive, chopped his feet off before the eyes of his friends, beheaded him, and chopped him up while others were captured and left there. They tortured them and, while they were still alive, chopped parts off their bodies. When they were going to kill them, they didn't shoot them but first tortured them; they died because of the pain and the lost blood. The most horrible thing was when we had to pick up several of our companions who were all torn apart, chopped up, riddled with bullets, and torn apart by grenades. We had to collect them in hammocks and take them from one place to another far away.

In the sector where we were, we listened to the radio broadcasts of the guerrillas. There is a radio station at the border between Colombia and Panama. We listened to the voice of the revolution of the Bolívarian guerrillas. There we listened when they announced that they had captured paramilitaries and soldiers—I don't know how many—and that they had recovered weapons and eliminated several enemies.

When I joined the self-defense group, the first operations were in Dabeiba[6] because there the guerrillas were at home. There was a neighborhood occupied by them. We had to do intelligence to be able to get the guerrillas out of there. We did intelligence the way we had learned from the army and as the paramilitaries had taught us, and so with great skill we captured several guerrillas. We were talking to the women and with all the men. We entered and brought them *panela*,[7] some food, because there people are very hungry. This way people got accustomed to us. We took pictures with them. Often they sent us the kids to give them something to eat.

We observed, we reported back, and the commanders decided what to do. They decided who was a guerrilla, but they also knew that because of evidence; we knew a certain person was a guerrilla. A guerrilla is easy to distinguish. When a guerrilla calls you, he addresses you as "colleague" or "companion" because [this language] is ingrained in them. It's like us, who call one another "lance" instead of "soldier." That's why they fall most of the time. So we enter [into a neighborhood] and we investigate. We realize [who is a guerrilla] because most of the time, these individuals change their clothing and go out at night. During the day, they are peasants, while at night they dress like guerrillas to go abuse people. This is how we realize who is who. We take pictures and we meet with them, without asking questions directly but rather by winning over their friendship. That's how we get them in our pocket. We don't ask them anything in return—we only give them something to eat. And each one of them surrendered because they realized we were not bad people— we really wanted to do something [positive] for the country. Other guerrillas were embedded in their ideology and wanted to fight against us and harm us.

Many of the guerrillas we caught told us that on that same night they were going to kill us, they had already told all their companions that we were giving them food, that they were aware who we were. We kept catching guerrillas and killing them. Eventually, the village of Dabeiba lived in peace. People farmed strawberries and fruit, and the village is now called the gate to Urabá because it's the beginning of this area. People don't want to be with any of the armed groups there. When we got there, everyone wanted to join the self-defense groups. Since these people were killing us and dismembering us, we did the same when necessary. But we didn't torture anyone. We interrogated them. It's more like therapy. One gives them something to eat and some water because when one captures one of these [guerrillas], you see they are very thin, because that's how you are when you are close to death. They feel thin, like they were not in the world—like if they didn't have feelings—and so you know something is going to happen. We didn't torture them . . . *sino que le damos psicología* [we manipulated them].

Several of our commanders were former guerrillas, and they surrounded the battlefield. They gave themselves up with all their weapons, and we welcomed them into the organization. We took their weapons away and gave them our own weapons. We treated them as ours. Eventually, they became very committed, and they want to get rid of the guerrillas.

I remember one guerrilla in particular. He was black. He was placing land mines against us. We caught him, and he said he was not a guerrilla, that he had fought with his woman and that he was there wandering. We did a thorough investigation. We realized he was a guerrilla, and we were going to take him to a commander for interrogation, but since he tried to escape, we killed him. They killed him. This is the last guerrilla I saw being killed.

When a guerrilla gets captured, we do an investigation. First we treat him well, we give him something to eat, we talk to him, and if he wants to collaborate and wants to stay with us, we give him an opportunity. Of course, we ourselves are the ones doing the investigation of the guerrillas who want to come work with us. They see the chance of a better life, and they become paramilitary since the guerrillas tell them that if they cross over, they will die together with their families. They find refuge with us, and they send their parents to a different place with the money they get from the paramilitaries, so the families are displaced to the cities. And so people who don't know how to cross a street because they fear the cars have to escape and go to the city. But many of them don't care about the paramilitaries, or about life for that matter. They only care about serving the people because of the manipulation to which they are subjected every day.

At the beginning, we in the self-defense groups abused people a lot because at the time, the guerrillas were just everywhere. We were behaving very badly because there were lots of people who liked the guerrillas. But now this has changed. For example, we don't kill any more if someone gives food to the guerrillas, unless he does so in front of our eyes. For example, if someone who has two children buys food for ten people, we know he is providing food to the guerrillas, and therefore I would make him a military target. But now, if someone is forced by the guerrillas to collaborate, we don't make him a military target anymore.

After working for a while, they told me I was a good paramilitary. They assigned me to a different group, a counterguerrilla bloc that was arriving in that area. So I went to a different area of Urabá. There one did not see anything but mountains everywhere, swamps, large rivers, and people sick with *paludismo* [similar to malaria]. I saw men without feet because of the land mines used by the guerrillas.

As a paramilitary, I began working very diligently, carrying out orders, and so time passed by. My work in general was to be a sentinel, prepare food, and walk a lot. Every day, we walked about four to six kilometers [two and a half to three and a half miles]; we stopped here and there, had some breakfast, and then we kept walking. When we arrived at a different place, we had lunch, and we kept walking until it was dark. We were between four and six hundred, walking along a path or in the mountains.

When I got sick, I decided to change my life and return to Medellín. I was sick with *paludismo,* which is something one gets because of too many mosquitos and from drinking dirty water. We didn't know how to purify the water. You start getting a high fever and feeling pain in the bones, and then you tremble when you lie down. You get a very strong tachycardia, and this lasts for days. The trembling in the body is unbearable. You don't want to eat, and you get dehydrated.

In Medellín, I saw again the friends whom I had left. Here I had many to greet, and they had informed me, even before I came from Dabeiba, that the Cacique Nutibara bloc was here. I told [the Cacique Nutibara] that I was coming from the mountains and that I was a paramilitary. They recruited me, and I started working in the Comuna 13.

A *comuna* is made up of several neighborhoods, and in each neighborhood, there is a self-defense group. These groups were made up of ten to twenty kids—young people from the same barrio who belonged to a gang and were happy to be with us. Since we didn't display our arms or give any reason for people to say anything, they adjusted to us and we to them so that we were together. In a *comuna,* each barrio has a commandant. They put a person in charge who knows how to manage people and who is not abusive so that he can make sure the only thing the kids do is defend their barrio. We tried to control people so that they didn't kill each other, so that they didn't have problems.

At the time, the Frank gang were still fighting. They were guerrillas and vandals who were afflicting the population. Everyone had to buy at the granary owned by the guerrillas because whoever did not became a military target. If someone wanted to build a house, they had to go to their warehouse. They came and imposed extortion and protection money on shops. Nobody progressed, and everyone lived in poverty. When they were crazy, they abused the girls. They abused women a lot.

The self-defense groups were the opposite of these people [the guerrillas]. We realized that, and so we led operations until we expelled the guerrillas from there. In the sector where I was, we had to expel people who were guerrillas. Many escaped, others were killed, and we remained with their belongings in the homes that they had previously occupied. I was in a large two-floor apartment. It had belonged to a guerrilla, and that's where the guerrilla died. The guerrillas had these homes that they had taken from people. They furnished them, put everything in, and had parties every night. We were not like that. We had our beds there, a jacket, a change of clothes, and nothing more. We didn't do *farras*—parties to get drunk. We occupied these homes that belonged to the guerrillas, and it was there that we formed a group. We had our base, like a command post, where there had been guerrillas before.

With respect to the Orión Operation[8] in the Comuna 13, this never happened. I mean, you always had these groups sent by the government to fight against the guerrillas, but you didn't recognize the guerrillas or the paramilitary, or the bad or the good; all people are the same. When [the government] arrived, people all hid the weapons in hideouts so that the government would never really be able to fight against these people. Sometimes they even passed by the hideouts; they got to their homes, saw a few people there. But when we entered, we expelled all those people, searched for the hideouts with weapons, with ammunition, with guerrilla flyers, with lots of stuff. Neither the army nor government groups were capable of doing this because they needed a warrant and permission to break in.

When I arrived there, they told me that my target was to [eliminate] what was left of La Banda Frank [the Frank gang]. "Frank" [who used only one name] was not there anymore; they had already annihilated a lot of his people, but some were still left. So we had to fight against them on the lower side of the *comuna*. We already had the top under our control, so we started to expel people who did damage and belonged to the guerrillas. I remember once, there were four individuals in an apartment and they didn't want to leave. They started to shoot like crazy. We fired back until they were all dead. Then we sent in someone to throw the bodies away. They disposed of them in the garbage or in the river, or in some other place where no one could find them.

Once we had taken over an area, we did not go after anyone, nor did we do anything. We were there to guard the barrio. We were going around in civilian clothes, and if we saw anything strange, we verified what was going on and if the thing could be settled or not. If a man didn't want to pay back [borrowed money], we told him he had to do so because those people needed money, too. If that person was a decent man, we would help him. There were men who did wrong, and we did not kill them but told them to leave and search for a different place to live. So people preferred to leave. We always talked to them so that people could get the message, because we didn't like to be bad and preferred that they collaborate us.

We had women coming to us who told us, "See, my husband is hitting me, can you please help me because I don't want to live with him anymore?" Or they said, "I want to live with him, but tell him to leave us in peace, not to abuse us." So we went and spoke to people and told them that if they didn't love their family or if they were tired of them, they should not harass them but go someplace else. Since we experienced a hard time in our own homes, we didn't want other people to go through the same experiences we had— that people harass you without being able to say a word.

People respected us a lot. There were many lovely women who told us, "My son, if you don't have someone doing your laundry, I can do your laundry. I will do it at a cheap price for you." Since they knew we had money, we helped them and gave them our laundry. Many times, we were tired of eating the same thing for breakfast, and so we bought breakfast someplace else.

The worst I saw is [one of my] companions who went crazy because when the militias were present, there was a guy who had abused [my friend] a lot when he was still a child and had killed some of his relatives. So, when we conquered the territory, this guy was captured. My companion hated the guy so much that he dragged him across the entire barrio while he was tied to a horse. He didn't kill him at once; while he was dragging him, the guy was still moving a bit, and then when he was done dragging him, [my companion] killed him. This for me was very impressive.

At that time, since we belonged to the Cacique Nutibara, we had to fight against a different paramilitary group, the Bloque Metro.[9] The commander of this bloc didn't behave correctly and preferred to run away with the money and abandon his guys. They turned against the people, practicing extortion, the same as the guerrillas. That's when the Bloque Metro fell apart.

We heard about the demobilization when one of our commanders told us that our commandant, Adolfo Paz [drug kingpin Don Berna], had sent a communication to one of our commanders to be responsible for the entire bloc. [Paz] showed his face on television and asked everyone to reach a peace agreement, and then the [government's] peace commissioner spoke with him.

[Our leaders] assembled us in different locations, not just in one place, so that we were not too many at once. They told us that we had to collaborate, that they were going to give us jobs, that we would be able to keep living in our neighborhoods like good people not living in conflict, without warrants and with good jobs.

When we had started working up there, in the Comuna 13, we had taken the house of guerrillas to live there. We had not been lacking food, because the organization would provide it to us. They had been giving us money on a regular basis, and we didn't have problems with anybody. Now instead, since they had taken away everything from us, we were left without money or a home, and we didn't have the opportunity to follow the organization because now whoever was part of a self-defense group became a military target and could be imprisoned or killed.

I liked it very much when I received my salary [before demobilization], partly yes, because you get into things and then you start liking it. Many at first like it when they have weapons, but when you are in the army, you realize that weapons are neither important nor essential. Most everything else both I and the other kids were part of is because it represented a job opportunity and survival. Now we had no money, nowhere to live, and only worries, because we continued to have the same expenses, the same stuff.

I see my future as I saw it when I was a child, a teenager, and now an adult. I have no future because I never had opportunities. I just don't have them. If I'm alive, it is because I hid, because I put myself in a position so that I would not be hungry or die at the hands of the state or society. I am a man who, at the end of the day, has repressed dreams. For example, I'd like to finish my studies. I can never do that. One thinks of all of this. There is no future.

Throughout my fieldwork, I remained in contact with Jorge Andrés. At one point, he shared a small and shabby room in the upper hills of Medellín with his girlfriend, who had just given birth to their son. Jorge Andrés was complaining that despite the fact that he was demobilized, his former commanders were still counting on him for vigilante work and inviting him for the occasional beating up of some petty thief. Jorge Andrés's story, a daily struggle for survival and dignity, made me recall those Auschwitz prisoners who, in the interpretation provided by Primo Levi, made up a hybrid class of people who "were poor devils like ourselves, who worked full time like everyone else but who for an extra half-liter of soup were willing to carry out these and other 'tertiary' functions" (1989, 44). Last I heard, his girlfriend had left Jorge Andrés to escape his beatings, taking their son with her.

LUNA

It was a friend and social worker who introduced me to Luna during my stay in Medellín in the summer of 2005. At the time, Luna was a demobilized paramilitary and, with another former combatant, he was staying at my friend's apartment for a few days, sharing her family's life. The first image of Luna I saw was him sitting on the floor of the apartment's terrace, back against the wall and playing with a toy car with my friend's ten-year-old son. I knew Luna had joined the paramilitaries in his early teens, and I wondered if this image was like one of his lost childhood. I wondered, too, as Georges Bataille suggested, that if in the pleasure of inflicting death and torture, there is also a quality of childhood, of a life "unbounded by civilized properties" (2004, 33). Later the two played with a kite, and I joined in their attempt to fly it high into the blue sky of Medellín. I wondered if Luna was somehow mirroring himself in the restless kite, which tried to climb the height of heaven, an impossible dream because of the thin and almost invisible nylon string binding it to the earth. In the days we spent together, I recognized Luna's struggle to move from a life engraved by violence to some sort of imagined good life. In his words, there was often nostalgia for the known world of weapons and violence, and illusions about and hope for the unknown life of an (im)possible future. But wasn't this search for a good life fueled by the desire and will that always had propelled Luna's life? Wasn't Luna's life the product of what Lauren Berlant (2011) defined as cruel optimism?

I met Luna for the last time in July 2006 in a small, poverty-ridden town in Northern Antioquia. He had abandoned the demobilization and reintegration program and was now back in the cocaine business (as I will detail in chapter 4), following his dreams, fantasies, and passions, always trying to escape and overcome a life of marginality that he, paradoxically given his violence, helped to perpetuate and deepen:

> My family was quite split, and that was because of my father. You know how in the past they liked alcohol a lot and a lot of stuff gets into your mind, strange ideas, because if your dad goes to the town and he starts drinking on a Thursday and comes back the following Tuesday and there is no food at home, that's very difficult, especially when there is no reason for it. In fact, I thank God my grandfather had left a huge inheritance to my father, a great ranch, but my dad didn't do much. My dad was getting drunk and hit my mother. We were very small, but one remembers these things. One day he was drunk, and I was already with the [paramilitary] group, and so I took out the gun and put it against his head and told him that if he was going to hit my mother, I was going to kill him. He left, and since that day we have not spoken. One remembers all of this and grows up with lots of resentment.
>
> We were seven kids, four girls and three boys. The girls were the first to leave, but my brothers left home when they were still pretty young. I left home when I was eight years old. At first we went to Urabá because my uncle was one of the founders of the EPL[10] [the Ejército Popular de Liberación guerrillas], and later he started working with the self-defense groups. He was my father's brother. When the parents of my father died, my father was adopted by my uncle's family. My uncle, since he was young, liked the violence. Beginning when he was young, he was with the guerrillas. My cousins on my father's side are all members of the guerrillas as well. My other brothers are in the military. My family is very much a fruit salad: We have guerrillas, *paracos* [paramilitary members], soldiers. It's a very split family. We never could have a family reunion. It's a family where we don't like one another very much.

I asked him, "How do you explain that your family members ended up in different and opposed armed groups?" He replied:

Because of the areas: [one group was] living in an area dominated by the guerrillas, and that's all there was, so they chose the guerrillas. We lived in an area dominated by the self-defense groups, and therefore when my uncle was arrested, he was confined in the high-security prison of Itagüí. When he got out, he joined the paramilitaries. *Fue la misma ley que lo sacó* [It was the same state officials who let him go].

"Why did he switch from being a guerrilla leader to being a paramilitary?" I asked.

Because they made him a better offer. When he was arrested, many of the EPL took their support away. That's what happens when you get arrested. But the paramilitaries, seeing that he was a good man, started helping him to see if they could get him out. When he got out, he did not continue with the EPL, *sino que se voltió* [he flipped] because they gave him better chances. He arrived at home escorted by the Sijin [law enforcement agency]. From there, he went to a ranch when Carlos [Castaño] arrived, and they put him in charge of the finances. From there, he made a career in the Bananero paramilitary group. He was very inflexible. If someone messed with us, he would kill him, and it didn't matter if it was a family member. On December 31, 1999, he killed the husband of my sister. He didn't do anything particularly bad and was killed. We found him after two days, and we were not able to recognize him except for a tattoo of a Virgin Mary that he had on his chest. [My uncle] was a very cruel man.

When we lived in Urabá, we had to run away because the people of the EPL were going to kill us all. We had to leave and leave everything behind. My sister, one of the eldest, went to live with one of my uncle's workers, and that's when I started to like weapons. I lived with them; I started liking arms, and I started the thing with the groups. I preferred the right-wing [groups] because of the ideals they were working for, because if the guerrillas were going to continue with their ideals, everyone would have just left. I liked the ideals they had initially, but the ideals changed a lot. Do you know what their ideals are?

"Tell me," I replied.

To help peasants a lot. They worked above all to help peasants, which is also how the AUC [Autodefensas Unidas de Colombia] begun. They had lots of good stuff. There were not a lot of massacres. It was a very good group when they started. But today no group is good. They don't care anymore about their members, but all they are interested in is the weaponry and land, which is money. The more villages you have, which means you own land, the more money you have, and thus the ideals were already gone and they were interested very little in the peasants.

Being part of a self-defense group is like a job. Most of the people take it as a job option. For others, it's ingrained in them. Some join for a personal cause, others for family reasons. One's childhood can be very tough. There are young men who don't want to get orders from their family. The father might tell him he has to study, and he doesn't want to, and so the father tells him he has to leave home and so the kid joins the group. There are many reasons to join, but the majority do it because it's a job. There is much unemployment in the country. In my case, I was just born for it. For me, the group represented everything. It was my life. I was born for it. I liked very much to be part of it, and it has been tough to have to get out of it.

I started very young. When I was a child, I wanted to be a sacristan. I was part of a group in my parish. I was twelve years old when I started working with the [armed] groups. It was in 1994, I believe. The massacres in Urabá had begun, and I was going everywhere with my brother-in-law. I drove the bike, and he did the killing. He was giving me the *liga* [payment]: "Ah! We have to kill so-and-so at that location." I would go there with the motorbike and wait for him, and when I saw him coming I would drive up to him. Once he killed the guy, he would get on the bike behind me, and I left with him. That's how we were working.

I wasn't part of any group, but I was smeared, and in 1994 or 1995, I started being part of the [paramilitary] group. I started in Urabá as a *urbano* [a para-military member working in urban areas], working in [social] cleansing. It is like being a hitman, but at the same time you are part of a group. And the people in a town collaborate with you. You make them your friends, you turn them into a support for the group. You help the population, and the people are like an arm of the organization, which you use to ask favors. It was not out of the ordinary that in December the *patrón* would arrive with five trucks of livestock so people could have a barbecue. These are details that "make you fall in love," as the people said. These are nice gestures that the groups have. But they have other details that are very tough, like when they arrive in an area, and to gain respect you have to kill; you have to penetrate [the area] by killing. Urabá, the banana area, is one of the areas where they killed the highest number of civilians. They paid you *bonificación* [a bonus according to the number of people one killed]. Everything is by *bonificación*, and so, let's kill! That's how I started, killing lots of people. One had to kill a lot in Urabá, but it was a good life.

The first man I had to kill was a commander of mine. He was a very tall man. We were four bodyguards going around with him. He had an accident with a carriage driven by two elderly people. He was drunk and had injured his hand, so he took the gun and killed the two elderly people. The boss learned about what happened, and one night we had to kill him. That was the first job that I had to do, and I wasn't able to sleep for about twenty days afterwards. To pull the trigger the first time is very hard.

I worked there for one year, and then my superiors moved me out from there because they were going to kill me, and I ended up in Caucana with the

Minero [paramilitary] group.[11] I remained there for five years. It's a big, big group, and they pay very well and on time. They gave you the money in an envelope without taking away one peso. When it's payday, they call you and say that the "moral" has arrived, or the *dolorosos*. It was a very good experience because I liked arms very much. Only now have I started forgetting them. One tries to change, but it's difficult. It doesn't happen overnight but only over time, especially in my case, since I didn't have a childhood. My childhood was with weapons—that is to say, not a normal childhood where one goes to school.

While I was in Caucana, I also met my girl. I had met her when she was still a little girl in her hometown, and she didn't pay attention to me. But when I got to Caucana, I had already a rifle. Now she is twenty-three, and she has been with me in good and bad times. Now that these are bad times, she is with me anyway. She has been with me in the [paramilitary] group. She knows how to handle all kinds of weapons and knows how to drive a car and a motorbike. I taught her all of this. At times we were together, and at others we were separated. The women who are part of the groups, it's like religion: if you have a woman, you cannot lend her to anyone. She cannot be with anyone else because otherwise she will die. That is to say, if the commander realizes that the woman of a patrolman sleeps with someone else, that's a death sentence. And even you, if you have a wife and you are sleeping with another woman, that's a death sentence for you as well. [In the life of the paramilitaries,] one gets to know lots of women, and that complicates things. Women like *paracos* a lot. They go after them. I know women, prostitutes, who walked for hours to get to where we were. Because where there are *paracos,* there is money.

I remained in the Minero group for five years, and I had to fight lots of battles. It was intense. I had very tough experiences and a tough drill. For a few months, they give you a weapon of wood, and you cannot leave this piece of wood. If you lose it, they kill you. You have to stay with the same piece of wood for months, and you cannot abandon it. You have to bring it with you wherever you go. For the drills, you go to a base, and if you don't pass the tests, and they realize you are really bad, *va pal hueco de una vez* [you go six feet under]. During a training, the *patrón*—the boss—killed a kid for entering the dispensary to steal a can of tuna because he was hungry.

I remember the first combat. They sent helicopters from the army to get us and bring us to the battlefield. The first time one is in a battle, he practically doesn't fight but tries to hide himself and not be killed. It's the seniors who fight and are killed. The novice hides, and it is the senior *que tiene que meter el pecho para todos* [who has to offer his chest for everyone]. That's how I got shot in my back, during an intense fight with the FARC, which had surrounded us.

That ruined my career as well, because being with the paramilitary is like a career. You begin as a patrolman. Later, if they like you or if you are a good element, they put you in charge of a squad of ten kids, and a squad becomes like your family. Later they say, "Ah, this guy is very good." More than everything else, one manages the *bara*. The *bara* is when a commander likes you, calls you all the time, recommends you, and, through him, gives you an opportunity. He says to the *patrón,* "Hey, this guy is good, help me, and let's make him number two." The *patrón* is the one who gets the money and is the owner of the [paramilitary] bloc, and there is no way you can touch him. Once you are number two, you can be tough; you are already in a good position. The number two is in charge of forty men, whom he commands through four commanders of squads. I was commandant of the counterguerrillas.

It can be a very tough life. At times, one is patrolling and remains without food. I'm not telling you stories—sometimes we remained without food for eight or ten days. One day, they brought food for two blocs, and the commander gave food to only one of the blocs, and we remained without food. He left us to endure hunger. That's something that kills your motivation, and you even want to cry. One sees himself as very tough, but you want to cry.

The longest operation that I did lasted ten months. From the Caucana, we ended up in Yolombó.[12] It took ten months. The army collaborated a lot with us. They collaborated with us because we were the self-defense groups—that is to say, we are like the military but illegal. But we were like the army, and we worked hand in hand with the legal group. In operations against the guerrillas, if we killed ten, fifteen, or twenty men, we gave them over to the military, who in turn presented them as their accomplishment. If they were fighting and they needed backing, we provided it to them. We shared the same ideology: to fight against the guerrillas. The only difference is that we were illegal. The advantage of being illegal is that when you identify a guerrilla member you can just kill him. If, as a soldier, you capture a guerrilla and you send him to a jail, chances are that after a few days he will already be free and give you the finger. Instead, when they [the paramilitaries] capture a guerrilla member, they extract information from him and then they kill him. But it is also true that the ideology [of the paramilitaries] changes. Now the ideology is power, and it changed into [serving the interests of] narcotrafficking. The ideology that we had is over. Now there are many ideologies, and this has become nothing more than a job.

There are very good relations between the *patrones* of the army, which is the state, and that of the paramilitaries. They meet, they have their ranches, go on vacation together, and go to drink together. They have meeting places where it's safe for them to meet and nobody sees them. They have ongoing communication, even daily. For example, one can call Don Berna[13] and say, "I have my guys from the army there, and I need a guide," and so Don Berna can call the commander of that area and tell him, "Hey, get me a guide to such-and-such commander of the army who is there and in that brigade." It's very normal communication. To me, the state is a very corrupt group. The state sells you out at any price.

That operation in Caucana didn't go too well. We lost rifles and men. We attacked a guerrilla squad where there was a guerrilla woman with a baby, and in the exchange of shots, the little girl was killed. It was very tough. People say we have no heart, but that's not true. One has a heart, and often a better one than people who are not part of the group. What happens is that at times your heart becomes very hard. Because you hold a weapon in your hands, you think you are a big shot. As a patrolman, you have to follow the statutes to the letter, but as a commander, you don't follow the rules. Very few commanders follow the rules—maybe one in every hundred.

I liked our political work, and I was about to go to take a course in politics, but it didn't happen. The self-defense groups have a base in Boyacá, which is the political-military base. I was going there, because my *patrón* was going to give me the opportunity, but he was killed, and that's where my dream stopped. There are groups in which the "politician" [the paramilitary who has a political role in a given area] stays in a town and drinks, and that's it. But there are groups where the politician has to go fight to gain respect. As Don Carlos [Castaño] told us, if you want to be a man in your life, and a great one, *tiene que poner el pecho* [you have to show courage], because if you are a commander and you don't show leadership, the patrolmen overrun you. If instead they see that you are fighting, then they follow you. There the nicest word you hear is "yes," never "no." There everyone says, "Yes, sir." You might have been without food for a couple of days and the boss will ask you, "Are you hungry?" and you say, "No, sir." People there get well educated. I believe that's one of the best schools in Colombia [laughs]. Everyone learns, the experience is good, and the living together is good as well. Being a commander is not about giving orders but about knowing how to command. You have to lead by example.

In the group, they say that the commander has to have two breasts: one with milk and the other with shit. First, one gives people the milk and tells them, "Let's do this, and let's do that." That, of course, becomes annoying [for the subordinates,] and so it happens that one abandons the guard position and goes drinking and shows up late. That's a death sentence as established by the statutes. But the commander is a good person and gives him the breast: "I pardon you this time, but don't evade again." But if that happens again and again, then you give him the shit, and you sanction him. One of the worst punishments [besides death] is that they tell you to stay four months without a salary. That is, you will fight for four months in the mountains [without getting paid]—that is very tough because you sweat a lot for that money.

When I was sent to Medellín as the commander of a group, I was not doing the killing anymore. I left the sport, so to speak. For many, [killing] is a sport. I left the sport because I was getting psychologically ill. When you are in charge of other men, you have to send them every day to kill many people. Thus I left the sport and sent other people to kill. Only once in a while, I killed someone so as not to lose the habit, but one has to give up the bad habit.

They got me out from Caucana because I got very sick due to the bullet I got in my back and the great heat. So one day they told me, "Get ready, you are going to Medellín." I arrived in front of the bus terminal in a barrio called Moravia.

Once I got there, they told me we had to fight against the Bloque Metro. "We had some problem with them. We are the Cacique Nutibara; we just started and we had a problem with the Bloque Metro." And then we started, and they brought us rifles.

To the kids we said, "We will give you two days to think about it. Either you work with us or we kill you." After a couple of days, the *patrón* gathered ten people. We started to fight and gain terrain. There were lots of gunshots, but what was bad was that the police arrived often and didn't let us fight. This was in the middle of Medellín. They didn't have the militia we had, because we had come from [fighting] in the mountains, while they [the members of the Bloque Metro] were vicious kids from the street.

And so we entered, caught seven of those kids, we tied them up in the soccer field and killed them. That's when I went to prison; it was my first time in a jail. We were fighting in a soccer field that Pablo Escobar had built. The guys were running away, and we were following them. They were running because a police patrol showed up and told us to stop. We were going to fight them, but the man [one of the police officers] said, "No! No! Don't get yourself killed. We will help you." They handcuffed me and took me to the police station in Belén.[14] We remained there from Friday through Monday, and on Monday the same man who had arrested us came and said, "You are free."

I remember that the guy who was on duty asked him, "Why are you letting these guys go?"

"Because they are of the Cacique [Nutibara]," he responded.

"Ah, fine then!" They had been paid to free us.

When the Cacique Nutibara demobilized, we started working with the Héroes de Granada[15] group. We started being Héroes de Granada from that moment. We continued with the same ideology [of the Cacique Nutibara]. The only thing that changed was the name and the armband. We threw away the armbands we had. Several gave themselves in [that is, they demobilized], but the majority of us became the Héroes de Granada. We continued working in the same area. We didn't move. Those who wanted to go home demobilized, while those who wanted to continue did so [under the new name].

There are people who are afraid of killing. The truth is, the first time you shoot someone in the head, you think a lot about it. The first time, you have to think twice about it, while later it's nothing. But the first time, you have to think a lot about it because it's a human being. Later one gets addicted [to killing]. One doesn't care anymore. One gets into the habit of killing and killing. It's your body that asks you for it: "So-and-so needs to be killed."

"Where?"

"In such-and-such place."

"Okay, let's do it."

I had a friend who was one of the commanders in Medellín. When I killed someone, he would come to me, almost angry, asking me why I was doing it all by myself and why I didn't call him to share in the killing: "You killed him on your own, and you didn't call me." I had a companion, and all he did was kill. The organization eventually had to kill him because he annoyed the boss, because he was not paying attention to the boss and had turned crazy. That was very tough.

One day, I killed a man for something stupid. I was with some influential friends from Medellín. I was also with my wife and my son. I killed this man in front of my son. Can you believe it? We were there, drinking with our women. My friend was dancing with my girl, and a drunk man came over and wanted to take her chair. "Leave the chair there. Don't look for trouble," I told him. I was already a little bit drunk. I told him not to take the chair, and when my girl sat down, this guy made her get up. He made a mistake, and so I put the gun to his head and discharged it because I liked to discharge it. I killed him for a stupid reason.

My boss called me and told me I had overdone it because I was drunk, and he almost killed me. He told me I was violating the statutes, because one cannot mix alcohol and guns. This is the first thing they prohibit in the organization, and I had mixed them very badly. In any case, that man had lacked respect. He didn't know who I was, and he bothered my girl, and my girl is my life. What's bad is that my son saw me killing this man, and now he knows I handle weapons, and the first thing he asks me when I call him is "When are they giving you a license? When are you visiting?" He tells his friends that I have a gun and that I kill criminals. He says that when he is bigger he wants to have a gun and a bike. I adore my son. He has been with me a lot, and he knows a lot about the war already.

My boss was like a father to me. I was always very good with my *patrones*. They put trust in me. They always liked me a lot. They are good individuals: they teach you discipline, and discipline is everything. Without discipline, one is nothing. With my last *patrón,* we cared a lot about each other. We made a pact: if I heard that they were going to kill him, I'd tell him, and the other way around. At times, we disregarded our own code of conduct. One day, my boss told me, "Let's go to collect some money at the ranch." We went, he opened the suitcase, and he gave me two million pesos and told me, "Go home. Let's leave Loco and another guy in charge here, and we will go for some rest. I will bring this money to our *patrón,* and we'll take off for a few days." And that's why they killed him. The money was extortion money, and one day, they caught my boss and Loco, and they were going to kill both of them, but then Loco said that on that day, I had been with the boss and not with him.

The day they killed my boss, we met and spoke [beforehand]. We went on his bike to have lunch, and he left me there at the restaurant. The following day, I called him. Every morning, I called him to report myself. I called him and called him, and for days he didn't get back to me. At some point, I was told that he had been transferred to a different group, which I found very strange. Then one day, his brother informed me that my *patrón* had been killed. That was very hard to swallow.

Because of this, I had to leave the group. I didn't leave the group because I grew tired of it. I liked the arms, but I had to [leave] after they killed my *patrón*. They called me for a meeting in Medellín. The appointment was at a gasoline station near Bello. I had to come and hand over a hundred million pesos. I didn't transport money on a bike, to avoid being frisked at a checkpoint, but I always took a bus, often together with my wife. The gasoline station was our meeting point, and I never stole a penny. A friend told me that they were going to kill me. So I didn't go to the appointment, and I entered the demobilization process.

I'm trying to change, but it's not easy. One of my friends, who now commands a group in Caucasia, told me, "Come work with me. I will pay you well." To work with him as a bodyguard, one can gain 2 million pesos [about US$1,000]. And I'm here [in Medellín] doing nothing. But in any case, one has the idea to change, and so one has to continue with the process. I've already been in this process for more than one year, and interrupting it to go back to the same vice is tough. This is practically an addiction like drugs. Sometimes I was on a twenty-day permit, and I was waking up in the middle of the night frightened because I didn't feel the rifle; I didn't realize I was at home. This is a vice that one gets and become addicted to. I got it when I was still very young. I know I will not get to be old—that I will not get to know my nephews. One more or less foresees that death will come soon, and so one does not give it much importance. Because when you kill someone, one already knows one has died as well.

A couple of years later, I heard of Luna for the last time. I was having dinner with my friend and social worker, the one who had introduced me to Luna. I knew she was in touch with him at times, and I asked if she had heard from Luna recently. She grew pale and fixed her gaze for a moment on the red wine resting at the bottom of a large glass. Then she lifted her eyes, and without betraying any emotion, she said, "My sister read in a newspaper that Luna was killed."

"And you didn't verify it?" I asked.

"No, I didn't," she responded.

I took my cell phone from the inside pocket of my jacket and typed Luna's full name on the small keyboard. A few seconds passed until the link to the news we were hoping not to confirm appeared. Luna had been killed not far away from Yarumal,[16] where his wife and her eight-year-old son were living, in a cottage not far from where I had once visited him and met his family.

My friend and I remained silent. Several moments I had shared with Luna came to my mind. I remembered the words he once wrote me while we were chatting over the Internet. I was in New York, and Luna was further losing himself in following the false promises of the wealth that cocaine never gives to people like him: "If I'd have been able to study and the circumstances had allowed it, I would have loved to be one of your students."

I responded that I had shared with my students some of what I had learned from him and that, in this way, he had become their professor as well. He wrote, "I'd like for them to learn that war is not something good and that there is nothing better than having a life with your family and living in peace." This was Luna's dream of a good life, but it turned out to be cruel optimism.

DOBLE CERO

My August 2003 meeting with Doble Cero (see the prologue) had happened at a crucial and difficult time for him and his organization. He was facing a major military offensive by his former allies from the AUC, led by Carlos Castaño, and by the Colombian army, which—so the public secret in Medellín said—had previously always been on his side, protecting and supporting their own former official. The infighting had begun when Doble Cero refused Castaño's order to demobilize and join the negotiation with the Colombian government. The leader of the Bloque Metro had asked for a separate negotiation forum because he refused to sit down with major narcotraffickers such as Don Berna, the founder of the Cacique Nutibara paramilitary group, which was now after Doble Cero and his men.

In the area where I had met Doble Cero at the end of August 2003, the fighting between the two rival factions of the paramilitary had started in May, provoking the displacement of over six hundred peasants. The Bloque Metro was increasingly losing territory that it had dominated for over seven years, and only a few municipalities remained under its control. Moreover, over five hundred of his men had deserted and joined the rival Cacique Nutibara. When we sat down for our interview, Doble Cero was losing the war. By the end of September, his group had been annihilated, and the leader had succeeded in fleeing, taking refuge in the Santa Marta area, on the northern coast of Colombia.

I proposed that Doble Cero write something to me about his life. Over a few months, the leader of the Bloque Metro shared his testimony with me.

At times, his emails were long and frequent, while at other times, they were short and sporadic. Our conversation continued until just a couple of days before he was killed on a street of El Rodadero, near Santa Marta, on May 27, 2004. He was thirty-nine years old.

Doble Cero's testimony is unique because of the role he played during the years the paramilitary expanded their domination across Colombia. A former official of the military and educated by the Jesuits in Medellín, Doble Cero had been the right-hand man of the Castaño brothers and a confident of Antioquia's elite, who had supported the formation of self-defense groups.

The life of Doble Cero shines a light on the purgative thinking that inspired Colombia's Dirty War. What follows is an abridged version of the emails that Doble Cero sent me over a period of about three months.

My great-grandfather on my father's side was a Conservative general during the so-called Thousand Days' War.[17] This was a confrontation at the end of the nineteenth century and the beginning of the twentieth century between Liberals and Conservatives. The war lasted three years, and the most notable consequence was the separation of Panama from Colombia. My great-grandfather's name was Laureano García Rojas. He was a Conservative and lived at a time when military ranks were given not based on your tactics and strategic skills, but rather based on the land you owned and your level of participation in the party. The Conservatives were in power, and they opposed a revolution by the Liberals, who were in disagreement with the constitution enacted in 1886. It eventually lasted until 1991, the year when it was changed for the current constitution. The Liberals at the time, led by Rafael Uribe Uribe,[18] one of most brilliant thinkers and military leaders the country has ever had, were defeated because of a lack of unity and internal cohesion and because of personalism and envy prevailing within the party. [Once the war was over,] they allowed Uribe to participate in politics, and later he was killed.

My grandfather on my father's side, the son of this man, got an education [like the one that] the elite received at the time, at the Universidad del Rosario in Bogotá. He became a doctor of philosophy and literature, and he dedicated his entire life to education. He was the founder of the Gran Colombia Universidad, which is today a prestigious private university. His name was Julio César García, and in addition to being a philosopher, he was a historian, a journalist, the director of the newspaper *El Colombiano*,[19] and the chancellor for some time of the Universidad de Antioquia, and for a while he was in charge of the ministry of education during the military dictatorship of the Conservative Gustavo Rojas Pinilla.

My mother's family was middle-class, made up of land settlers who later became landowners. But they were Liberals at a time in Colombia when one adopted the political affiliation of the family. My father, a Conservative, and my mother, a Liberal, met while they were studying law at the university at a time when political sectarianism through education was disappearing and remained only in the minds of ignorant peasants, manipulated by their political leaders who used them as cannon fodder.

My brothers and I were born in the bosom of a middle-class family with a past that made us proud of the moral values shown in the course of their lives. One [part of our family] was dedicated to educating younger generations at the expense of themselves. The other [part of our] family was dedicated to commerce and providing for their own family, but they did not have a good education. My parents, having this very clearly in mind and taking advantage of the good individual and family connections we had, got us into the Jesuit school of San Ignacio. Of course, since I was the youngest one, my brothers went a few years before me.

When I started in 1972, the Jesuits had begun to practice a new method in education as an experiment. It was the Ford educational method, or personalized method. It was based on the Hegelian dialectic as a knowledge theory. At the time in Colombia, it was something innovative. The method was that a student was given a statement, with everything he had to know within a given time frame, and he was also given all the needed resources. This was the thesis. Then, after this phase was completed, the student was confronted with the knowledge of the professor in an interactive class. This was called the antithesis. From the clash between the two, the synthesis became a source of knowledge and at the same time a basis to continue with the process.

At the time, we were living in an artificial bubble in which we were not aware of what was happening around us. My brothers were expelled because their grades were low, and so my father turned to a priest friend of his who had a school in one of Medellín's *comunas*. It was a community school where children from the unprivileged class went. That was where my brothers went as punishment for being expelled from the best school in town. It was hard on them initially, but little by little they adjusted.

One day—I was in fourth grade—I went to see my brothers' new school, and I found myself in a reality that was always there but that I had never seen before. I realized that all this time I had lived in a bubble, that I didn't know anything, that everything was false and artificial, that things were not as someone saw them in the bubble. All of this left me wondering, and later on I decided to get out of the bubble, to get to know reality, and to prepare myself to engage with reality, since within the bubble one was trained to remain in it forever.

I changed schools—I left the best school to go to a community school. There I met more humble mates who had to work hard in order to be able to study. I met with the phenomenon of drug addiction, which I did not fall into, but one of my brothers did. I met with the social issues of the time, including the insurgency, which almost absorbed me because of the rebellion that characterizes one at that age. The guerrillas rejected me because they said that I was a representative of what they called the little bourgeoisie, that what I was looking for was adventure and nothing more. And they probably were right.

So I did fifth and sixth grades in this kind of environment. My other friends continued living in the bubble, and I never heard from them again; they were also not interested in my fate.

The life of the people who live in what I have called the bubble was a different kind of life in the sense that there we had everything we needed and, to a certain extent, everything we desired. We had clothes, food, transportation, books, professors, and an entire education infrastructure at our service. We especially had the sensation of the security and solidity of it all. It was a solid life project, and this was projected onto us. We knew there were people who were much poorer and that we had to practice charity, which is what the priests inculcated into us. We looked at our situation and stability as the most normal reality, and we didn't think you had to struggle to gain things. We were like in a state of sleepiness in front of certain realities that we were not aware of.

Life outside the bubble was real life. It was the life of our community schoolmates who had to wake up at dawn to look for something to eat, study from 7 A.M. to 2 P.M., and then go to work to make money. Our mates outside the bubble felt the uncertainty that you didn't feel while within the bubble.

One might say that I had the idea of the military within me. It was like an interior power that drew me toward everything that had to do with it. It became like an obsession. Everything that had to do with it interested me enormously: the weapons, the uniforms, the military discipline, the mysticism, the patriotism, the fighting. It was a great desire to be a soldier. In the last year of school, I applied for the cadets' military school, which is where those who aspire to become officers of the Colombian army are educated. My parents, desiring the best for their kids, didn't support my decision to join the military.

When I joined, I had just turned eighteen. The change from a civilian to a military life is traumatic. First was the absolute loss of freedom. During this process one is deprived even of the freedom of movement and of physiological necessities. For any movement, no matter how little, one had to ask and obtain permission. It's a process of mental subjugation. Eventually, you control and direct yourself according to how the institution has formed you.

During the years I was at the school, between 1983 and 1985, the political situation began to get complicated. In 1983, the narcotraffickers killed the minister of justice. It was the time when they began to play hardball against the state; they believed they had great power and challenged the oligarchy and the state itself. This was also the time when the self-defense groups put themselves at the service of the drug lords and became their mercenaries, while the guerrillas got more serious with their political and military expansion across the entire country.

The guerrillas dominated the entire countryside when Belisario Betancur, a Conservative, became president, with a program focused on making peace with the guerrillas, giving them political and military concessions so that they would remain without a political base for their fight. This created discomfort among the military and was reflected in the instructions we were given by our superiors. It was inculcated into aspiring officers that the army was the fundamental pillar on which the democratic system rested, as did individual freedoms. All of this was threatened by enemies outside and inside the democratic system, and it was because democracies are imperfect that a president like the one we had at the time could become president. And so this is why, on certain occasions, we had to temporarily transgress the rules imposed by the same system; it was [done] to defend our own system, our democracy, which was one of the oldest in Latin America. The army was the defense fortress [of democracy].

In 1984, we went through more of the same: mercenaries of the narcos, in cahoots with the official authorities, killed leaders of the party of the FARC. They killed prosecutors and judges because they opposed narcotrafficking and had open investigations against narcos; there were guerrilla attacks across the entire country and killings of officers, noncommissioned officers, soldiers, peasants, and farmers. There was the silent displacement of the peasant middle class to the cities because of the pressure and the action of the guerrillas. What affected us in particular was the death of several military leaders, some of whom had been our superiors and instructors.

In 1985, the same went on, but worse. Little by little, Eastern Antioquia became a powder keg of social battles. With great skill, the guerrillas manipulated the population to recruit the entire youth of the region. At the time, the guerrillas were still very clandestine. One could still travel through the municipalities of Eastern Antioquia with no danger. In that year, M-19 guerrillas assaulted the palace of justice [in Bogotá]. During its recapture by the military, more than a hundred people died, including all the judges of the Supreme Court.[20] Some of [the judges] were family friends because they had studied with my parents. That day, as had become almost routine in those days, they put us out to patrol the streets of Bogotá, and thus we could experience, though from afar, what all Colombians felt during those days.

I then chose to be sent to Puerto Berrío.[21] I arrived there at the beginning of 1986. Starting in 1982, the Middle Magdalena region had gone through a horrible war inflicted by the guerrillas. When I arrived, there was already an investigation into the alliance between members of the military and counterinsurgency groups [paramilitary groups] that had ties to narcotraffickers, who at the time were seen not as a threat to stability or generators of social problems, but as wealthy cattle ranchers, entrepreneurs, and investors who had come to the region to help clean it of Communists, generate jobs, and help the region to progress.

The superiority of the guerrillas was overpowering. The army's lack of resources made it look like an army of poverty-stricken men. There were no uniforms, and the weapons were old and almost didn't work. That's why one looked with sympathy on these groups of civilians fighting, with better arms and equipment than the army had, against the guerrillas. We knew that close by, in Puerto Berrío, [the paramilitaries] acted as if they owned the place, and they were allied with the military in operations against the guerrillas.

In certain circumstances, one didn't fight on behalf of his ideas to defend democracy and all that discourse, but rather to save his own life and that of the people who depended on him. During a fight, a sort of camaraderie is established, and one is aware that the lives of his men depend on the decisions one makes.

The state had sent us to fight with few resources and means in an area then controlled by the enemy. One's survival and that of his men did not depend on the support the state might have been able to provide, like for any Colombian soldier today, but it depended exclusively on one's own skills. In those moments, in the forest and without knowing the terrain, one had the great dilemma between acting based on the rules of engagement—and thus most probably becoming one more statistic among the soldiers who died during an ambush—or putting aside the rules to give more flexibility to the operations by getting more intelligence and knowing the terrain. This could have severe implications for the résumé of an officer, but in those moments one's own life is much more important than a piece of paper, and it is better to be alive with my men than to have an impeccable CV and an after-death promotion.

According to the rules, what I was doing wrong was capturing some civilians and obliging them to be guides and informants over a period of between eight and fifteen days. This was giving me good results because the hostage, in order to save his life, ended up telling us everything he knew about the guerrillas. Every person who remained in the hands of the troops was looked on with suspicion by the guerrillas, and, most likely, he had to abandon the region once the army left the area of operations. I was aware of the legal consequences of my actions, as well as those for the hostage. But our attacks against the guerrillas were significant, and it didn't take long for the guerrilla commanders to discover my survival strategy. They mobilized all the peasants from the areas of Remedios and Segovia to abandon their land, and in a peasant exodus, they moved to the municipality to protest en masse against our presence in the rural areas, to demand that we leave the area and that a national government commission should investigate our supposed abuses. A few months later, the military tribunal called me, and I was suspended. I knew that with such a sanction on my career I would not ascend in the army, and so I started thinking of retiring and continuing my law studies.

Then a retired mayor proposed an opportunity [for me] to meet with friends who were civilians but were against the guerrillas. He wondered if

I could give them military advice. I liked the idea, and I agreed. I thought I could help them while I was continuing my studies. It was a way to follow my ideas and to help people in the rural areas to free themselves from the slavery of the guerrillas who subjugated them. My friend took me to a villa in an exclusive neighborhood of Medellín, where I interviewed several people. That's when I realized I was talking with, among others, the Castaño brothers, though they didn't tell me [their names]. Since I had been in Amalfi,[22] I could recognize several of the people there. They talked about Fidel as *el patrón,* the boss, and they didn't share much information about how I could assist them because Fidel was not in the room and he was the one calling the shots. That's when I first met Carlos, the younger brother of Fidel. The first impression I got of him was that of a rebellious and immature kid with lots of power in his hands, more than he could handle.

I went back home, continuing my own business, and I really thought this would not turn into anything concrete. One day [the Castaño brothers] called me and they invited me to go and see them in a house in El Poblado [the wealthiest neighborhood in Medellín]. I went, and Carlos was there with a group of men. He immediately said, "This is the new lieutenant who is going to assist us in the operation. Let's go." On the road, he told me they had information on the location where the guerrillas were going to show up to get some extortion money, and they we were going to ambush them. The operative was going to be in San Carlos.[23]

We drove through Granada, and a little bit further from it, they gave us weapons. We stood there three days waiting for the guerrillas, but, noticing something strange, the guerrillas didn't pass by where they were supposed to. We went back to Medellín and Carlos told me, "Lieutenant, go home, and when we need you we will call you back." This was my first operation with the group of Fidel and Carlos Castaño, before it was called a self-defense group. Rather, it was a private justice group or vigilantes or something like that.

Later they called me back, but this time it was not because of an operation. They told me Fidel wanted to talk with me and, while waiting for his arrival, they wondered if I could provide security to the house where we were staying. We waited for eight days. Luckily, I was able to call home and tell them that I was on a trip with some friends. When I saw Fidel, I had the impression that we had met before. He didn't ask any questions, but only told me to follow him. Fidel was an adventurer and a skilled negotiator who was still very young. He had left his home and promised to return only when he was a millionaire. Fidel always saw in the narcotraffickers a source of wealth for himself. He was a friend but never took orders from them or let himself be corrupted by their money in the sense that they never could buy him.

We got into the car, and after a while we arrived at the upper side of El Poblado at a very luxurious home filled with armed guards. Fidel got out of the car and entered the villa. A few minutes later, a caravan of cars arrived, and individuals got out whom I had never seen before or, rather, I had seen only on television.

Later, they all came out and got into the cars. Fidel said to me, "Just follow us." We left, and we crossed the entire city in a caravan. We got to a very luxurious farm on the outskirts, and once again everyone got out and entered the hacienda. I was again outside observing all of this. After a while, a new caravan of cars arrived, but it was different. The majority of the people arriving were very young, armed with all types of automatic weapons. When the main guy got out, I understood that I was getting into something that was not as simple as I had thought. The [main] man who had just arrived was Pablo Escobar. At the end of the day, I not only discovered my new task, which was to be Fidel's bodyguard when he was in Medellín, but I also started to discover a world of powerful people and forces, which until then had been unknown to me.

In 1990, Fidel decided to create an expeditionary force to fight against the guerrillas in the province of Chocó.[24] He didn't want to create a paramilitary group, in the sense that it would work in cahoots with the police and the army, but a group that would fight against the guerrillas with its own means in an extremely [difficult] area. This was a sort of mission impossible, a suicidal mission: to get into the jungle, into its heart, where the enemy is, far away from one's own resources and means of support and without counting on the help of the state and its forces. Fidel made this proposal to me, because that's what I was doing when I was with the army. This was nothing unusual for me, or at least this is what I thought. So, in 1990, I stood for an entire year with twenty-five men, fighting the guerrillas in the jungle without any support or contact with external forces.

At the end of 1990, and within the framework of peace negotiations between the government and the guerrillas of the Ejército Popular de Liberación, Fidel decided to make his own contribution by demobilizing his group, disarming, and giving ten thousand hectares [24,711 acres] of the best land of the Río Sinú valley to peasants. Fidel asked me to lead the disarmament, and I did. In a ceremony, I handed over all the weapons to the government. I thought of going back to Medellín, but this was not possible because I had some enmity there with several people who applied pressure to prevent my return. In fact, when I had gone to the jungle, many had thought I was not coming back alive, and they rejoiced because of that.

One of those who didn't completely understand me was Carlos, because I was not participating in his parties and I didn't celebrate everything he was doing like the others who were with him did. I limited myself to observing, analyzing, and being quiet.

I started working for a company commercializing bananas around the entire world. It had five big factories in Urabá and exported fruit to Europe and the United States. I was in charge of the security of all the factories. I worked there for the first eight months of 1991. I was the boss of the general services department. What impressed me was that I met several people who had studied with me during the years that I called the "bubble." I thought that because we had shared those years it would generate acceptance and recognition, but this was not so. These people acted as if they had never met me. They were in positions of responsibility, supposedly at my same level, but there was an invisible barrier, a sort of class wall, and they saw all the people who worked in general services as servants, as inferior beings, so I was like the butler of an English lord. This was another thing that impressed me.

I served as the personal bodyguard of the owner of the company for more than a month. I was with him from dawn until late at night, and during the entire time, he did not once talk to me directly. Whatever he had to communicate to me he did by sending me a message through an employee who was submissive to him. I really realized that these kinds of people look down on people below, as if these same people were not the reason that they are wealthy and powerful, but rather are baggage that they have to endure and a necessary complement for their capital. Many details made me resentful of people belonging to the Creole oligarchy who believe that to do something good is to give alms to people who are at their service and are slaves of their capital. This is why when [in 1991,] Fidel, who was a humble person of peasant origin, who was working hand in hand with the peasants, invited me to work with him. I didn't think twice and said yes.

In August of that year, Fidel called me to his hacienda, Las Tangas. Since I was in Urabá, it was easy for me to go to Córdoba. He asked me how I was doing, if I was happy about my job, and he asked me why I was not going back to work with him as his personal assistant. He said that he was not at war but was engaged with agrarian reform in collaboration with the communities and social projects of the peasants. I thought that this was all good and filled with good intentions, and over the two days I stayed with him, he showed me the projects. So I decided to resign from my job at the banana company and go back to work with Fidel in the construction of a new social fabric in Córdoba. I felt very happy because I felt like I was at home, with my family, free to leave behind the environment of those people [who had previously employed him]. Fidel was a visionary and charismatic leader, a person who, despite being able to assemble some wealth and capital, did not lose his humility and simplicity. Though he did not study much and barely knew how to read and write, he had a great practical knowledge of life, and one could learn a lot from him. Of course, he had also his dark side.

We spent the rest of 1991 and the entire year of 1992 working with the communities. When Pablo [Escobar] fled from his prison,[25] Fidel got very worried because Fidel thought that as long as he was in prison, it was possible to somehow control Pablo, but that outside the prison he was going to be very dangerous. When Pablo escaped, [the government] formed a search unit in Medellín, which had the support of the United States. During the last months of 1992, each of Pablo's enemies—that is, Fidel and Carlos, the search unit, the government, the Cali Cartel, and the North Valley Cartel—tried to fight against Pablo independently. But it was really Pablo who had the initiative, and the rest hid before him or turned against him because of his actions. It was Rodolfo Ospina Baraya, alias Chapulín, who unified all these initiatives to form an ad hoc organization against Pablo Escobar. I'm not sure that I was part of these meetings, since I was only Fidel's personal assistant for the social work that we were developing in Córdoba, but of course I was aware of everything that was happening. That is when Los Pepes, those persecuted by Pablo Escobar, were formed.

With respect to Los Pepes, the national government participated both directly and indirectly. The narcos of the Valle [cartel],[26] always interested in finding solutions to the their problems due to narcotrafficking, got into contact with President Gaviria and with the general prosecutor, Gustavo de Greiff, through their contacts with politicians. They agreed on benefits and immunity for the members of the Cali Cartel in exchange for collaboration in the arrest or death of Escobar. Little by little, because of what happened at the time, the reality we have today was woven. Los Pepes were established by the narcos of the Valle [de Cauca] province with the government, the direct participation of the general prosecutor, and the heads of the police. Fidel and Carlos came in later, when the agreements were already made. These are Colombian politicians: they make alliances even with the devil, but all under the table, using everyone who wants to be used, thinking that one day there will be some payoff, but that's not the case. One is simply thrown away, and that's it.

In December 1993, Pablo Escobar was killed, and on January 6, 1994, Fidel [was killed as well]. I was scheduled to meet with Fidel on January 10 in Urabá to talk with him about the FARC invasion of those territories where we were developing our social work. Fidel's other two brothers, Carlos and Vicente, asked me to organize the defense because of my military experience. This is when we established the ACCU [the Peasant Self-Defense of Córdoba and Urabá]. I was in charge of fighting against the guerrillas with the collaboration of peasant communities and of managing an open and democratic organization. Carlos's initial idea was to put great military pressure on the guerrillas and later negotiate a mutual respect agreement and a nonaggression pact, an initiative that later I had to submit to the guerrillas following instructions from Carlos.

Between 1994 and 1998, we expanded [our domination] in the north of Colombia, but with the idea of not getting involved in narcotrafficking. But in 1998, the narcotization of the AUC began, at the time when the government of President Andrés Pastrana, with the support of the United States, began negotiations with the FARC guerrillas. Someone had sold the idea to Carlos that to have political weight in a negotiation, he had to seize control of the narcotrafficking, of the drug routes, and of the laboratories. And this was the biggest mistake that Carlos made.

I received the last email from Doble Cero on May 24, 2004, just four days before a hitman put an end to his life. Responding to a question I had sent him, he explained why he had parted from the AUC: his opposition to the presence of drug kingpins in the organization. "What we continue to profess after we parted from United Self-Defense of Colombia," he wrote, "is the search for an alternative to overcome and resolve the conflict, instead of being the defenders of the indefensible." The bullets that killed Doble Cero also interrupted the narration of his life history, thus switching off and truncating his confession. One wonders if, beyond punishing him for his treason, the leadership of the paramilitaries and his political allies had wanted to mute a man who had been witness to how the paramilitary project had expanded and consolidated through its intertwinement with other powers, such as political and economic ones, in the 1990s. Because of his death, many questions remain unanswered, especially those concerning the establishment of the Bloque Metro, which he led, as well as the war between the Bloque Metro and the Cacique Nutibara, which was led by Diego Murillo Bejarano, alias Don Berna, the drug lord and head of the Oficina de Envigado Cartel.

Limpieza

THE EXPENDITURE OF SPECTACULAR VIOLENCE

Like wolves hankering after prey, men in military fatigues, armed with semi-automatic rifles, their faces masked, dropped into towns across Colombia. Like angels of death carrying out divine violence, the paramilitaries extended their shadow of terror over the targeted population. There was no show of mercy, no second thoughts, no hesitation, but only spectacular death. When they retreated, they left behind corpses lying still warm on the pavement and towns frozen in fear, windows and doors shut. In the paramilitaries' spectacle, the guilty verdict pronounced upon the town was displayed for all to accept, and on their knees. Such events played out across Colombia over the past three decades every time the paramilitaries "broke a territory," carried out killings that "set an example," or engaged in massacres and acts of *limpieza,*[1] that is, in the cleaning of a town stigmatized for being a guerrilla nest, a *pueblo guerrillero.* Their spectacular violence was an act of purification and reeducation.

The violence was performed by paramilitary groups, which had turned into powerful and well-organized regional armies. Their development and expansion were the result of the leadership and initiative of Carlos and Fidel Castaño, brothers originally from the town of Amalfi, in the department of Antioquia. Fidel, the older brother, had accumulated considerable wealth as a drug trafficker in Pablo Escobar's Medellín cartel, which he then invested in a private art collection and large estate properties in the department of Córdoba. Carlos instead began his career in the criminal world as a hitman and collaborated both with his brother Fidel and with Escobar. Their father's kidnapping and killing at the hands of the FARC in 1981 fueled their hatred of the guerrillas and sparked their personal war against the FARC, and served as a foundational myth for the establishment of the paramilitaries

(Rondero 2014). Eventually the paramilitaries turned into a nationwide counterinsurgency project, for which they had the support of cattle ranchers as well as a population tired of FARC harassment. While the paramilitaries, which had formed in the Middle Magdalena region at the beginning of the 1980s, was primarily a local self-defense group protecting the interests of cattle ranchers and multinational companies and boosting the counterinsurgency efforts of the army, the paramilitary groups that the Castaño brothers established in Córdoba and Urabá resembled a private army supporting a seminal political project. Gustavo Duncan, in his book *Los señores de la guerra,* has referred to the role that the landowner Rafael Garcia played in introducing the Castaño brothers to the elite of Córdoba and in developing a political program underpinning the political-military project of the paramilitaries (2006, 300). And, in a book-length interview, Carlos Castaño has called Garcia his second father (Aranguren Molina 2001, 183). As I mentioned in chapter 1, the Castaño brothers called their army the Autodefensas Campesinas de Córdoba y Urabá (Peasant Self-Defense Forces of Córdoba and Urabá), known by the acronym ACCU. Yet at the outset, the Castaño brothers launched their military campaigns to protect and to advance the economic interests of Urabá's banana plantation owners, who saw a threat in the guerrillas' violence against them as well as in the labor rights demands advanced by exploited banana workers. These workers had represented the insurgency's social base since the beginning of the 1970s.

Among the leading paramilitaries who started campaigns in Urabá was Hérbert Veloza, known as H. H., who began his career as a *raspachín,* a coca gatherer, but became one of the most influential paramilitary leaders and eventually played a key role in the killings of Doble Cero and Carlos Castaño. After he had declared his intention to reveal the relations among the paramilitaries, politicians, and the business community, Veloza was extradited to the United States on March 5, 2009. I met him one rainy and dark afternoon in New York, in a bare room of the Metropolitan Correctional Center, which rises as an impregnable fortress behind the courthouse building just a few blocks away from City Hall. Escorted by a guard, Veloza, a short man wearing a khaki prison uniform, appeared subdued and stripped of all his might. The man who had led paramilitaries to carry out massacres throughout several areas of Colombia told me how he now spent his days: sweeping the floors of the prison's cafeteria and attending hearings. We spent four hours together, and while I was not allowed to record the conversation, I was able to take notes.

Veloza was born in 1967 in the town of Trujillo, in the Valle del Cauca department, but the family moved often, following Veloza's father's job opportunities. "My father lived like a gypsy," Veloza told me. At one point, they settled in Urabá. Observing how his older brothers were making money as coca collectors in San José del Guaviare, Veloza dropped out of high school and joined them in their work. In a handwritten note titled "How I got to be a paramilitary," which he sent me a few weeks after our meeting, he wrote: "Seeing that my brothers were coming back loaded with money and that they were able to buy all kinds of things, the insect of adventure [*el bicho aventurero*] bit me. And one morning, instead of going to school, I went to San José [del Guaviare]." There he worked in the coca fields in the morning and in a clandestine laboratory in the afternoon to produce the cocaine base.

When Iván, a friend of the family and a former guerrilla fighter who had deserted and whose sister was married to a cousin of Fidel Castaño, proposed that they join the paramilitaries, Veloza grasped the opportunity and traveled with his friend to Medellín to meet with the Castaños:

I went with him to Medellín. Flaco Panina, who was a cousin of the Castaños, came for us. He picked us up at a gasoline station, which is on 65th Street at San Juan. I was very frightened because I knew that once I spoke with these people, afterward I could not regret it and go back to driving a truck. They brought us to a house in El Poblado [Medellín's upper-class neighborhood] that later I learned belonged to Arutu, one of Pablo Escobar's hitmen. Vicente Castaño [the third brother of the Castaños] and Carlos Castaño waited for us there.[2]

They welcomed us, though I was more frightened than a recently caught monkey. They explained that they needed people who knew Urabá because they had a project to establish a self-defense group in that area. Vicente introduced himself as "the Professor" and Carlos by [his real name,] Carlos Castaño. We thought [at first] that Vicente was Fidel Castaño. Each one of us told them what we know about Urabá. They proposed to pay Iván five hundred thousand pesos monthly and me two hundred and fifty thousand pesos. I already knew I could not regret [being there], and therefore I accepted the job.

They gifted each one of us with one million pesos and told us to report to Valencia, Córdoba. There one of Iván's cousins had a shop. We went there, and later "Mobile 5" and "Marabilla" picked us up to take us to Las Tangas farm; Mobile 5 was one of the Castaños' most trusted men, and Marabilla was a cousin on their mother's side.

At Las Tangas, we met [Vicente and] Doble Cero, who was the Castaños' military commander. They explained to us that the banana plantation owners [*los bananeros*] were tired of the guerrillas because they controlled the workers' unions and kidnapped and blackmailed the *bananeros,* who therefore wanted a self-defense group to face the guerrillas. They asked us if we could recruit more people. Iván called some members of the EPL guerrillas who, like him, had deserted. I called some friends in Cubarral and El Dorado in Meta [department].

Veloza thus became one of the founding members of the so-called Group of 20, the paramilitaries that had begun the penetration of Urabá. They were able to accomplish this by working hand in hand with the Colombian army. "With us we had an army corporal whom we called Kike as well as other soldiers," Veloza wrote me in his note. A long and dark season of terror and death began in Urabá. Around 1995, the annual homicide rate was five hundred in every hundred thousand residents, and in 1996 Urabá was declared a "Special Area for Public Order." This allowed the army to operate with a free hand and to ignore the paramilitaries' systematic killing of Communist Party and Unión Patriótica opposition members as well as union and human rights activists (Romero 2003, 195). As the 1990s went on, Veloza gained the trust of the Castaño brothers, especially Vicente, and eventually became the leader of the paramilitary Bloque Bananero in Urabá.

In a document that he prepared for court hearings, Veloza described the expansion of the paramilitaries throughout Colombia. With regard to Urabá and his own role, Veloza mentioned the support that the paramilitaries received from banana plantation owners and then wrote:

> The order that we received was to be present in the banana farms and to prohibit labor strikes, with the sole objective of reactivating the banana economy in the region.
>
> We started operating in all the municipalities of Urabá, in Antioquia, to debilitate the urban structure of the guerrillas. . . . I became the commander of the group in Urabá in March 1995.
>
> In a war, you don't only kill, but you also forgive. This was a strategy that we started to implement because the enemy is not only someone you fight against militarily and politically, but also someone you forgive.
>
> We welcomed into our ranks guerrillas who had deserted, and thus the results against the guerrillas were the best.

The success of the Castaño brothers' military campaign in Urabá, which eliminated the presence of the guerrillas there, provided Carlos Castaño with the legitimacy to invite other self-defense groups across the country to confederate under an umbrella organization, the Autodefensas Unidas de Colombia (United Self-Defense of Colombia), or AUC. which was officially established in April 1997. In 1999, the government of Andrés Pastrana, whom Colombians had elected as president the previous year, started peace negotiations with the FARC and agreed to establish a demilitarized zone the size of Switzerland for the guerrillas in Southern Colombia. The negotiations deeply worried the political and economic elite in the country, and there was a spreading fear that the guerrillas would seize power. This fear convinced key members of the elite, many of whom had been victims of kidnappings and extortion, that only a heavily armed and well-trained paramilitary army could counter the guerrillas and keep them from overthrowing the government. This was the time, and these were the circumstances in the country, when Carlos Castaño established the AUC, which spread like wildfire.

Financing for the expansion of the AUC, though, came primarily from powerful drug kingpins. In fact, as Tate (2007) highlighted, what distinguished Colombian paramilitaries from other such organizations in other parts of Latin America was the injection of significant financial resources from drug trafficking. When I met Doble Cero, he provided me with his interpretation of the role that drug cartels had played in the AUC's establishment—the kingpins, he told me, were frustrated that the alliance they had established with the FARC in Southern Colombia had not turned to their advantage by the time that the Pastrana administration agreed to peace talks. The cartels were not invited to the negotiation table, and this taught them a lesson: they now understood that a political discourse might protect their interests and provide the opportunity to negotiate with the government in the future. This is why Carlos Castaño found the North Valley Cartel to be a strong ally in providing funds for the establishment of the AUC (Civico 2009). And thus the justificatory counterinsurgency discourse of economic and political groups that favored expansion of armed self-defense groups merged with the interests of drug kingpins. In other words, counterinsurgent language became the blanket that covered and rationalized the murky alliance between the army and the paramilitaries and between Colombia's political and economic elites and the drug kingpins. Doble Cero told me the following during our meeting:

> While we were fighting on behalf of the communities, [Carlos] Castaño
> started selling the leadership and the control of the organization to the drug

traffickers because the traffickers wanted leadership and control. But [Carlos and Vicente] Castaño said, "If you want leadership and control, this is not going to be for free." They started to sell the leadership and the control of the organization and to put the narco at the head of it, narcos like Don Berna and Macaco, like Cuco. . . .

That's when the first ideological disagreements began with us. . . . One asked oneself, "For whom are we working? Are we working on behalf of peasants as part of an independent process of a society fighting against the guerrillas because of the state's weakness, or are we working on behalf of mafiosi so that they can buy land at a cheap price while the peasants are being displaced to the big cities and inflating the belts of misery?" Somehow we ended up helping the guerrillas because we [the paramilitaries] generated large estates. This is what we started seeing in Urabá . . . "my friends" of the North Valley Cartel arrived there, and they were not only able to own a small farm, but they also wanted to have a competition [to see who could own the most] land. . . .

This was [our] strategy: from a military point of view, to search for the guerrillas and eliminate them; and then, after security was established, a political and social process would begin. But when [the narcos] arrived, they accumulated land, and they wanted to accumulate it rapidly. Within this strategy, they didn't distinguish much between who was and who wasn't a guerrilla. There were excesses in the attempt to gain space and to rapidly gain land to grow coca. We put [this issue] up for discussion in 1998 within the AUC, saying, "We can't do this."

They told us, "You are just an idealist."

Castaño's vision was to turn antiguerrilla groups owned by feudal lords into an army with national reach. As the journalist Mauricio Aranguren Molina wrote, "Carlos Castaño led the effort to convince each of these solitary and diverse forces of the necessity for unification, with a single commander, a single armband, a single uniform, and a political north shared by everyone" (2005, 199). Self-defense groups from regions across Colombia, from Middle Magdalena to Santander, from Cundinamarca to the Guajira, from Putumayo to Caquetá, responded to Castaño's invitation, and along with Castaño himself, paramilitaries such as Salvatore Mancuso, Don Berna, Doble Cero, Ramón Isaza, and Botalón became the AUC's leaders (ibid.). The formation of the umbrella group was not a smooth process, however. Local self-defense group leaders who did not share Castaño's vision were killed, and fragmentation, tensions, and rivalry among the top leaders of the AUC remained an unchanging factor, to the point that even talking about a proper and effective AUC "general staff" is an overstatement.

The AUC was a nationwide organization with an independent political-military project representing the interests and aspirations of its leaders. In a report drafted by the Colombian Ministry of Defense during the peace talks with the FARC, the government recognized that "the illegal self-defense groups were the ones that developed and expanded most over the last few years" (2000, 1). According to the report, the numbers of paramilitary combatants grew from 850 to 5,900 between 1992 and 1999. In 1993 and 1994, they registered a growth of 79 percent; in 1998 and 1999, the AUC recruited 1,415 new combatants (ibid., 4). After the demobilization of the AUC began in 2003, more than 30,000 paramilitary members disarmed.

The expansion of the AUC from Córdoba and Urabá to other regions of the country was announced in July 1997 with one of the country's bloodiest paramilitary massacres, which occurred in Mapiripán, a village in the Meta region of southeastern Colombia where the FARC guerrillas had a significant presence at the time. With the assistance of the army and the police, over two hundred paramilitaries were flown in from Urabá and Antioquia, and over five days, they killed a total of forty-four people. Mapiripán, as well as Salado, La Rochela, and Pueblo Bello, is now among the names of previously little-known towns and villages that mark the well-known geography of paramilitary terror in Colombia. They compose a landscape of violence (Tate 2007) and bring up memories of massacres, public executions, mass graves, large forced displacements of people, and paramilitaries working in cahoots with the state, which often either acted as an accomplice or preferred to look the other way while the slaughter occurred. The Grupo de Memoria Histórica (Commission for Historical Memory), which is part of Colombia's Comisión Nacional de Reparaciones y Reconciliación (CNRR), has published reports on some of the most brutal paramilitary massacres over the past few years, highlighting the experience and testimony of survivors as well as pointing to parties within the state responsible for these episodes. The work of the commission is an encyclopedia of terror in Colombia, in which the systematic and spectacular violence of paramilitary death squads is exposed. To sketch how paramilitaries used systematic and spectacular violence in the territories they conquered and dominated, I summarize below the experiences of two towns, San Carlos and Granada in the department of Antioquia, as they were presented in the commission's reports, and then compare them with my own fieldwork in the same area.

Oriente (or Eastern Antioquia), the geostrategic region where both towns are located, is a microcosm of the dynamics that have characterized Colombia's armed conflict in the past few decades, during which the population was subjugated to violence perpetrated by a variety of armed actors, from the guerrillas to the paramilitaries to the state. Most of the stories that I collected from both victims and victimizers are drawn from this area. Oriente is also representative of Colombia's experience of paramilitary violence because it is the subregion where Doble Cero's paramilitary group had been operating until it was annihilated by other paramilitary groups of the AUC. It is also the home region of El Doctor, whom I portrayed in chapter 1. For three decades, Oriente's residents were the target of forced and massive displacement, disappearances, massacres, selective killings, sexual abuse, kidnapping, and extrusion perpetrated by a variety of armed groups: the guerrillas of the ELN and the FARC; the paramilitary groups of the Middle Magdalena such as the ACCU, Bloque Metro, AUC, Cacique Nutibara, and Héroes de Granada; and the army and law enforcement.

Strategically located near Medellín and appreciated for its rich biodiversity, its wealth of natural resources, and its great agricultural potential, Oriente became the focus of an ambitious modernization effort from the 1960s onward that the state, in alliance with regional elites, imposed on the population without previous consultation and without evaluation of its environmental, social, and economic impacts (Grupo de Memoria Histórica 2011, 50). Three mega-infrastructure projects were implemented in Oriente: the construction of the Medellín–Bogotá highway, the building of the Rionegro international airport (the country's second largest), and the installation of a hydroelectric power plant that now produces energy for a third of the country. The execution of these three projects meant, for the rural population, the expropriation of land and forced relocation. Furthermore, the state militarized the area, establishing several bases to protect economic interests linked to the modernization process. The projects also caused the influx of several thousand workers, who had a significant impact on the demography and culture of the local population (ibid., 26, 48).

In reaction to the installation of the hydroelectric power plant in the 1970s, a civic movement arose to resist forced relocations and to advocate for the rights of locals adversely affected by the projects. Groups organized several strikes (paros cívicos) and asked local authorities to redress their grievances. This civic movement, as Mary Roldán highlighted, "built broad cross-municipal alliances. Issues such as displacement, threats to local subsistence production, and poor energy access and service affected a broad range of people in ways that cut across partisan and even class lines" (2009, 282–83). At the end of the 1970s and the beginning of the 1980s, the movement gained momentum: "Different sectors of civil society (merchants, students, teachers, and peasants) made up the movement. They developed a deep sense of belonging and high levels of commitment with their cause and fight, which translated through their initiatives into an active and united participation" (Grupo de Memoria Histórica 2011, 55). An Oriente resident explained the protest of those years to me by saying that the civic movement

> was the expression of the communities' frustration, because they knew they were rich, that they were producing or were going to produce energy for the entire country, [and yet] the majority of these communities didn't have potable water, electric power, or roads to facilitate the commercialization of peasant products and food. [The movement] generated an important political space, which later became the entry point for the guerrillas.

The success of the movement suggested that an alternative political project was possible, particularly after the elections of some members to local municipal assemblies demonstrated that the movement could become a part of the political process. Such successes critically challenged the historical and traditional political hegemony of the Conservative party in Oriente, which worried its representatives, and the challenge became even more significant after a new law, passed in 1988, allowed for the popular election of mayors, who previously had been appointed by local governors. The movement's civic initiatives soon met with such extreme repression that "in the memory of the region's residents[, violence] was directly linked to development, to which they attribute in part the beginning of the chain of horror and barbarism they lived for decades" (ibid., 26).

Threats and rumors began to spread, and on October 27, 1983, a movement activist named Julián Conrado David was killed in San Carlos. This event marked the beginning of the wave of terror that would shape the history of Oriente and its people: the repression of the civic movement served guerrillas as a Trojan horse that they used to penetrate the Oriente, and they eventually borrowed the movement's discourse and its cause. Though guerrillas had been present in Oriente since the 1960s, it was in the mid-1980s that the influence of the ELN in particular emerged as part of a larger strategy to dominate areas of strategic economic interest across the country. At the end of the 1980s, FARC guerrillas also established their presence in Oriente and imposed their domination through forced displacements, kidnappings, and selective killings. Some of the civic movement's leaders were accused of siding with the insurgency, and this in turn became the justification for violent incursions by Middle Magdalena paramilitaries led by Ramón Isaza. As a result, many of the civic movement's leaders were killed (ibid., 58–59).

The paramilitary occupation of Oriente began in 1998, after Carlos Castaño had established the AUC and was envisioning the takeover of other strategic departments in the country from the organization's strongholds in Córdoba and Urabá. Paramilitaries belonging to Doble Cero's group, Bloque Metro (which at the time was under the ACCU) carried out the first paramilitary raid in Oriente. On the early afternoon of October 27, 1998, about two hundred paramilitaries in a caravan of SUVs left the municipality of San Roque, where I later met Doble Cero, and headed toward San Carlos. At the bridge of La Holanda, a strategic intersection where roads lead off to other towns and villages, among them Granada, the paramilitaries set up a checkpoint. Over the next few hours, about one thousand people were stopped and frisked. Several local leaders, including members of the civic movement, were accused of being supporters of the guerrillas. The paramilitaries killed and beheaded them on the spot, leaving their corpses for everyone to see. At the same time, paramilitary death squads penetrated the town of San Carlos. With a list of targets, they went door to door, picked up their designated victims, and executed them, leaving the bodies on the pavement. The Grupo de Memoria Histórica quoted in its report the testimony of a woman from San Carlos, who recalled murders of several residents of her own town:

> The paramilitaries broke through, and they began, bam, bam, bam. We went to the window and we watched from the window, and there was the sign [reading] AUC. . . . They picked a certain Don Graciliano out from there . . . close to the police station, and they killed him, they killed him there. . . . And they were just roaming the town when they picked up Rocío and they killed her here. This happened in 1998, at the time of La Holanda [the bridge massacre]. This was the worst [of the massacres] because they killed a lot of people. I remember it very well because that's when they killed Chucho Orrego, when they went to the mayor's office. . . . Chucho Orrego was trying to escape from the roof, he was able to pass by his wife and his kids, and when he was almost at the top, they pulled him by his feet and there they killed him. They threw him in the middle of the street, and they reduced him to nothing, to the point that the wife did not recognize him and said it was not him. She went to search for him, because they took lots of people and they threw [their bodies] along the road.

This is when [the killing] of Rocío happened; it is when they beheaded Victor Velázquez, who was a leader of the civic movement in the town. Also Don Mariano, who owned the coffee shop, as he arrived home, they picked him up. This was so terrible. This man, the father of the young woman who works at the Culture House, they took him away, too. He worked at the hospital and they picked him up at the hospital.

They went for everyone in their homes. It was impressive. They knocked on the doors. (Ibid., 117)

More spectacular violence followed in Oriente as still more massacres and selective killings were carried out by Doble Cero's paramilitaries. Men and women known for their political and social leadership were disappeared or killed outright, their bodies cut into pieces with axes, chainsaws, and machetes. In San Carlos, the paramilitaries took over the Hotel Punchiná, the best hotel in town and previously owned by El Doctor, and turned it into their headquarters, where executions, sexual violence, torture, and disappearances were carried out. Here, in 2002, the paramilitaries took a fifteen-year-old girl, Leidy Johana, whom they sexually abused, tortured, and killed. They disappeared her body, which was found and recovered only years later. Local people called the hotel the *casita del terror,* the "little house of terror"—the diminutive rendering the horror even more horrific. The following two testimonies give a sense of the fear in which the population lived under the paramilitaries:

There was a time when, after 7 o'clock in the evening, no one went out, out of fear they were going to pick you up. A van or something like that would come by, pick one up, and that's it. At that time, nobody wanted to sleep in their own homes. We all wanted to stay at a different place . . . one didn't want to be there when they knocked on your door. Many of us became the support for others and others became our support, but here it was a tragedy every day at every hour. This was already a ghost town. Every afternoon you would see people with their blankets and their pillows looking for a place of refuge, in other homes; many young people slept in the mountains. . . . The moment came when we saw so many innocent people fall that we all felt threatened. With the disappearances, one knew that after one disappeared, the entire family was slowly going to die. (Ibid., 146)

[The paramilitaries] were heartless people who strongly conditioned the town [*metiéndole una psicología muy verrionda al pueblo*]. There you mentioned the paramilitaries, and everyone was running, worse than if the devil had come; it was worse because I believe the devil comes only for the one he needs. (Ibid., 121)

The terror perpetuated by the paramilitaries displaced about 20,000 of San Carlos's 25,840 residents to other urban centers around the country. Almost half of the outlying municipal areas belonging to the San Carlos municipality were completely abandoned by their residents. As mentioned in chapter 2, the violent rivalry among paramilitary groups later provoked further displacement of the local population: in 2003, Oriente became the battleground of the fight between Doble Cero's Bloque Metro and Don Berna's Héroes de Granada, which won the war and occupied Oriente until it demobilized in 2005.

In 2000, it was from San Carlos that paramilitary death squads, following the orders of Doble Cero, launched a raid into Granada, twenty miles (thirty-two kilometers) away, and began that town's occupation. I first learned in detail about the paramilitaries' spectacular violence in Granada when, at the outset of my fieldwork in the summer of 2003, I collected the testimonies of people forcibly displaced by paramilitaries from that town, which is just a couple of hours' drive from Medellín, to the capital itself. The people I met and interviewed had found refuge on a hill overlooking Medellín's river that was once a trash heap. They were living in precarious conditions, in shacks made of wood with tin roofs, struggling for survival and wondering how they could pick up their lives again in the aftermath of violence.

It was through their victims that I first met the paramilitaries; that is, through their victims' testimonies as well as their occasional silence and our movements from one location to another perceived as more secure to share their tales of terrors. It was through these stories, silences, and brief displacements that the presence and power of the paramilitaries were truly revealed to me.

In particular, I recall an old and tiny peasant, in his early eighties, who had been evicted from his land by the paramilitaries and had been displaced, along with his much younger wife, to a shantytown in Medellín. Still dressed like a *paisa* peasant, with a black sombrero and a folded white poncho—signs of a life now gone—he was making a living by selling tropical juices and cigarettes from a shack that he had turned into a small bodega. He invited me in, and his wife offered me coffee in a small plastic cup. While I sipped, the old peasant, in broken sentences, called back his memories. His thoughts were interrupted by pauses and sudden changes of topics driven not by amnesia, but by fear. When I realized this, I suggested that we continue the conversation on some other day, in some other place. Both the old man and his wife agreed, and a few days later I picked them up at the gateway of their barrio. Together we took the subway to the other end of Medellín, and finally we sat down in the living room of the apartment where I was staying. Here, at last, he finally told me how the paramilitaries had evicted him from his own land, threatening to kill him and his wife.

I also met Juan Fernando, a peasant living in a small Medellín shack with his family. They had left Granada to flee the paramilitaries' violence. His testimony echoes the experience of millions of Colombian peasants uprooted from their land by the guerrillas and the paramilitaries and forced to move to urban areas. Following the penetration of the paramilitaries, almost half of the residents of Granada left the municipality to resettle in Medellín or other cities across Colombia. Juan Fernando summarized his own experience and that of other victims forced to reinvent life in urban areas:

> I was a peasant. It was a family tradition. I cultivated coffee, plantain, and beans, and I worked as a day laborer on farms. I had my cow for milk, some chickens, and so on. It was very good, and my children helped me on the farm to harvest coffee and crops and take them to town. I have dedicated my entire life to the land and to work as a peasant. This was a good destiny for me. I'm forty-two now, and it's the first time I have come to know a city. Since we came to Medellín, it has been a severe drama, a very difficult one. To leave the rural areas and come to the city is very difficult. Here one gets lost. Once you come here, you are scared to move from one corner to the next. It's very difficult. Life has been very difficult.
>
> When I arrived here, I bought a small piece of land in a squatter zone, and I built a small shack with money I borrowed from a cooperative. Now the government or the mayor is telling us that they are going to send us away, and I don't know what will happen to us. I'm gonna lose everything we did here to build this shack, which I put together with my own hands. And now they tell us they are going to evict us because this is a squatter area. I don't know what's gonna happen, because we can't stay there [Granada, from which they were displaced] or here. For now, I don't know what to do.
>
> In the countryside, we had to coexist with the guerrillas, though I never got involved with them. It was normal to run into them. Then the *paras* came and the confrontation started. The guerrillas started pressing us to collaborate with them, and if we didn't want to, we had to leave. We had to go to the town and get stuff for them. And sometimes they force you, and you do it out of fear they are going to kill you if you don't help them. They recruited many minors—kids who were twelve or fourteen years old. They brainwashed these kids. They did lots of things. It was horrible to coexist with these people.

I always remained neutral. I was seeing them, I greeted them cordially, but I never helped them. I never liked to get involved. That's why lots of us had to leave, because we didn't collaborate. I just wanted to do my work with no problems. Eventually, thank God, I was able to come here with my children.

The paramilitaries arrived in the year 2000. We had the bad reputation that we were all guerrilla members. So they arrived in the town shooting indiscriminately. The day they entered, they killed eighteen people. Early in the afternoon, I arrived in town and saw all those dead bodies. I was in fear. I hid in the church and prayed. People were confused and didn't know where to go; they were crying. You don't know what to do. Eventually we left the church, went back home, and locked ourselves up in our homes. That's when things got complicated. In December, the guerrillas retaliated. I was in the fields, and I heard the bomb explosion. There were many deaths that day, many injured people. That's when people became even more fearful and when [residents] started to leave. It had been terrible. We had to live through a lot of fear over there.

I went on working, but always with this tension of knowing the paramilitaries would show up and wondering what would happen. One already didn't have much motivation to work. I felt like I was retired. With this tension and fear, I was not able to work well. It was when these massacres started that we began to be fearful.

The home of both these interviewees, Granada was founded at the outset of the nineteenth century. As a whole, the municipality covers about 120 square miles (311 square kilometers) and includes 52 rural areas *(veredas)*. Coming from Medellín, one reaches Granada by turning off the highway to Bogotá onto an 8-mile- (13-kilometer-) long road that the residents of Granada—after the paramilitaries took over—have named *el camino del terror,* the road of terror. Between 2002 and 2003, the paramilitaries executed over 300 people on this road. Before the paramilitaries' violence, Granada had a population of over 20,000 residents. Today, because of massive forced displacement, it has only 9,818—less than half of the population it had prior to 2000.

I drove to Granada in 2003 with a resident who had agreed to take me to his town. As we approached, we saw abandoned buildings, some of them in rubble, with the acronym AUC (for Autodefensas Unidas de Colombia) spray-painted in blue or white on their walls—"AUC es presente. Muerte a los sapos" (The AUC is present. Death to snitches). In a clearing was a small, low building, which was once a small restaurant; its name, Fonda Che, in honor of the revolutionary leader Che Guevara, was still engraved on its Coca-Cola sign. On its closed, dark rolling shutters, the paramilitaries had written, "AUC presente en la zona. Desertate guerrillero. Confíanos tus dotaciones" (AUC is present in the area. Defect, guerrillas. Surrender your weapons). The two inscriptions on the façade of that small restaurant reflected the history of Granada's domination from the time of the guerrillas to that of the paramilitaries. I was arriving here just a few months prior to the demobilization of the paramilitaries, which began in late 2003, and the paired inscriptions were a reminder of who was dominating the area: they made the paramilitaries' presence felt, though it was perhaps invisible to the naked eye.

I hesitated to ask questions or corroborate stories that I had heard from displaced people in Medellín. Instead, my trip was an experience of permanent and conscious surveillance. I saw no display of weapons or military camouflage on the road to Granada; neither did I run into a paramilitary checkpoint. Yet the fear of encountering the paramilitaries' force was constantly present.

At the end of the year 2000, the paramilitaries had taken over the town of Granada one morning with the force and speed of lightning, but in the months leading up to the takeover, they had begun enforcing a checkpoint at the start of the "road of terror," stopping buses and selectively killing individuals accused of being guerrillas or collaborators. A woman whom I had met during my fieldwork in Granada shared her testimony about the gradual penetration of the paramilitaries and how fear had changed the town's way of life, including even residents' perception of time:[3]

For my generation, life in the town was very good. The kids played sports and at night. One felt safe. People partied without any problems. You never thought about violence. We knew that the guerrillas were in the rural area, but we didn't feel constant fear or terror. You respected them, though you didn't agree with them, but you did not feel the terror that we feel now. Mothers were not afraid of letting their children go out. Life was peaceful in our town.

I believe that everything began in 1999 or 2000. Things began to get tense. One began to hear that someone had been killed. People started leaving. The bus schedule changed, and there were no buses before 6 A.M. or after 6 P.M. going to Medellín. You saw that people were afraid. They started saying that 6 or 7 P.M. was already very late, as if it were 1 or 2 at night. You were afraid, you had this fear living within you. You listened to rumors—to commentaries—and this made people averse.

During this time, shootings would begin when you least expected them. I guess it was the guerrillas shooting from the hills that surround the town.

Another thing that made you afraid was hearing the noise of motorbikes roaming through the streets at night. Since it was nighttime and people were in their homes very early, one wondered who it might be—things began to change. Friendships and camaraderie faded away. Once we had a cultural week, with plays and all of that, but it was cancelled.

Traveling from Granada to [the adjacent municipality of] Santuario or Medellín was a tense experience because you always ran into a guerrilla or paramilitary checkpoint. They would have the bus stop; we all had to get off, they frisked us, and they separated some people from us, all of whom turned up dead the following day. I think there are several people who just didn't travel anymore.

The first time that I had to get off the bus, I was very afraid. I believe I went through all of the prayers I knew. It didn't matter if you didn't do anything, because that's how war is—something bad can happen to anyone regardless, simply because the other person has such a desire to kill, and if he doesn't find the individual he is looking for, he simply kills whomever. That's very nerve-wracking.

Not long afterward, on a Friday morning in early November 2000, three paramilitary squads, descending from Santuario, entered Granada from three different entry points, walked toward downtown, and indiscriminately killed those who were in the street, mostly adolescents and the elderly, a total of seventeen people. Armed with semiautomatic rifles, the paramilitaries shot everything that was moving, aiming at people's heads or backs. Up to seven bullets impacted each of the people killed while trying to escape. The massacre was intended as a moment of truth—a sentence, punishment, and public execution for the entirety of Granada—because, according to the paramilitaries, it was guilty of being a *pueblo guerrillero* (guerrilla-supporting town). The sentence of guilt was embodied by the corpses that remained lying on the street until they were removed late in the afternoon.[4] This also was a moment of the spectacular: sensational in appearance and thrilling in effect.

The former ombudsman of Granada provided a detailed account of the years of paramilitary terror:

> I was born in Granada, and I began my career working with Antioquia's energy company, and this gave me an opportunity to get to know the entire municipality. After college, I became Granada's municipal ombudsman.
>
> The problems in Oriente began in the 1980s when people from the Middle Magdalena region were displaced to our area because of the paramilitaries. In the 1990s, the problems were manageable. The guerrillas of the ELN and FARC had their presence, but the situation was relatively manageable. It was

easier to negotiate with the ELN because they are more political as an insurgency as compared to the FARC, which is more of a military organization.

In 2000, the AUC made its presence felt with the Bloque Metro group. At the beginning of the year, [the Bloque Metro] established their presence in Santuario, but they first launched a concrete and very tangible incursion into Granada on July 30, 2000, when they established a checkpoint on a site called the Alto del Palmar. On this particular day, they killed three young men from Granada, and they sprayed buses with ink. That's how the Bloque Metro announced its presence. That's when Alto del Palmar became a site of terror. The thirteen kilometers [eight miles] between Granada and Santuario were known as the kilometers of terror, because along those kilometers you could run into the legal forces of the state and the United Self-Defense Forces of Colombia, and, closer to town, you could run into the FARC. In other words, all of the armed forces were present on that road: the extreme left, the extreme right, and the state. This made the situation very tense. Selective killings were a constant, perpetuated both by leftist *and* right-wing groups.

He continued, offering his own description of the November massacre:

On November 2, 2000, [the paramilitaries] killed a man only three kilometers [about two miles] away from the town, and on November 3 at 11:55 A.M., an incursion by the Bloque Metro killed nineteen people, among them a teenager and an elderly person who was over eighty years old. The town took a huge hit. In the media, they said that the people assassinated were all militants of the guerrillas, but this is a total lie. We had to issue a denial.

It was like Dante's *Inferno*. Though the people were killed at noon, we were only able to remove the bodies at five in the afternoon because the ELN reacted and in retaliation killed two people whom they had previously kidnapped. The prosecutor and the judicial police weren't able to get to Granada, and we, with our poor means, had to remove the bodies in the afternoon.

On December 6, 2000, at 11:20 A.M., the FARC carried out a bomb attack with about 400 kilos [880 pounds] of explosives in a vital area of the town on its main road. They wanted the bomb to explode in front of the police station, but it exploded a few blocks away. On this occasion, 24 people died. More than 120 apartments and 50 stores were destroyed.

In Medellín, I met a displaced woman who had survived the paramilitary massacre in Granada and left town the following day with her husband and other family members. And yet she had not been able to escape the horror of violence:

I remember this day very clearly: November 3. I was there, and the following day we left. It came as a total surprise because [the paramilitaries] had not announced an incursion. They came through the street where we lived. My husband had been out of town, and he arrived right when the shooting took place. He knocked at the door asking me to open it. It didn't last long, and I couldn't believe they had killed so many people. One could have never imagined that something like this would happen.

I was there with my husband, who made a living repairing household appliances. We were there, and although we left [town], he went back. That's when they killed him and my brother. They killed them both on February 20[, 2001]. They had planned to come back [to Medellín] the same day, but they didn't. I waited for them on Monday and Tuesday. On Wednesday, a police officer called me from Granada and told me that they had found the bodies of two young men. I asked, "Why? What do the papers say?" He told me they didn't have any papers, nor did they have watches, money, or shoes, but he said it was my husband and my brother. I asked what clothes they wore. He described the clothing and I said, "Yes, it's them." It was very, very difficult when they told me. I thought that I was going crazy, but other people and God help you to keep going.

We went for the funeral, and we came back here [to Medellín]. I don't know why they killed him. I had a six-month-old baby, and when my husband was killed, [the baby] got sick. The doctors told me he was not going to survive, but he is still here. My daughter also has a problem—she is deaf.

Before [the paramilitaries' arrival,] life was good. I was working as a home helper, and I had a lot of work there. Life was good because there was peace and tranquility—you had everything, and you got work. After the massacre of November, I started to feel afraid. After the massacre, one couldn't eat because there was so much fear.

What do the two ethnographic examples of the paramilitaries' takeover of Oriente discussed above suggest about the paramilitaries' practice of violence in marginal areas? The discourse of the paramilitaries suggests that an antagonism exists between the guerrillas and the state, which are seen as opposing forces competing for domination and control of the resources and people of a given territory. The notion of "counterinsurgency" itself suggests the existence of this antagonistic dynamic, in which the paramilitaries become a reactive force. The justificatory narrative employed by the paramilitaries also echoes a broader interpretation of Colombia's history as the story of a fragmented land and an unfinished national project, of a nation plagued since its independence by irreconcilable and violent rivalries, which the enmity between Francisco Paula de Santander and Simón Bolívar—the generals who led Colombia to independence from Spain in the nineteenth century—

embodied first, their conflict later engendering the permanent antagonism and competition for hegemony between the Conservative and Liberal parties. This rivalry turned into a chain of civil wars that lasted until La Violencia in the mid-twentieth century. Present-day violence is often understood as the continuation of this long and linear history of violence—the effect of an original and irreconciled fracture that has shaped the destiny of the country. In other words, the narrative suggests an original sin that generated a rift, from which violence has been permanently flowing like blood from a wound.

In his analysis of political violence in Northern Ireland, Allen Feldman explained how a tale of a similarly original and immutable partition engendered the historic antagonism between the Catholic and Protestant communities: "Linearity and repetition, metaphorized as history, are deployed in these tales to repress historicity" (1991, 18). He suggested that understandings of Northern Ireland's violence as grounded in ideological and/or socioeconomic explanations have prevented an interpretation of that violence as a semantic modality capable over time of mutation that ultimately reproduces itself: "Novel subject positions are constructed and reconstructed by violent performances, and this mutation of agency renders formal ideological rational and prior contextual motivation unstable and even secondary" (ibid., 20).

While space and spatial symbolism in Northern Ireland represented, as Feldman argued, a structural mechanism for the reproduction of ethnicity, in Colombia, and specifically in the case of Oriente, space became "a power and an animated entity" (ibid., 28), produced as an exteriority and inhabited by unruly people who had to be reined in and dominated in order to be modernized, civilized, and brought into line. The existence and the permanence of such spaces are the consequence of Colombia being an unfinished and fragmented project. Not only a complex history, but also a hostile geography—with three cordilleras dividing up the country in a way that renders Colombia's conception of itself as a single and united nation even more difficult—has contributed to the reproduction of a narrative that conceives of untamed spaces as areas where the state has been weak, if not absent.

Rather than offering an analysis of recent paramilitary violence as an additional link in the linear chain of Colombia's history of violence, an alternative interpretative strategy suggests that we pay close attention to the praxis of violence, which indicates that it is not so much the absence or weakness of the state that legitimizes paramilitaries' presence and violence in the liminal spaces where they act, but rather their actions express a form of violent power that is immanent to the state's function of capture. As such, the paramilitaries are the driving force of an imagined order populated by tamed and docile subjects, and their violence is the cipher of a pacification aimed at producing that order. As Foucault (1994) observed, war is the cipher of peace.

The case of Oriente thus suggests that the state's intertwinement with paramilitaries does not prevent state formation, but rather mirrors the state's practice in spaces that are produced as liminal, thus legitimizing paramilitary violence.[5] This violence does not reflect the absence or weakness of the state; nor does it mirror the early stages of the state's evolutionary process in a continuum from violence to nonviolence, from disorder to order. To the contrary, it unmasks the driving force that lies at the foundation of the state: it is not the absence of the law but the power of the law to be suspended that allows the production of liminal spaces and the legitimization of the arbitrariness of power.

The legitimized violence of the paramilitary has been referred to by both victims and victimizers as *limpieza*. The word designates a violence that cleanses and purifies a space that leftist insurgents as well as so-called *desechables* ("the disposable people"), such as junkies and homosexuals, have polluted with their ideas and vices. The idea of *limpieza* suggests a notion of dialectic spaces, constructed as either pure or impure, which provide the social structure for the reproduction of violence (Feldman 1991; Taussig 1987). Purity and impurity are akin: there is no discontinuity between the two opposites, but rather a transmutation from one into the other, since the pure presupposes the impure and the impure contains the possibility of the pure. This ambiguity, as Durkheim highlighted (1995), is immanent to the sacred, and on it rests the legitimacy of paramilitary violence, whose attribution as an act of *limpieza,* of cleansing, confers the character of the sacred on its intention. In the justificatory discourse of the paramilitaries and their advocates, *limpieza,* rather than being a violence that destroys, is one that purifies, that transforms, that makes anew.

Death lists, selective killings, disappearances, tortures, and massacres are all expressions of paramilitaries' *limpieza*. In his narration, Luna—the informant who had shared his life history with me (see chapter 2)—defined *limpieza* as the act of sweeping the floor and putting out the trash. Killing is therefore a form of extreme cleaning:

> The guerrilla is the dirty thing, and then one goes to clean it up. One takes the broom to sweep the dirty and to leave everything clean. For something to be clean, there has to be someone who removes the garbage. The cleaning is done for guerrillas, bands, thieves, and vicious people. I began cleaning in Urabá, killing a lot of people. There were a lot of *gamines* [street children]. We also cleaned it up of those gays who were there; there were about three hundred, and we began to kill them. *Gamines* used to walk on the street gathering cardboard. We started killing all of these too, and the town was left clean and healthy.

Some years later, when I returned to these and other statements about *limpieza* while working on this book, I took a stroll to refresh my mind. At the time, I lived in the Manhattan neighborhood of Hell's Kitchen, which, I was told, had once been a nest of crime, prostitution, and gang violence before Rudolph Giuliani became mayor and promoted his zero-tolerance policy, which spearheaded the gentrification of urban areas such as this one. Now, instead of sex shops and gentlemen's clubs, there were restaurants and luxury apartment buildings. As I walked down the street, I saw a bearded black man wearing a blue-collar worker's uniform, separating waste and putting used soda cans in a huge transparent waste bag. The man worked calmly, selecting with care and scrutinizing the disposed cans. I observed that he was engaged in an act of cleaning and ordering the chaos of urban waste. To the eyes of a city dweller, a sidewalk that is filled with smelly and ugly waste is unpleasant and off-putting. Cleaning up is called for, desired, appreciated, and, most of all, needed. "Keep New York City Clean," I read on a large green cylindrical trashcan installed by the city's department of sanitation. In Colombia, paramilitary death squads worked like a department of sanitation of sorts, cleaning up—or "sucking up," as they said in Argentina during the Dirty War—from the streets the guerrillas as well as petty criminals, drug addicts, prostitutes, and people who had a way of thinking that did not fall in line with a fixed notion of order: a work that was, for some, considered desirable, needed, and appreciated. "Exterminator!" says the main character in William Burroughs's short story of the same name. "You need the service. . . . Just plain ordinary sons of bitches. That's all they are," he says of roaches and bedbugs, which are metaphors for disposable people (Burroughs 1973, 7). *Limpieza,* too, is the work of exterminators. This is how a paramilitary, who for several years was a member of a *limpieza* squad in Antioquia, explained the paramilitaries' job as exterminators to me:

The *limpieza* that the self-defense groups carry out has several meanings. If you are an individual living in a different country and you arrived and started to commit robbery, abuse people, hit women and all the girls in town, whom you treat like hustlers, that is recorded in a book; they are going to take notes of all the bad things that you do until they gather thirty or forty kids who did shit, and they hold a meeting in the village and ask, "So-and-so: How has he been behaving?"

"This guy does shit, this guy is so-and-so, this guy doesn't have respect for no one, this guy is a thief, and so on." They ask about each of the guys they rounded up.

Then [the paramilitaries] say to them, "We are not gonna do anything to you. We just wanna talk to you." And to each one, they say, "Brother, you're gonna behave or we kill you."

A chance is given to them to change. If they see that the kid is changing, they take him out of the book. If within a month you haven't changed, you are going to die. They give them a month. Some remain [in the village], while others leave. Then one day, they kill two or three of them. The following day, they kill four or five. And they continue killing all the [bad] kids until a nice cleansing of the village has been done. You clean the town of those people who don't deserve to stay in town. Sometimes [the paramilitaries] recruit them as part of the self-defense groups, or they tell them to enroll in the army. If they see the kid is reluctant or doesn't leave, then they kill him. It's like the cleaning of a home, the aim of which is to have a clean house. Likewise, killing has the aim of cleaning up the neighborhoods. As a result, you don't hear of robbery anymore. The one who wants to commit a robbery thinks twice about it because he knows that chances are, they are going to kill him. And so kids take a good turn in their lives. They try to change their lives. Of course, the day that you relapse, they are not gonna forget, and they kill you. So people start behaving well, and that's how you clean a town.

I was working in *limpieza* within a town. I remained there for eight months. They gave me a house for my ten comrades. We had cars and motorbikes. Previously it was a guerrilla town, but we, with the help of God, ejected the guerrillas a while ago. We started collecting information that the peasants themselves gave us. The list of people to kill is formed with the information that the people themselves give us. The people guide us. They come to complain about someone, and we take notes. We tell the women [who complain] that we are going to talk to their husbands, and if they rebel, we kill him. They told us where the guerrilla was, and little by little we expelled the guerrilla, and we are left governing this town. I did a very nice cleansing there, because no guerrilla was left. Now it's a very healthy place. If there are killings now, it's because someone did some shit. Every day, we killed up to seven or eight people.

When the self-defense groups take over a village, they circle it with four or five hundred of their men. Then they send three to twenty people to do an exploration and start talking to people. They ask if there is a guerrilla in town, and people tell them, "So-and-so is a guerrilla; in that house lives a guerrilla," and so on. At the beginning, you leave things quiet, as they are, and then, when they least expect it, they enter and kill everyone. You start killing until the guerrilla can't deal with it anymore; you establish yourself there and start dominating that territory. When we do the *limpieza,* we leave behind twenty to thirty of our men and withdraw nearby. To carry out *limpieza,* they choose men whose hands don't tremble when they have to kill.

When you're going to kill a person, you never talk to that person, and you never look them in their eyes. Nor do you let the person talk. There are many people, especially women, who soften your heart because they start crying or beg you not to kill them. So you can't let them talk to you, and you can't look a person in the eyes. When you are going to kill someone, you kill them without looking them in the eyes because it's like . . . I don't know . . . but a certain sadness stays with you.

Acts of cleansing are a reminder that a particular village or neighborhood lives under the jurisdiction of the paramilitary, which, more often than not, enjoys the collaboration of the police and the army. In particular, it is the ambiguity of the paramilitaries' intertwinement with the state that offers a sense of sovereignty to their violence and confers a divine quality to its manifestations, thus reflecting a primitive right to make life-and-death decisions and exercise them in an absolute and unrestricted way. As in Oriente and elsewhere across Colombia, populations subjugated by paramilitaries are, as Elias Canetti observed, like believers submitting to God, aware of that they are in his power and subject to his sharp intervention: "It is as they were already in God's mouth, to be crushed in the next instant" (1984, 282).

When I first began my fieldwork among the displaced population in Medellín and later in the Oriente, I did not know that I myself would become the witness of a paramilitary death squad act of *limpieza.*

It happened in a few minutes on a hot and humid Sunday night in a town in the Bajo Cauca area of northern Antioquia. Children, young people, and families crowded the town's main square or strolled through the streets surrounding the square. I was in a car with Luna, whom I had previously met in Medellín when he was a part of the paramilitary demobilization process. Now he was back in town and very much a part of the cocaine business.

Approaching the square, we saw a medium-sized truck parked obliquely, and to my inexperienced eyes, it looked like an accident had occurred.

But Luna made me stop. He understood that something was going on, something was about to happen. The truck was obstructing the passage of a Toyota Prado van, and someone was talking to the truck driver. Then there was a commotion. A few men, maybe eight, were surrounding the vehicle and forcing the driver to get out. Their silhouettes suggested that they were robust adults. One extracted a revolver from under his shirt and pressed it against the driver's head—a tall man, around forty, his slim torso in a white sleeveless T-shirt and his long toothpick legs in blue jeans. The gun shone in the dim light. "Those are the *paras*," Luna told me with some excitement.

The men tugged at the poor driver, who was screaming and clinging to the wooden frame of the truck, hanging onto his life with desperation. He cried out for help and for the intervention of the police, whose station was only a block away and just around the corner. But everyone, including the police, played deaf as he yelled, "Police! Help! Police!" Everyone knew—including myself—that no help we could offer could reverse the deeds of paramilitaries in action. The street and the truck had turned into a scaffold. A horrifying silence swept the area. The only sounds were the moans of the truck driver, the paramilitaries' heavy punches slamming into his body, and the clunk of the revolver when it slipped from the hands of a paramilitary and fell to the ground.

My heart was pounding heavily, shooting blood to the extremities of my body. Eventually, someone opened the trunk of the paramilitary van, into which they threw the weakened driver. The paramilitaries disappeared into the darkness at high speed, leaving the town. "Now they are going to kill him," Luna said.

I was still shaken. Luna suggested we go to a bar, where we might find information about what we had just witnessed. Other young people arrived, ones who, like Luna, were involved in small trades of cocaine paste. Everyone ordered beer and acted normally, as if no major event had happened. News came in. The operation was apparently carried out by the men of a cocaine-base vendor who was linked to a paramilitary boss, and it was retaliation for the disappearance of two of the vendor's men the day before. "Such an operation can only be carried out with the blessing of the paramilitaries," Luna explained. The truck driver was a *sapo* ("a snitch"), who was probably collaborating with the armed forces by handing over competitors in the drug business. That morning, in fact, the military had spread thousands of flyers from a helicopter, asking anyone with information about drug dealers to share it with law enforcement. Protection and immunity were assured. This method sought to encourage complaints and betrayal. "One first talks and later gets killed," a passerby had told me when he saw me reading the flyer that morning. He had anticipated what I would later witness.

"No doubt this was coordinated with the police," Luna commented. We went back to the car and looked for one of his friends who, according to Luna, was the local commander of the paramilitaries. The situation was *caliente.* Apparently, the truck driver was Luna's neighbor, and if he had shared information with the military about Luna's illegal activities, then Luna was in danger of bring apprehended. Luna decided to leave town immediately, and I took advantage of the situation and left as well, driving back to the town of Tarazá, where I would spend the night, something that I had wanted to do from the moment I had witnessed the kidnapping of the truck driver.

When I woke up in Tarazá the following morning, I found my hotel surrounded by men armed with rifles. I turned to Jader, a former paramilitary who knew the area and who had accompanied me from Medellín, for some explanation. "These are all the security forces of the *patrón,* who is having breakfast at the restaurant," he responded. The *patrón* was Cuco Vanoy,[6] a drug kingpin and a demobilized paramilitary leader who, in 2008, the government of Colombia, would extradite to the United States along with thirteen other paramilitary leaders.

I went to have breakfast with Jader and my friend Ana. Inside the restaurant were about ten armed men crowded around a larger table while the *patrón* sat at the head of another table in a corner. Stuffed into his jeans was an Italian Beretta handgun. People took turns talking with him. At one point, Mi Sangre, the paramilitary commander of Tarazá, showed up in a white van. He went straight up to Vanoy, sat down on his left, and, interrupting a conversation that the boss was having with another individual, whispered in his ear while fixing his gaze on me. The situation felt awkward and threatening. Both Mi Sangre and Cuco Vanoy got up, got into the white van, and took a short drive, apparently to avoid indiscreet ears. They returned to the table after a few minutes.

Not much time had passed when a police patrol arrived at the restaurant. The police were also heavily armed. The captain, escorted by a few of his own men, went up to the *patrón* and greeted him. He then walked up to me and greeted me formally. He asked me where my car was. "In the shop, to repair the brakes," I said, indicating the shop just next to the restaurant.

He asked me if I was a foreigner, to which I replied, "Yes."

He turned toward Jader and asked him for his papers. "Are you Luna? Do you know Luna?"

Jader denied it. At this moment, I knew that we were in trouble. The police asked Jader to follow them, and they took him away to interrogate him. They left a police officer to watch Ana and me.

Fear took over. What was going on? Why were they looking for Luna? Why did they link Luna to my presence here? Who did they think I was or what my role might be? Fantasies and images linked to what I had witnessed the night before abounded. Would the police or paramilitaries come back and ask me again about Luna? Feeling the gazes of the police officer and the paramilitaries upon me, I tried to read the newspaper, pretending to be relaxed and fine. In reality, I was sweating.

Luna suddenly showed up, arriving on a motorbike with a friend. I was terrorized and felt my heart sink. The police and paramilitaries alike were after Luna, but here he was, appearing on a scene filled with armed men. Fear is a strange and dominating feeling. The perception that one's life is in jeopardy causes the expenditure of a great amount of energy and provokes a conflict between the rational and irrational, between thought and instinct. My brain constantly processed, interpreted, and combined present and past information in an infinite number of combinations, images melting into a single nightmare. As Linda Green (1999) observed in Guatemala, fear and terror can become a shared experience, the grease that lubricates the gears of an entire society. Fear is the state of emergency that becomes the quotidian normality; it is the reality that lingers on beyond the event of spectacular violence. Fear is hidden, not immediately perceptible, but it is always present and commanding behind the gazes, smiles, and greetings that people living in despotic spaces share every day. It leaves its mark in the many microdecisions that they make daily. Fear is the organizing principle of such spaces.

My legs felt an urgency to run away, and yet I sensed that the best move was not to move at all and to feign serenity. Instinctively, the nail of my right index finger scraped the skin of my thumb. When I became conscious of this small nervous tic, I tried to control it. Yet It took a great amount of effort to stop a tiny gesture that could reveal a great deal of information. After a few moments, instinct prevailed, and I automatically got up and walked toward the nearby car shop where a mechanic was fixing my brakes. One of the *patrón*'s bodyguards, a heavy man with a gold chain around his neck, followed me.

Luna saw me and followed me as well. "Go away right now," I told him in a rush of words from behind the car when he reached me. He turned white. "Everyone is looking for you!" I told him.

"Everyone who?" Luna asked, looking surprised.

"The police. The *paras*. Just go!" I told him with urgency.

Luna ran out of the shop, got on the motorbike, and vanished. I went back into the restaurant, waiting for Jader to return and for my car to be repaired

After about two hours, the *patrón* eventually left the restaurant, and Jader finally came back. He was visibly exhausted and tired, and we returned to the hotel. "This time, I was sure they were going to kill me," he said, throwing himself on the bed in my room. The officers had first, he related, brought him to a police station where a hooded man, probably an acquaintance of Luna's, assured the interrogating paramilitaries and police officers that Jader was not the man that they were after. Later they brought him to a hospital where another man, who had hit by a bullet during a gunfight, did not identify him as Luna either, and so they let Jader go. We packed our luggage and we left the area. This was the last time that I ever saw Luna.

In this event, I experienced one manifestation of what Doble Cero explained to me as the paramilitaries' military tactics. In fact, when I met with him in the area surrounding San Roque, from where he had coordinated the penetration of San Carlos and Granada, I asked him about that morning when his death squads had entered Granada and killed people, and about that spectacular display of violence in their acts of *limpieza*. He responded:

> It is a sort of counterterrorism that needs to be aimed at the minds of the people, since their minds are filled with the terror of the guerrilla. What you try to do is show the capacity for disputing the domination of the guerrilla.... It is a demonstration of force; it is a demonstration of power, which you normally need to do in the initial phase [of paramilitaries' domination].

While providing his explanation, Doble Cero drew, with a ballpoint pen, a stylized body on a piece of paper and then crossed out the small circle representing its head, thus sketching the meaning of *limpieza* as an act of erasure, of deleting what is prohibited. It was a definite act, one that shaped the body in a way that was definite and did not allow for any reshaping. Doble Cero had drawn a body as an ideological construct on that sheet of paper: it was the body of the radical Other, which, because it inhabited a determined and external space—equally an ideological construction—was produced as the body of the enemy, a detached body. As such, it had to be disposed of through violence. The violence inscribed on that body also transformed it into a political text that allowed the paramilitaries to produce otherness and enmity and, in turn, legitimized their acts of *limpieza*—a violence that doesn't destroy for the sake of destroying, but one that pretends, through purification, to educate.

Thus the corpses publicly exposed, such as those in the massacres of San Carlos and Granada, became the bearers of a political message. In the public spectacle of violence, a whole economy of power, as Doble Cero pointed out, is invested in its excesses. In the bodies of alleged guerrillas and petty criminals that are left behind after execution in public squares or soccer fields, their guilt is exposed and the sentence becomes legible to all. As Foucault emphasized, the spectacle of punishment "made the guilty man the herald of his own condemnation" and "established the public execution as the moment of truth" (1995, 43).

The paramilitaries' acts of *limpieza* can thus be interpreted as a political ritual in which power is manifested and expanded. They are acts that, through punishment, affirm a truth. As such, they are intended to educate. The *limpieza* is not only about subtraction; it does not only eliminate. The cleansing is meant to be an act of transformation—it is part of a process of deterritorialization and reterritorialization. The focus of our analysis, though, should not be on *limpieza*'s effects and consequences, which would merely consider violence as a means toward an end. Justificatory discourses tend to offer utilitarian explanations of violence and its spectacularity. Doble Cero's explanation of the spectacular character of violence falls within a utilitarian framework, but it is worthwhile to consider the meaning of violence's spectacle in itself, and to wonder if Doble Cero's prestige and rank, like that of other paramilitaries, were rooted not in the effects of violence but in the expenditure of violence itself. It is here, it seems to me, that Bataille further clarifies what Foucault observed about the scaffold and the spectacularity of violence. It is not in the restraint of violence, but in the excess and spectacularity of its discharge, that the truth effect of *limpieza* is affirmed. Acts of *limpieza* can thus be seen as sacrificial acts in which the sacrifice of the victim, as in Bataille's (1991a) analysis of the Aztecs' myth, is necessary to the life of the sun. In other words, for power (as for wealth if we follow Bataille), it's the expenditure rather than the accumulation that matters. The accumulation is only the delay of expenditure: "Energy finally can only be wasted" (ibid., 11).

Accordingly, it is not in the effects of *limpieza* that the power of the para-militaries is revealed. *Limpieza* is not the act that precedes domination and opens the gate to hegemony. Rather, it is *limpieza* itself—as a violent discharge of energy, as an expenditure, as violence done for the sake of violence—that both contains and reveals the power and the exuberance of the paramilitaries. *Limpieza* is not a necessity but something more like luxury, something like spectacles, games, and sexual activity, all of which have no useful purpose but are an excessive expenditure done for their own sake. This is an insight that Luna, the paramilitary who started to toy with guns and killings when he was only twelve years old, provided to me when he spoke of killing as an addiction and a sport:

> When you go out to kill a person for the first time, it is very difficult. When you bring your finger to the trigger, it's very difficult. But soon after you pull the trigger, you are taken by the taste of it, and you want to continue holding the finger [on the trigger]. This turns into a sort of addiction, like a drug. And if you kill three, four people, then you get even more addicted. One has already lost control. In Urabá, many were killed. We were paid on a piece-rate system.

Luna went on to share how he once had had to kill a young woman. "She was very beautiful, but I had to kill her," he told me. He had an order to follow, and "when the boss came, I already had her head in my hands." He then dwelled on an explanation of the different tools, such as chainsaws and machetes, used to dispose of a body after it was killed and told me that there are individuals among the paramilitaries who train one on how to appropriately cut a body into pieces. "Chopping up [a body] is a delirium," Luna admitted.

When he became the paramilitary commander in a neighborhood of Medellín, he told me, he no longer carried out as many killings as he had before. "I gave up the sport," he said. He simply gave orders to kill designated victims rather than executing them himself. "I was killing very little—just once in a while—so as not to lose the habit," he added.

In Luna's confession, killing was done for fun and sport. It was killing for the sake of killing, violence for the sake of violence—it was "delirium," sport, pleasure, or entertainment. It reminds one of Bataille's Bluebeard and how he strangled a child while sexually stimulating himself: "He relished seeing the blood" (1991b, 14).

In the process of purification and pacification, the spectacularity and expenditure of violence are essential features. In liminal spaces where law and order are suspended, civilization and barbarism conflate. Benjamin suggested that "there is no document of civilization which is not at the same time a document of barbarism" (1968, 256). What seems interesting to me here is Benjamin's emphasis on "at the same time," by which he means the simultaneity of civilization and barbarism rather than the evolutionary and linear evolution of history from barbarism to civilization. History instead happens in the now, in the conflation of margin and center, primitivism and modernity, barbarism and civilization.

The spectacle of paramilitary violence in Colombia, then, should not be narrowly interpreted as an instrumental violence, a violence that is merely geared toward an end. Rather, paramilitary violence in Colombia suggests that we consider the simultaneity of barbarism and civilization as immanent to the notion of modernity and the state. It is a simultaneity that is expressed in the state's ability to decide to impose a state of emergency, which, as it suspends the law, awakens the savage that lies within it, only apparently dormant. Giorgio Agamben, in *Homo Sacer,* used the metaphor of the werewolf, a monstrous hybrid divided between the forest and the city, to represent this quality of the state. "The state of nature is not a real epoch chronologically prior to the foundation of the City but a principle internal to the City," he wrote (1998, 105). In other words, the state is not the reasonable remedy to the state of nature, as the classic theory of state has suggested. Instead the state is simultaneously interiority and exteriority, reason *and* state of nature. It is at this threshold that Colombia paramilitaries are called into life and operate with impunity.

4

An Ethnography of Cocaine

On a sunny Saturday morning in July 2006, I left Medellín, where I was based, to head north toward Colombia's Atlantic coast. I drove on the main road that had enabled Medellín to become the industrial and financial heart of Colombia. Along this road—one that first passes through the steep and sinuous contours of the Central and Western Cordilleras, then follows the Río Cauca until it reaches the town of Caucasia and finally turns gently toward the Caribbean Sea—town-villages have been forming like clots of blood in recent years. Compelled by the promises of the country's nascent market economy, their residents, desiring a good life, have settled in these small urban centers, which, during the sixteenth century, first formed around gold mines. Today these places grow up near coca fields, where money is frantically exchanged and miraculously multiplied by the apparently divine qualities of cocaine. Equally attracted by the allure of this lively commodity, I resolved to travel to a coca-growing area to explore and attempt to convey the texture of social life in the cocaine-driven Bajo Cauca region, a subregion of Antioquia that lies at the base of the Western Cordillera and expands north toward the regions of Córdoba and Bolívar.

Traveling with me was Jader, whom I mentioned in the previous chapter, a twenty-two-year-old demobilized paramilitary who had provided me with some initial insights about life in cocaine-producing areas of Colombia. When puberty struck, Jader had lost his grandfather, who had served as his surrogate father. Surrounded by the disorder of both his own existence and that of his country, Jader, still a minor, decided to join the paramilitary at the age of fourteen. When a platoon stopped by his grandparents' property, he joined them. After an intense and demanding three-month training, and with a rifle in his hands, a heavy rucksack on his young shoulders, and the dream of soon becoming "someone," Jader began his life as a combatant. He served in many groups, fighting guerrillas in the mountains, carrying out assigned killings and massacres, and escorting shipments of cocaine across Colombia's northwestern border into Panama. Over the years, he attended several *patrones*—that is, the bosses and the owners of right-wing armed organizations. Jader told me that in Bajo Cauca, he had been the commander of a forty-man paramilitary unit—a battalion—in charge of watching over the coca fields and laboratories belonging to a boss and keeping guerrillas out of the territory. For some time, Jader told me, he had been one of the bodyguards of his last *patrón*, Cuco Vanoy.

I had first noticed Jader in April 2006 in a shelter for forcibly displaced people in downtown Medellín. He had come to the city after his group had disbanded as part of the larger demobilization process. Jader had unwillingly handed over his rifle—along with the life that he had known up until that point in time. At the shelter, Jader hardly talked to other guests and spent a good deal of time on a balcony overlooking a street corner, watching passersby and smoking cigarettes. He would barely return a greeting or a smile. His pale-brown eyes were icy. Over time, having sat down with many paramilitaries, I had learned that this cold and lifeless look distinguished people who had witnessed much bloodshed and for whom death was a regular companion. Handsome and slim, with broad shoulders, Jader wore the proper outfit of an urban paramilitary: trendy sneakers, blue jeans, and a colorful T-shirt. Other typical emblems were his high-and-tight military haircut and, most importantly, his pencil mustache.

"He doesn't look like a displaced person," I said to Clara, the affable social worker who takes care of people abruptly evicted from their homes.

"You are right," she smiled back, with some pleasure at my intuition, "but the law grants everyone the right to declare oneself a 'person in a situation of displacement.' It is up to the state," she concluded, "to define their status."

Once declared part of the "displaced population," the displaced must leave the shelter within a couple of days and reinvent their lives from scratch, aided by some money granted by the state. Acción Social, the government agency designated to attend to displaced people, rejects many applications, but Jader's tale sounded credible to the officer who had collected his testimony, and he was granted status as a displaced person. His deeds, and those of his paramilitary group, had no doubt caused the displacements of peasants and rural communities, and Jader certainly possessed knowledge that made his account sound credible and coherent: he knew about the dynamics of displacements, including the fates of uprooted people and the places where and when such displacements had occurred. Thus, in addition to getting state support as a demobilized paramilitary, he was also given state assistance generally granted to the displaced population.

"If I don't find a job within a few months, I will go back to work in Bajo Cauca," Jader told me when I approached him at the shelter to ask about his future.

"Are you going back to work for [your paramilitary] group?" I dared to ask.

Surprised, Jader widened his eyes and smiled. "How did you know?"

"Just by looking at you, I can tell you are one of them," I said in a conspiratorial tone.

Jader laughed, astonished but probably also happy to remove his displaced-person mask. The ice was broken. From that moment onward, we spent a great deal of time together. Over time, Jader would loosen up his iron demeanor, revealing himself to be a frail young man with a lost childhood.

My idea to travel to Bajo Cauca came one night while I was talking with Jader over dinner in Medellín. As our conversation developed, he became increasingly collaborative. Up until that night, he had been reluctant to disclose details of his paramilitary life, and I had had a hard time gaining insights into his experience. Now I had the impression that in planning the trip, he was finding a way to show me his expertise and prove useful to my research. That night, I witnessed the unfolding of an informant, and we became partners.

Jader assured me that he was still on good terms with his former companions and superiors and that the regional commander was his close relative. In phone conversations with comrades, Jader would proudly refer to his relative as *mi sangre* ("my blood"). Though officially demobilized, the group still looked after the cocaine business of the *patrón,* the demobilized paramilitary leader and drug dealer Cuco Vanoy. In addition, one of Jader's uncles owned a medium-sized coca field. The trip, which we planned to last a week, was an opportunity to take a close look at some of the ongoing dynamics in Colombia's internal conflict and its links to the ever-growing cocaine business.

Our trip from Medellín to the Bajo Cauca region reversed the journey taken by the Spaniards in the sixteenth century. From the belly of Antioquia, we drove north as if attempting to connect the past and present, the now and the what-had-been, in a link that could make sense of a world shaped by gold yesterday and cocaine today. The village-towns that we drove through were landmarks of Colombia's pioneer gold-mining years, which plugged Antioquia into the capitalist market at a time when the global division of labor between Europe and the rest of the world was established. In Antioquia, as in the rest of Latin America, this process started when the Spaniards subjugated the Indians. In fact, Colombia, soon called Castilla de Oro, became a significant gold producer, supplying most of the 185,000 kilograms (about 407,850 pounds) of gold shipped to Seville between 1503 and 1660 (Wolf 1982, 135).

Spaniards launched the conquest of Colombia at the outset of the sixteenth century. Conquistadores first landed on the Caribbean coast, spreading their presence from the Darién to the Guajira region. The conquistador Francisco Pizarro ordered Sebastián de Belalcázar to penetrate north from Quito, which he had founded. Belalcázar sent lieutenants into the region that today corresponds to the Valle del Cauca and later followed them, founding the town of Cali in 1536.

Penetration into the interior of Colombia proved to be difficult. The Spaniards ventured into the country's interior from the Gulf of Urabá, through the Río Magdalena, or from the Valle del Cauca. Their attempts were often repelled by the indigenes and their poisoned arrows, which were the weapons most feared by the conquistadores. Diseases, mosquitos, ticks, and a hostile geography also often defeated the Spaniards. Yet Belalcázar's troops reached Antioquia in 1539 and began to establish settlements around areas rich in gold and silver. Gold, in fact, became the conquistadores' economic engine in the Cauca region.

They subjugated the indigenes and used them as workers to extract gold. As Frank Safford and Marco Palacios wrote, the gold mined from the veins at Buriticá in pre-Columbian times inspired the founding of Santa Fe de Antioquia, the capital of Antioquia (2002, 36). Once a gold site had been depleted, the Spaniards would move to a different area but took along the name given to the original settlement.

While still in his teens, the Spanish conquistador Pedro de Cieza de León, author of the *Crónicas del Perú*, joined the expedition that the Spaniards undertook from the port of Urabá into the interior of Colombia, crossing hostile and almost impervious territory toward Antioquia. Cieza de León reported on that journey in his chronicles and explained how the conquistadores had to walk through dense forests inhabited by herds of pigs, great tapirs, lions, bears, snakes, and tigers and cross chains of mountains "that horses neither can nor ever will be able to pass over" (2001, 43). He described those forests as a space fraught with perils in which tales of terrors circulated, not unlike the ones that, a few centuries later, were shared in the Putumayo and that Taussig (1987) interpreted to highlight how terror is mediated to us through narratives. Cieza de León wrote:

I must here relate a circumstance, which I hold to be certainly true, for it is attested by many men who are worthy of belief. It is that when the Lieutenant Juan Graciano was traveling by this road ... in company with certain Spaniards ... they met with a snake or serpent, which was so large that it measured more than twenty feet in length, and of great girth. Its head was a clear red, its eyes green and protruding, and, when they saw it, it leveled its head to strike at them, and, indeed, gave Pedro Ximon such a blow that he died. They found an entire deer in its belly. (2001, 43)

Not only wild animals, but also "Indians, who possess much gold" (ibid., 44) inhabited those spaces. The Indians were perceived as being no less dangerous than the wild animals, and thus equally terrifying stories circulated about them:

I heard it said that the lords or *caciques* of the valley of Nore collected all the women they could find from the land of their enemies, took them home, and used them as if they had been their own. If any children were born, they were reared with much care until their reached the age of twelve or thirteen, and, being then plump and healthy, these caciques ate them with much appetite, not considering that they were of their own flesh and blood. (Ibid., 50)

The Indians in Antioquia were followed by a powerful *cacique* called Nutibara, who inspired the name of Don Berna's paramilitary group in Medellín and its department. Cacique Nutibara, who traveled around the country sitting on a litter inlaid with gold and borne on the shoulders of his principal men, was revered and feared by his members of his tribe, who sent him gold and apparel as tribute.

Near the door of his house, and the same thing was done at the houses of his captains, there were many heads of his enemies whom he had eaten, which were kept there as trophies. All the natives of this country eat human flesh. There are many large burial places which much needs be very rich. They had, in the first place, a great house or temple dedicated to the Devil. (Ibid., 46)

When the expedition in which Cieza de León took part invaded the lands of Cacique Nutibara, the Indians there had already hidden their gold, following the advice of the "devil":

An Indian woman, who belonged to one Baptista Zimbron, said to me that after Cesar returned to Carthagena, all the lords of these valleys assembled and performed sacrifices, when the devil appeared in the form of a very fierce tiger (which in their language is called *guaca*), and said that those Christians had come from the other side of the sea, and that soon many more would arrive to occupy and take possession of the land, and that they must prepare for war. He then disappeared, and the Indians began to prepare, first taking a great quantity of treasure out of the burial places.... In truth, as these Indians have not faith, I am not astonished at this. (Ibid., 48, 51)

It was the rush for gold, and the desires and fantasies that it kindled, that lured Spaniards into Colombia's midland and motivated them to overcome the hardships and perils of a hostile nature as well as indigenes armed with poisoned arrows. Antioquia was a land rich in gold and silver—an engineer, Vicente Restrepo, provided an account of the early history of gold mining in Colombia in his classic *Study of the Gold & Silver Mines of Colombia,* a work that he considered "a patriotic labor" (1886, 12). He described Antioquia as a region whose "mountains are crossed by innumerable veins.... There is scarcely a stream, or brook, or river in which gold is not found, so that it may be truly said of this State, that it is like an immense net that holds in its meshes inexhaustible deposits, wherewith to enrich its industrious people" (ibid., 23).

Using rudimentary tools, the indigenes had already been mining gold along the Cauca, Nechí, and Porce rivers; after the arrival of the conquistadores, "numerous rich tombs have been unearthed, in which [the dead] were found buried with idols and ornaments, all made of gold, which they seemed to have possessed in great abundance" (ibid.). Antioquia was so rich in gold, Restrepo observed, that, "to use an expression of Fray Pedro Simón, it seemed as if the earth were vomiting forth the gold it could not suffer to remain in its bowels" (ibid., 24).

Once the Spaniards had subdued the indigenes, the exploitation of gold began in earnest. Settlements grew around lode mines, turning the Bajo Cauca region into the pulsating heart of Antioquia's economy. Restrepo reported that the people of Cáceres, Antioquia, Cartago, and Cali extracted large amounts of gold from the Río Cauca (ibid., 28). The expansion continued eastward along the Porce and Nechí rivers, where in 1580 the settlement of Zaragoza was founded. "Places so rich in gold were found," observed Restrepo, "that it was only necessary to pick up the soil and wash it in a trough, to satisfy one's cupidity with the sight of the glittering metal." He added: "As the people of Remedios used to say, it seemed as if mother earth had made her last will and testament, and had divided her treasures among her children" (ibid., 34–35).

The golden age of the Cauca region did not last forever. Between the eighteenth and nineteenth centuries, in fact, the mining industry underwent a crisis caused by extreme poverty, inefficient technology, a scarcity of slaves, and the high cost of sustaining slave labor. Only in 1820, after the war of independence, did the newly constituted Republic of Colombia again provide a strong boost to merchants and gold smugglers from Medellín, who would make that city very rich. The Society of Antioquia Mines exploited gold veins in Anorí, Bajo Nechí, Sonsón, Santa Rosa, and Titiribí. This wealth excited the desires of British bankers and later, French, German, and American engineers.

Between 1820 and 1830, Antioquia became the nation's principal auriferous region, and the prestige of its businessmen and merchants increased along with their fame as tenacious, diligent, and frugal entrepreneurs. The people of Antioquia, nicknamed *paisa,* still take pride in preserving that reputation. Even though the age of gold did not leave behind an enduring economy, those who gamble their lives in the cocaine business today revere the memories of a past laden with gold and with men who had found their El Dorado.

At the beginning of the twentieth century, after the Thousand Days' civil war, Bajo Cauca experienced a new migration wave due to a renewed surge in gold mining and the exploitation of land for cattle raising. Settlers moved to the region, which registered the locations of squatters, which over time grew to the size of towns. Towns such as Tarazá and Caucasia became important centers of commerce, but the influx of people fleeing the poverty of surrounding regions, and the consequent building of squatter districts, caused increased conflicts between settlers and cattle ranchers in the 1940s (García 1993). When sectarian violence between the Conservative and Liberal parties spread throughout the country, Bajo Cauca, like the Middle Magdalena region (see chapter 1), became a receptacle for refugees.

Later, at the end of the 1960s, the region experienced the penetration of guerrillas—in particular from the ELN, which led acts of sabotage against the mining industry and construction of the highway crossing the town of Tarazá. Furthermore, the ELN engaged peasants and workers in political formation and protest, and thus Bajo Cauca soon became the guerrillas' center in inland Colombia (ibid., 77–79). In 1977, for example, Tarazá hosted the ELN Guerrilla Assembly, with its major leaders in attendance. In the

1980s, the region also noted the presence of the other major guerrilla groups—in particular the FARC and the EPL. The state response to the guerrilla presence was to militarize the region, which increased the conflict and further disenfranchised the settler population.

The militarization of the region in later years favored the formation of paramilitary groups, which had their main supporters and allies among cattle ranchers, merchants, and gold-mine owners, in addition to the army and the police. Two paramilitary organizations, both linked to the Autodefensas Unidas de Colombia (AUC), operated in the region: the Bloque Mineros, led by drug kingpin Cuco Vanoy, and the Bloque Centauro. Vanoy was a former longtime emerald dealer, who had joined the Medellín cartel in the 1980s but eventually turned against Pablo Escobar. In Tarazá, he modeled his domination on the lesson he had learned from the legendary drug dealer, combining the spread of terror with the construction of hospitals and communitarian restaurants, the paving of roads, and the donation of grocery to needy families. Vanoy and the Mineros demobilized in 2006; over three thousand combatants gave over their weapons. Among them was Jader, my guide to the Bajo Cauca. In 2008, Vanoy was one of fourteen drug traffickers and paramilitary leaders extradited to the United States: the South Florida Federal Court sentenced him in 2009 to twenty-four years in prison for drug trafficking.

The voluntary renditions prompted by the Justice and Peace Law, which regulated the paramilitaries' demobilization process, unmasked how deeply ties run between legal and illegal forces in Bajo Cauca. For example, in 2006, during the demobilization process, Hugo Barrera, president of Antioquia's equestrian association, admitted that cattle ranchers had granted support to Vanoy's paramilitary group in Bajo Cauca. Barrera, who is accused of being a front for the drug kingpin, was also the mayor of Cáceres. The mayor of Tarazá was arrested in 2008 for his ties to the Mineros group.

When I traveled to Tarazá, I did not imagine that I would have the chance to run into Vanoy, who at the time was a formally demobilized paramilitary leader, but I did: I observed him at his work, and I grew aware of the ties he enjoyed with local police. His business continued as usual, despite the ongoing demobilization process.

On my way to Bajo Cauca with Jader, we came across several checkpoints marked by orange traffic cones aligned in the middle of the road. Nearby were young soldiers displaying their automatic rifles, flanked by yellow banners with the phrase "¡Viaje tranquilo!" (Travel without worry!). Such encounters were part of President Uribe's democratic security campaign,[1] which deployed soldiers to militarize main roads to give Colombians the opportunity to travel without fear of being hijacked, harassed, or kidnapped by guerrillas. Thus, running into soldiers was intended to communicate a sense of security rather than threat. As a result of the president's policy and the perception of restored security, movement of goods and people across the country was restored, and Colombians rewarded Uribe in May 2006 by strongly backing the constitutional amendment that allowed his reelection.

We passed many checkpoints undisturbed until a soldier eventually stopped our car once we had passed Valdivia. I lowered the window and heat and humidity enveloped us. The officer, barely in his early twenties, greeted me in a friendly manner, stretching to shake my hand. He did not request any identification or vehicle documentation, which I found surprising, but instead asked some routine questions, inquiring where we were coming from and what our destination was. "We are going to the coast for a few days of vacation" was my improvised response.

Then he asked the question that clarified the real motive for stopping us. "Would you make a contribution to get some sodas?" Sweat was running down the soldier's neck from under his helmet, soaking his green shirt.

At first, I reacted with surprise and confusion, unable to utter a word, but then I reached for some pesos stored near the car radio and passed them with a smile to the grateful soldier. With no further questions, we were able to continue on our journey. This sort of encounter happened two more times during our trip, and I wondered why it was so easy to bribe these underpaid soldiers serving their country under an unforgiving sun. What would have happened if I had refused to offer a "tip"?

Soldiers were not the only surprise that we encountered during our journey. We passed the town of Yarumal[2]—previously a guerrilla stronghold but today flocked with police and former paramilitaries and serving as an important center for the distribution of cocaine base. As we drove, we observed poor and shabby shacks put up at the border of the road. Living there, explained Jader, were people who had been evicted from their properties or from the mountains by guerrillas. Sent to look for phantom opportunities in urban centers, now they were all heading deeper into misery day by day. The icons of this misery were the small boys and girls lined up at the edge of the street in front of their barracks, stretching out their fragile, thin arms to beg for coins and compassion from passing cars. We drove by quickly, without stopping, thus contributing by our indifference and distraction to the mosaic of misery in which, forgotten and invisible, the majority of today's humanity lives. To watch this scene from inside the car was to observe reality from within a bubble. We could see, but we did not touch or contact the world outside.

These shacks were the offshoots of the larger shantytowns that had metastasized around the town-villages shaped and controlled by cocaine production and trade. This cocaine-shaped geography became even more visible when we arrived in Tarazá, one of Bajo Cauca's main towns. Bars, clubs, stores, gas stations, motels, and restaurants occupied the main road crossing the town from one end to the other. The circulation of money was readily apparent. Luxury vans with plates from Envigado and Sabaneta—two historic narco-centers at the outskirts of Medellín—drove through the town, accompanied by dozens of motorbikes. At night, paramilitaries escorting beautiful women assembled in front of the gentlemen's club Kamasutra or at one of the many bars where young people swarmed, consuming beer and rum to the beat of *vallenato,* the romantic Colombian music from the coast. When Mi Sangre, the town's paramilitary commander, an athletic-looking black man who beautified his neck with a gold chain, got out of his white Montero Jeep, the *paracos*—short for paramilitaries—all saluted. Late at night, down the street, a senior paramilitary accompanied by his little son was playing billiards with some of his friends. His bodyguards drank beer at the bar, hiding their guns under their shirts.

As I was observing all of this, I thought that my trip to the Bajo Cauca region was also a journey into the world that lies behind the taste and effects of cocaine, to paraphrase Marx and Engels.[3] In fact, the millions of cocaine consumers in the United States and Europe who inhale the white powder do not care to wonder, while they are getting high, about the relations of production to the system that produces, distributes, and consumes cocaine. The experience of the cocaine consumer is lived far away, and separated from, the experience of those, such as Jader and others, who grow coca plants and collect and transform their leaves into unrefined cocaine.

Colombia emerged as a country involved in drug trafficking at the beginning of the 1950s. Those were the years of the Medellín–La Habana Connection, so called because Cuba, under Batista, was an important hub for the shipping of cocaine to the United States, where the U.S. Mafia controlled the market. When Fidel Castro and Che Guevara overthrew Batista's regime in 1959,

Miami took over the role previously played by Cuba and became the strategic hub for drug trafficking between North and South America (Salazar 2001).

Yet the new and powerful class of drug traffickers emerged in Colombia only in the early 1970s. At the time, there was a defined distribution of labor among Colombia and two other countries of the Andean region, Bolivia and Peru, where peasants cultivated coca fields and produced cocaine paste, which Colombians bought at a cheap price and refined into cocaine hydrochloride in their laboratories prior to shipping it to the United States. Colombia's role in drug trafficking experienced a boom in the mid-1970s as a consequence of South American military regimes' crackdown on cocaine's routes toward the north. To expand and consolidate their new business in the cocaine trade, Colombians leveraged their experience in smuggling marijuana and the infrastructure that they had already created.

Around this time, Colombian textile fabrics were closing down, creating an unprecedented economic crisis and massive unemployment, Medellín, the city known for its entrepreneurial spirit, emerged as the strategic drug-trafficking center, later followed by Cali and Bogotá. As a class of new rich emerged in Medellín and other cities, they also began to colonize neighborhoods and streets in Miami, Los Angeles, and Queens, New York, putting Cubans—who until then had controlled the cocaine market—out of business. It was during this period that the pioneers of international cocaine trafficking established themselves in Colombia. These were people such as Gilberto Rodríguez Orejuela, José Gonzalo Rodríguez Gacha, the Ochoa family, and Carlos Lehder.[4] Among them, too, was Pablo Escobar, who grew up in the town of Envigado, on the outskirts of Medellín, who started his career as a car thief but later reached legendary status. Escobar is credited with transforming the Medellín Cartel into a multinational criminal corporation. Instead of using individuals as drug mules, which is how the business had worked prior to Escobar, the *"patrón* of evil," as he was nicknamed, had at his disposal fleets of trucks and aircraft that were able to ship tons of refined cocaine to the United States (Gootenberg 2008, 304–05).

By the early 1980s, Colombia had control of the entire cocaine chain, from the cultivation of coca fields to the production of refined cocaine to its distribution to the United States. Powerful cartels emerged, such as the Medellín, Cali, and North Valley cartels. The influence of criminal organizations—and their leaders—increasingly extended into other areas of Colombia's life, such as politics and the legal economy. Ownership of large estates—a signal feature of lives of excess and luxury that mimicked the privileges of the country's traditional oligarchy—became trademarks of the increasing power, as well as admiration and envy, enjoyed by drug lords and their associates.

In Medellín, a former paramilitary field commander who was still involved in drug trafficking told me that when he was a child, he and his friends were inspired by the young people in his neighborhood who worked for Pablo Escobar and wore trendy sneakers and shirts, surrounded by stunningly beautiful women and giving away money to the poor people. The expenditure of their wealth gained the drug kingpins the respect and support of the lower-income class, who benefited from the drug lords' philanthropic activities. In the poor peripheries of Medellín, for example, Pablo Escobar built low-income housing and soccer fields. Not only the poor benefited from Escobar, but also politicians, who turned to the powerful drug lord for funds to finance their political campaigns and get the electoral support they needed to win. Reported by *Forbes* as one of the richest men in the world, Escobar was elected as a deputy representative to Colombia's congress in 1983. Alonso Salazar has observed that drug traffickers exhibited their abundance and made gifts to the poor because these strategies enabled them to be recognized as powerful and merciful beings (2001, 61–62).

The targeted killing of Pablo Escobar by national police at the end of 1993 and the extradition of drug kingpins to the United States engendered a reorganization of the cocaine business in Colombia, which became more open and competitive (Gootenberg 2008, 315). New, smaller, but still powerful cartels emerged, in particular the North Valley Cartel and the Oficina de Envigado, a spinoff of the Medellín Cartel. In the 1990s, intertwinement between paramilitary groups and drug cartels became tighter, to the point where major drug lords such as Don Berna—the head of the Oficina de Envigado in Medellín—became full members of the AUC staff. Paramilitary death squads played a strategic role in allowing drug kingpins to accumulate land by dispossessing peasants and driving guerrillas out of their territories. Drug lords used their estates not only to establish lavish farms, but also to house cocaine laboratories and control drug-trafficking routes. As I illustrate in the next chapter, the anti-insurgency discourse that drug traffickers used to justify their private armies also allowed them to ally with the state's security entities, thus assuring their collaboration and guaranteeing their own impunity.

The Bajo Cauca region, through which I was traveling with Jader, is a case in point. Because of the presence of the guerrillas, this part of the Antioquia department is heavily militarized. This facilitates the establishment of paramilitary groups, which have, in cattle ranchers, merchants, gold-mining owners, and the army and police, their main supporters and allies. At the same time, as elsewhere in Colombia, the Bajo Cauca paramilitaries have also been the drug lords' private armies.

Two paramilitary organizations, both linked to the AUC, operate in the region: the Bloque Mineros, led by drug kingpin Cuco Vanoy, and the Bloque Centauro, led by another drug lord, Daniel Rendón Herrera, known as Don Mario.[5] Without cocaine, Jader told me in Tarazá, there would be neither paramilitaries nor guerrillas:

> There is no [paramilitary] group without cocaine. In fact, if the boss is sending [a shipment of] 50 tons [about 45,360 kilograms] of cocaine and it gets lost, we are left without uniforms, food, money—that is, with nothing. We are left naked, because money comes from cocaine. That's how we eat. That's how we can wear new uniforms. Because of cocaine, we have powerful rifles. And if there is no [cocaine], there is no money. Without cocaine, there are no armed groups—no guerrillas, no paramilitaries, no nothing. In fact, the FARC and the self-defense groups would not fight over a banana plant or yucca. No. They fight over coca plants, which here might not cost much, but in another place might be worth millions of dollars. That is why they fight against each other.[6]

Cocaine, and the desires, fantasies, and profits attached to it, is the main organizing principle of towns such as Tarazá. Like a god, it possesses the powers of life and death over the residents, whose social and economic lives are enabled by the securities and insecurities of living in areas of despo-capitalism. Cocaine is the substance that sustains their dreams of better lives, that fuels their desires and offers the illusion of someday fulfilling them. At the same time, these are areas of violence and terror, as I witnessed myself.

"Cocaine allows for a decent life," Luna once explained to me. After I had met him in Medellín, Luna moved to Bajo Cauca to return to work in the cocaine-smuggling business:

> It's a very nice town, with lots of opportunities. There people get jobs. There nobody lives on the street. [The *patrón*] provides houses where people can live. In other words, nobody has a bad life there, and there are lots of drugs. In this town, there is lots of cocaine. That's why people have opportunities. They progress thanks to cocaine....
>
> Where there are paramilitaries, there is money. That's why women who work [as prostitutes] go to these areas, because they know they will do fine.

These sort of women can live there for one or two months and make up to four or five million pesos because there are many people there, such as the *longos.* They are the *raspachines,* the ones who collect the coca [leaves]. There are about fifteen thousand of them who harvest daily. Plus, there are the paramilitaries and all of that. Therefore there is lots of money. In the town, people drink every day. This is why these women take advantage of it and go there [to work].

Jader, while we were driving through town, echoed Luna's words: "Here there are more paramilitaries than civilians," he told me to highlight their presence and domination in this area: they are the nervous system of this despo-capitalism space. Everyone living here, he clarified, makes a living from cocaine:

> Everyone in town lives off the cocaine industry. "Everyone" means *everyone.* In fact, the farmer lives off cocaine. The collector lives off cocaine. The stores make a living out of cocaine. If I am a collector, I need to go to a shop and buy stuff. And where is the money [to buy] coming from? From cocaine. If I need a guarantee [to rent an apartment], they give it to me because they know I have money from cocaine. Everyone makes a living with cocaine. Where does a bar make money from if not from cocaine? Everyone in town is making a living because of cocaine. And since there is lots of money in circulation, there is an additional concentration of prostitutes. If, as happens at times, the town remains without money for a period of two or three months, the prostitutes leave the town because there is no money. When they hear that money is back, then they come back. They too are propelled by money. Therefore, how do these prostitutes make a living? With cocaine. If a [coca leaf] collector sleeps with a woman, he pays her [with money coming] from cocaine. Many, many people live thanks to cocaine.[7]

Though these quotes emphasize mainly the economic benefits that the cocaine trade provides, cocaine is a total fact here: it produces identities, affections, and fantasies, capturing individuals and spaces in a network of shared desires. Cocaine, in spaces such as Tarazá, is both a desire-production and a social-production machine.

As such, cocaine produces a reality in which having links to the drug—its production and commercialization—is a given. There is nothing wrong with it. Not one of the several people I met disguised his or her ties to its production and trade. This fact is something that customers at a shabby bar on a dusty road talked about with ease as we sat around a table covered with empty bottles of Clarita, the cheap local beer. People openly admitted that they worked as coca-leaf collectors or as employees in laboratories built next to the fields, producing the unrefined cocaine from which highly paid chemists, like magicians, extract cocaine by the ton.

A young mother whom I interviewed once opened a 2-pound (0.9-kilo) package of cocaine base that she and her husband, a midrange paramilitary leader, had hidden in a closet in their run-down bedroom. Their two-year-old son witnessed the moment of disclosure.

"Where did you get it?" I asked.

"From my mother," the young woman responded. Her mother, I soon learned, was working in a cocaine-base laboratory in a town just across the river. For about two million pesos, or a little more than US$1,000, the woman whom I met was going to sell the package to the local paramilitary boss and narcotrafficker. "You've never seen cocaine base?" the woman inquired in disbelief as I coughed, my throat irritated by the vicious odor of gasoline and acids.

During my stay in Tarazá, I had the opportunity to visit Jader at the coca field owned by his uncle. The field was not far from the main road crossing the region. A fragile wood canoe that would carry us to the opposite bank of the Río Cauca waited behind a small shop where Jader's uncle and his wife sell beverages, chips, pirated music, and cigarettes. At the edge of the street, I noticed a small, isolated stand of coca growing next to the shop. What is striking here is the overlap between the everyday lives of people buying and selling imported American drinks and the illegality of coca fields and laboratories that transform the ancient leaf into white powder. There is, in fact, no clear boundary between the legal and the illegal, and one is forced to ask: Who defines and imposes law in this part of the world? Who sets the rules? And who enforces them? What does sovereignty rest upon here?

To reach the coca field, Jader and I, together with his uncle Don Luís, walked for about an hour, crossing a swampy plateau, fields of guavas, and the remains of an old gold mine. After a few minutes, we were thirsty and bathed in sweat because of the thick humidity. Along the path, we ran into small groups of young coca collectors carrying machetes at their waists.

Once we arrived at Don Luís's fields, he showed me short, young coca plants that had been planted only recently. They belonged to the White Peruvian species, he explained, which is the best one because it produces many leaves. Behind a curtain of trees, we arrived at a larger coca field. Don

Luís owns eighteen thousand plants, which look like shrubs, and he harvests them every two months. After they are picked, the coca leaves, with the help of chemicals spread at the bottom of the stems, grow back at great speed. The most recent harvest was two weeks before my visit, and already the elegant green leaves were sprouting again.

The cultivation of coca plants is only the first step in the long chain of cocaine production. Luna, the former paramilitary turned drug smuggler, had described to me in detail how green coca leaves are transformed into powdered cocaine. Harvesters, called *longos,* collect the leaves starting at dawn and work until noon or two in the afternoon. Once collected, the leaves are brought to a hut called a *caleta,* the processing plant. At the end of the day, each harvester is paid 200 pesos—about US$0.10—for each pound of leaves collected. In the *caleta,* the coca leaves are processed with strong acids. The *longos* chop the leaves until they are all shredded. "The leaf is soaked with urea and water, and all of the *longos* stomp on the leaves with their feet for about an hour to an hour and a half," explained Luna. Thereafter, the leaves are treated with gasoline and sulfuric acid before being fried and dried.

Once the cocaine base is ready, the peasants bring it to the village, where buyers employed by the drug lord collect it and pay its producers. More sophisticated laboratories then transform the base into the white crystallized powder that is then ready to be commercialized and exported. The production and commercialization of cocaine require a monopoly system strictly enforced by technologies of punishment. The drug trafficker is the despot of the areas under his dominion, where the paramilitary forces function not only as an army, but also as the boss's private police, making sure that the *mercancia,* or merchandise, as the cocaine is nicknamed, arrives safely at its destination. Luna explained to me how this system works—it is a despotic monopoly enforced with a violence that tolerates no competition or any form of cheating:

> Here they don't charge [you] the *vacuna* ["vaccination," or protection money]. The only thing that is demanded is that you sell the drug to the *patrón;* that is, drugs finance the group. You have to sell the drug, everything you do, and they buy it. They don't steal your money. If you arrive with fifteen or twenty kilos [thirty-three or forty-four pounds] of cocaine base, they pay you right on the spot. But you cannot take out a kilo from this village and sell it [to someone else]. You have an obligation to sell it here. You cannot take it to another village and sell it. No. You have to sell it to the *patrón.* In the village,

the [paramilitary] group does not buy the drug directly. The *patrón,* in order to give people jobs, has offices where buyers can get cocaine at a price fixed by the narcotrafficker. The buyers sell it, then, exclusively to the *patrón* at a different price.

This system is strictly enforced, Luna explained:

> [Once] we had [paramilitary] checkpoints. There were two at night and two during the day. We searched the cars. We were wearing good-looking uniforms. There the first thing that was requested was a good presence. In order to be an urban paramilitary, you have to be very serious and have a good presence. You have to be a gentleman with the people. Thus, [at the checkpoints,] there were always two of us with machine guns. You had to search every car that came into or out of the village, and if you found drugs, you sent them back [to the boss] right away. If you confiscated five kilos [eleven pounds] for a value of ten million pesos, two and a half million went to each of the patrolmen and five million went to the boss. The boss paid you for seizing the merchandise. You actually got paid.

In a land where the law of the *patrón* has replaced the law of the state, despite the violence and terror that have resulted, a system of transgression is in place, said Luna:

> From the laboratories in Caucana, we had to take [the cocaine base] out and bring it to another town in order to get it to the proper laboratory. The van was shuttling two or three times during the day [from town to town], and the police knew that it was transporting cocaine, but ... nothing [happened] ... because there the police get paid in order to remain silent and live well.

When the police occasionally seized a few tons of cocaine, I was told, it was because the narcotrafficker himself handed it over voluntarily; the drugs can be shown to the public as positive results in the war against drugs. Yet even when the police take hold of a couple of tons, Luna assured me, another eighty or a hundred have already slipped out of the country, with law enforcement's blessing:

> [The traffickers] get together, and they give the drugs to the police so that they can do their operations and be successful. That's why the police have so much money right now. Only very few don't have [any money]. A police officer can make 2 to 3 million pesos [a little more than US$1,000] every week. When a police officer who is barely making a living runs into someone with marijuana or other drugs, he immediately asks: "How much will you give me to let you go?" If he realizes that someone [who is guilty] is not giving

him a sufficient amount of money, then he arrests [that person]. If instead he sees that the money is good, he lets him go right away and gives him back everything without seizing anything.

There is a huge amount of corruption. Everyone lives in peace because it's only a very small number of police officers who actually do their duties. Everyone can walk with a gun or with lots of money. If they stop you, you just say, "Look, agent, don't arrest me, I have given you so much." And that's it. They only confiscate the gun in order to sell it [on the black market]. In other words, [the police] are very vicious.

During my stay, I had heard rumors of army helicopters raiding and burning cocaine-base laboratories. I asked Don Luís about it:

The last fumigating plan was five years ago. Right now the army is burning down some hiding places, but we're not concerned about that. We [the cocaine growers] had a meeting among ourselves, and we collected 60 million pesos [about US$30,000]. That amount we gave to the army commander. They went [fumigating] to another side, and this field remained healthy. All of this *vereda*[8] remained healthy. The army is working somewhere else, but not here. For the next crop, I had to bring 250,000 pesos [about US$130]. This is not money—it's like paying insurance. Here multitudes of people have jobs [in the cocaine business]. The only money that one makes around here is from cocaine, just cocaine. Just look around [and see for yourself].

Where there is a norm, there is transgression. Sacred and profane, virtue and sin, legal and illegal, Nietzsche warned us, go hand in hand. The world shaped by cocaine is no exception. I became aware of it one night while conversing with Luna in the town of Bajo Cauca, where he was living in a run-down home owned by the local paramilitary commander for whom he was working.

Within the cocaine circuit, Luna works as a freelancer, or a "pirate," as they say here. His task is to steal cocaine base from a territory across the river that is controlled by a rival paramilitary group and narcotrafficker and sell it to his paramilitary friend in his village, who works for a different drug lord. People such as Luna move quickly from one village to the next, traveling by motorbike across invisible boundaries drawn by drug lords, stealing and selling cocaine paste to various paramilitary groups or smuggling it to Medellín and other cities. It is very dangerous job whose consequences, if the freelancer is caught, may include death. "I am working legally here but illegally over there," explained Luna. *Legally* means that he works with the authorization of the *patrón* in one area and does not interfere with his interests. *Illegally* means that he steals cocaine paste from a rival drug lord who dominates a different territory.

Driving around the town, Luna sometimes stopped to talk to people and ask them for cocaine-related job opportunities. Eager to make money, he was constantly looking for commissions to smuggle cocaine base into other villages or to steal it from rival laboratories. "If you know something, give me a call," he told a robust man who sometimes provided him with work.

"Another paramilitary?" I asked.

"No," responded Luna, "another like me." That is, another pirate, someone working in the underworld of the underworld. Thus I discovered that Luna is a double-crosser: With his friend's complicity, he works not only for the local paramilitary organization but also with the (illegal) network of "pirates."

A large network of teenagers, housewives, and double-crossing paramilitaries exists in the area. They work even deeper in the shadows, cheating the *patrones* and their paramilitary groups. They all compete among another and with the *patrones* to steal cocaine base and sell it on the black market. As they travel, they hide packages of cocaine in their underwear or in gasoline tanks, and the police, at times, arrest them.

Don Luís admitted to selling some of the cocaine base he produces to the black market "illegally," thereby transgressing the rules of the narcotrafficker:

> Let's suppose I produce 5 pounds [2.25 kilograms] of cocaine base. I sell just 2 pounds [about 1 kilogram] [to the boss]. I still have 3 pounds [1.4 kilograms]. Thus I pirate 3e—I can sell each pound for 1.5 million pesos [about US$750] instead of just 1 million. That means that [in selling to the black market], I gain 1.5 million more pesos. I pay the workers, and I still keep 3 to 4 million pesos. Near [my coca field] is a guy from Medellín. He produces 6 pounds [2.75 kilograms] of cocaine base. He delivers 3, and he [illegally] brings 3 with him to Medellín.

People are gambling with their lives, since the paramilitaries punish pirates with death. Luna had told me of such an incident when I interviewed him in Medellín:

> There everyone was betraying the boss. We had to go and get them. They were buying an average of 250 kilos [550 pounds] [of cocaine base] per day. They would hand over 200 [to the boss] and keep 50 because they had a laboratory in another village where the [paramilitary] groups were not present. All the buyers had a laboratory, and they produced cocaine there in order to send it

somewhere else through different means. The boss heard about it because a cocaine cargo was intercepted, and we had to arrest all those people. [Among them] was the buyer the boss trusted the most, the one with the most money. He had a hiding place as big as a supermarket where he would hide the drugs that he was stealing. At night, people would gather at this supermarket. Under his desk, he would push a button [to open a safe], and thus we seized rifles that he owned. [Possessing weapons] was not permitted; only members of the [paramilitary] group could carry weapons there, and nobody else. There was lots of money. We got everyone, and the boss sent [his people] to kill the majority of them because they were betraying him.

Cocaine is a lively thing that shapes, defines, produces, and consumes the lives of many Colombians living in the area that I visited. People involved with the cocaine trade all seemed to consciously or unconsciously follow the laws linked to this commodity. The spirit of cocaine is the ruler of the town.

As cocaine enters the cycle of exchange and passes from hand to hand—from the hands of the coca grower to the hands of the collector; from the hands of the chemist to the hands of the drug lord; and from the hands of the seller to those of the consumer—its spirit produces a reality with innumerable interconnections. As gold did in the past, cocaine—not by chance nicknamed "the white gold"—today takes over the lives of people living in this area of the country.

In *My Cocaine Museum,* Taussig suggested the existence of a cultural continuum between yesterday's age of gold and today's age of cocaine, one marked by fetishized commodities that share a similarly ambiguous relationship with good and evil, God and the devil, and natural and supernatural forces: "Gold and cocaine are fetishes, which is to say substances that seem to be a good deal more than mineral or vegetable matter. They come across more like people than things, spiritual entities that are neither, and this is what gives them their strange beauty" (2004, xviii).

This strange beauty is the ability of gold and cocaine, which Taussig called "the devil in modern guise" (ibid., 4), to instill simultaneous attraction and repulsion, awe and fear, which are predispositions and affections that the sense of secrecy, danger, and transgression linked to these commodities make even more intense and meaningful. Peasants, as Taussig has discussed in his work on commodity fetishism in precapitalist societies—and as I myself recorded in some conversations with paramilitaries—attribute these qualities to the nature of the devil, taken as a metaphor for the lures, illusions, and subversive powers of capitalism, and express them as unnatural conditions, since "people tend to be seen as commodities and commodities tend to be seen as animated entities that can dominate persons" (Taussig 1980, 25).

One night during the same trip, Jader and I watched a TV program in the hotel room. Clips from a concert by a Colombian celebrity were being broadcast. Jader watched intensely and at one point calmly said, "I want to kill her." He said it almost to himself, voicing the thoughts that in that moment crossed his mind. He was almost in a state of trance. In fact, that afternoon Jader had shown me some photos from the time that he was a paramilitary combatant in an antiguerrilla unit fighting in the mountains. Some pictures portrayed him embracing semiautomatic rifles in Rambo-like poses. In one in particular, he was shirtless, with a cigarette hanging from a corner of his mouth, his chin tilted slightly upward, and his legs spread open, while he held a rifle in each hand, their butts resting on his hips. He had posted the pictures on the headboard of his bed frame and looked at them in silence, in a nostalgic and rapturous mood.

"Why do you want to kill her?" I asked Jader.

"Because she made a pact with the devil," he responded.

"How do you know?"

"Because she became famous overnight. That's possible only if you make a deal with the devil," Jader asserted. His words were a social commentary on the unnatural essence of capitalism, of which the entertainment industry is one expression.

During my short stay in Bajo Cauca (which was cut short due to the events described at the end of chapter 3), I had an opportunity to observe and experience facets of the paramilitaries' domination of one of their strategic areas. I had met *raspachines,* the workforce of paramilitaries' controlled cocaine business; like the gold-mining workers of the nineteenth century, they were wandering nomadically from town to town to look for work as coca-leaf collectors in the region's fields. I recorded several instances in which local police and paramilitaries worked hand in hand, blurring the boundaries between the legal and the illegal, the licit and the illicit. I witnessed the violence (in the attack on the truck driver) that paramilitaries use in the public sphere to punish and to assert their domination. I observed how money generated by cocaine overflows into the legal economy, supporting small shops, bars, restaurants, and gasoline stations, and how coca, as a commodity, had transformed rural areas of Colombia into thresholds between tradition and modernity, the past and the present, the periphery and the center. I thought about Taussig's early work on commodity fetishism and the almost

Manichean separation between the purity of the peasant world and the twisted capitalist mode of production. In Bajo Cauca, the distinction between use-value and exchange-value economies, precapitalist and capitalist markets, and pure and impure are also blurred. Cocaine, as a total fact, has become the reification of desire as a productive force, a will to power embodied by people and communities that perpetuate the old search for El Dorado. It seemed to me that gold yesterday and cocaine today were manifestations of the desire that, according to Deleuze and Guattari, produces reality: "There is only desire and the social and nothing else" (1983, 29).

During my fieldwork, I came to experience the Bajo Cauca region as an embodiment of a despo-capitalist space, the threshold where the repressive forces of the despot coexist with the liberating forces of capitalism. Fetishized as a commodity, cocaine in fact sets in motion fantasies and actions; it unleashes both the forces of liberation and infinite possibilities and the reactive forces that control, dominate, repress, and terrorize the very same impulses and predispositions that are enabled by desire. Deleuze and Guattari (1987) defined despotism as a reality in which codes of conduct, beliefs, and meaning are at the service of the despot. In spaces shaped by cocaine, such as Bajo Cauca, the ruler is not the drug lord, such as Cuco Vanoy, whom I met in Tarazá, or El Doctor, of whom I wrote in chapter 1, but cocaine itself: a totem that organizes the distribution of bodies, practices, objects, symbols, and words.

While sitting at the bar in the town where I had witnessed the paramilitary taking away a truck driver to kill him, I asked Luna about his hazardous job. I wanted to know what motivated him to be involved in drug trafficking. At first, his justification was economic. In Colombia, he told me, he might be able to find a job for minimum wage—about US$200 a month—but that was not enough to sustain his family, he claimed. "I felt very bad when my wife asked me what we had for lunch, and I had to tell her that we didn't have any money," he said in a justificatory tone. To be sure, Luna is not making big money in the cocaine business, either, though he risks his life daily. There are periods, he admitted, when he does not make any money at all but simply sits around waiting to carry out the next mission, hoping for a stroke of luck that would make him wealthy. "That will happen within a year," he predicted, "and I will quit, reach my wife [who at the time was living in a different town], and open a winery." For now, waiting for the big score to come, Luna remained on his cell phone, constantly calling his contacts to inquire about the next job. "I just have fun doing this," he told me at one point.

That latter brief statement provided a more valuable insight than had his previous, merely instrumental explanation. In fact, at the same time that he complained about his lack of money, Luna drove a Yamaha motorbike that had cost him about US$7,000—a figure that to people in places such as Tarazá represents a fortune. During another of our conversations, when he was discussing the paramilitary's main source of motivation, he used the word *ambición*. We were looking at a map of Colombia hanging on the wall of a rundown office in Medellín, where we had locked ourselves away to record our conversations undisturbed. Luna was telling me where and how paramilitary groups penetrated and occupied ("liberated," in his words) territories by mercilessly slaughtering people in villages and towns. When I pressed him for the motives for so much bloodshed, he came up with the word *ambición:* an illuminating synthesis of desire, greed, and conquest. In Luna's following statement, it is interesting to notice that, when talking about legal money financing the formation of paramilitary groups, he highlighted the fluidity between legality and illegality:

> The guy who establishes a [paramilitary] bloc is always the one with money who is involved in different kinds of businesses. It's people with money—legal money, owners of businesses—and they finance someone to put together a [paramilitary] group. . . . They do it because of the need to take care of their business. But they also do it for the ambition that comes with money. They desire to have more money, since the wealthy never get tired of accumulating money. It's their ambition. . . . If you have one hundred million [Colombian pesos], you want to have two hundred, three hundred, or four hundred [million], and so on. It's the ambition to have even more money. There are people who don't know what to do with their money anymore, and thus they invest it so that they get even more. . . . To have money is to have power.
>
> But an even greater power is to have rifles. It's a huge amount of power to have two hundred, three hundred [weapons]. With one hundred armed people, you have power. . . . One who has money in the pocket and rifles has power. . . . So [the owners of paramilitary groups] realized that power was bringing in lots of money. . . . Our ideals of fighting the guerrilla were once good. But this is no longer the case. Ambition killed [our values]. The knowledge that we have today is that we need to get rid of the guerrilla, but in truth, it is all about the money. This is what stays before us. . . . Thus even violence is [now] motivated by ambition. In truth, ambition is a disease.

As an organizing principle, cocaine is a commodity embodying the aspirations, dreams, and desires of those who worship it like a divinity, and worship in turn the forces and promises of total freedom and the unlimited possibilities of a capitalist economy. At the same time, the history of Bajo Cauca—from exploitation of gold to the production of cocaine—points to the fact that these commodities, endowed with the desires and ambitions of those who worship them, are forces of both liberation and repression. It is within this contradiction that the essence of the paramilitaries is revealed: they are a release and a reflection of the larger forces that carry the illusions and promises of a capitalist economy.

FIVE

The Intertwinement

In the summer of 2005, while I was doing fieldwork in Colombia, Leoluca Orlando, the anti-Mafia mayor of Palermo with whom I had had the opportunity to work in the early 1990s, came to Medellín, where I organized several meetings for him with organizations interested in his anti-Mafia fight in Sicily. One day, after we had listened to leaders of several organizations telling us about abuses perpetuated by the paramilitaries and were driving back to the apartment where I was staying, he shared an intuition that shed light on my understanding of paramilitaries in Colombia. It was not the Colombian drug cartels that were most like the Sicilian Mafia, but the paramilitaries, who resembled the Mafia as a historical, social, and criminal phenomenon. "Like the Mafia," Orlando said, "the paramilitaries are at the same time against the state and in favor of the state, outside the state and within the state. They are against the free market *and* part of the free market."

The mayor of Palermo thus pointed out the essence of the paramilitary phenomenon, recognizing the convergence of interests that engender a murky gray area where paramilitaries and state are enmeshed and sustained by a convergent justificatory discourse that describes the state as weak, absent, or even failed. In this convergence, he saw a reflection of the Sicilian Mafia's own interaction with the state. This convergence is the focus of this chapter.

To this point, I have focused on paramilitaries' violent practices, providing excerpts from the life histories of foot soldiers and the leaders of their death squads, interpreting the spectacle of their violence, and presenting an ethnography of their domination in coca-growing areas. Throughout, I have hinted at linkages between the paramilitary death squads and other entities, such as the police and the army. During my fieldwork, the more I listened to, observed, and learned about the paramilitaries' violence and dominion across

Colombia, the more I wondered about the alliances and linkages that allowed their existence and promoted their legitimization. Thus I increasingly questioned what the experiences of paramilitary members and the communities subjugated to them suggest about the articulations that allow such a phenomenon to flourish, as well as what they suggest about the essence of Colombia's paramilitary forces.

In search of an answer to this question, and prompted by Leoluca Orlando's intuition, I built on my own understanding of the Italian Mafia's nature, which I had developed during the early 1990s, when I lived and worked in Sicily. Looking at the experience of Colombian paramilitaries through the lens of the Italian Mafia phenomenon helped me to gain a better grasp of the complexity and breadth of paramilitaries in Colombia. The comparison helped me see the paramilitaries not as a criminal organization dedicated to violence, but rather as a process, mechanism, and political and economic project of domination that has enjoyed the tacit, as well as open, support of large portions of Colombia's population. In other words, the source of paramilitaries' power and legitimacy is external to them.

In particular, to understand the alliance of the paramilitaries with the state, I use as a heuristic strategy a term that is employed in Italy to describe the entanglement between the Mafia and politicians: *intreccio* (see chapter 1). The intertwinement is not simply a structural and functional alliance between organized crime and the state. *Intreccio* is more than a metaphor for the elements that compose this alliance—it is a reality in itself. In fact, as when fibers that are closely woven together become a new thread, one whose original strands cannot be differentiated, so too does the intertwinement between the Mafia and the state constitute a reality that is more than the sum of its parts.

Thus, at one level, the intertwinement reflects a convergence and synergy of interests between organized crime and other economic and political patrons that engender the support, sympathies, and impunity enjoyed by the Mafia. These patrons are referred to in Italian as *favoreggiatori;* that is, those who favor the Mafia. Italian anti-Mafia prosecutors first used the expression "convergence of interests" during the so-called Maxi-Trial against the Cosa Nostra in the mid-1980s (Dalla Chiesa 2010). What the prosecutors meant to highlight with the expression was the fact that the Mafia could not have committed its crimes without the impunity assured them by state officials and political leaders. They also meant to suggest that certain crimes were even prompted by individuals and realities that were external to the Cosa Nostra, in exchange for favors. Today Italian law indicts individuals who are external to the Mafia but collude with its criminal actions on the charge of "external complicity in Mafia association." The law was established to reflect the reality that individuals who do not have membership in the Mafia may still be willing to undertake behaviors that are functional to the Mafia, based on convergent interests (ibid., 11–12).

And yet this convergence is much more than an exchange of favors or a way to get business done. In their study of the Sicilian Mafia, Jane and Peter Schneider pointed to the reality of *intreccio* as an immanent characteristic of the Mafia and its relation to the state, writing that it "points to a vast gray area where it is impossible to determine where one leaves off and the other begins" (2003, 34). Intertwinement, then, is a complex convergence in which the relations between the Mafia and the state are organic and continuous.

A historical overview of the Mafia's origins allow a better understanding of the notion of intertwinement, not only as it refers to Italy, but also on the nature of Colombian paramilitaries' relation with the state, highlighting intertwinement as the immanent characteristic of such a relation.

Not unlike the paramilitaries in Colombia, the Sicilian Mafia developed and sent down deep roots in rural areas, and it has been characterized, as remarked by Charles Tilly ([1974] 1988), by the private and systematic use of violence as a means for control that is articulated via economic and political interests. According to the Italian historian Salvatore Lupo (2011), the notion of the Mafia arose in Sicily during the nineteenth century as part of a larger discourse of power employed by Italian state officials and representatives, who were from the northern part of the country and who constructed Sicily and Sicilians as belonging to a faraway, unruly, unreliable, and mysterious world that resisted modernization. Hence the Mafia has often been used as a metaphor for backwardness and underdevelopment and is seen as representative of a reality that was perceived as irreconcilable with the values embodied by the nineteenth-century modern liberal state. Originally, then, mafiosi were perceives as a class of bandits and ruffians who wanted to subvert the existing social order: "As such, [the Mafia] appears to be darkly intertwined with political subversion, and most importantly, it reflects a fear of the obstinate survival of the obscure and distant past, of a cultural context that is profoundly hostile to modernity" (ibid., 5).

After the unification of Italy in 1860, the notion of the Mafia evolved to indicate a new emerging class of peasant entrepreneurs, who did not hesitate to recruit ruffians and use violence to establish, consolidate, and expand their domination over a given territory. From its origins, the Mafia was a phenomenon characterized by control over a territory, with a repressive apparatus at its disposal and a relationship to political and economic institutions that enabled it to guarantee its own impunity and to safeguard the laundering of its finances. Since its origin, then, the defining feature of the Mafia has been its coexistence and articulation with the state. To characterize this articulation, anti-Mafia prosecutors, such as Giovanni Falcone,[1] used the Italian expression *convivenza* (connivance) to indicate someone's willingness to conspire or be complicit in a crime.

Historians trace the origin of the Mafia to western Sicily and identify its genesis in the local transition from feudalism to capitalism. In the nineteenth century, Sicily was a viceroy of the Bourbon kingdom of Naples. In 1812, a few years before Napoleon's defeat at Waterloo, and adjusting to the notion of the nation-state arising across Europe, the Bourbons abolished feudalism by decree in Sicily, transforming its feudal and ecclesiastic lands into private property and therefore into a market commodity (Gambetta 1993, 84). While their intention was to establish a modern centralized government and to democratize *latifundia,* in reality the new order favored the so-called *gabellotti*—the renters and leaseholders of large estates previously owned by aristocratic landowners. In addition to administering the large estates of the new landowners, who for the most part lived in the city of Palermo, the *gabellotti* were also at the junction of the relationship between the peasants and the new land barons, functioning as arbiters of their disputes and hiring the workforce as well as field guards—the so-called *campieri* who, often recruited among former bandits, were perceived as the embodiment of toughness. Anton Blok described the function of the Sicilian *campieri* in a way that recalls the function of the self-defense groups established by cattle ranchers in Colombia: "The campieri constituted a kind of private police force which, in the absence of an efficient formal control apparatus, climbed to maintain law and order in the countryside" (1988, 61). In other words, the *gabellotti* increasingly became a cornerstone of a power system based on patronage and backed by the use, or the threat of use, of violence, which, as during feudalism, remained the sole rule of social administration in the *latifundia* (Dalla Chiesa 1976, 61). Within this system, land was "the most important political asset—a primary source of power" (Blok 1988, 37), and the *gabellotti* emerged as a new elite, eager to mimic the lifestyle of the traditional aristocracy.

In short, the transition from feudalism to capitalism saw rural entrepreneurs emerge as a new elite, consolidating rather than dissolving the power system rooted in land ownership. The failed democratization of land resulted in the further subjugation and proletarization of the peasants, who expressed their resentment through rebellion (Schneider and Schneider 2003, 24). Led by squads of *guerriglie* (insurgents), the rebellions were fiercely repressed by counterinsurgency squads of the Guardia Nazionale, or National Guard. As Salvatore Lupo highlighted, during this period "individuals and groups became accustomed to resolving disagreements violently, linking them to broader contexts as suggested by the direction of 'large-scale' politics, arming, and making use of, and keeping under control what the sources of the time generically refer to as the class of the 'ruffians'" (2009, 38). It is in this violence-marked milieu that the Mafia arose as a phenomenon in Sicily.

The unification of Italy did not alter but instead strengthened the class of the *gabellotti*. Sicily joined the newly unified Italian nation in October 1860. Yet the notion of a center capable of enforcing law and order failed in Sicily, where the monopoly of the use of force, in the classical Weberian definition, reflected neither the reality nor the practice of the state. The growth of unemployment and proletarization brought unrest and witnessed the consolidation of brigandage, and the impoverished peasants, who during the nineteenth century had resorted several times to uprisings to vent their grievances, perceived the bandits as heroes. Eventually the peasants served as the social base for Garibaldi's expedition, which brought the Bourbon reign to an end and led Sicily to unite with Italy.

As both Blok and Lupo noted, the bandits were not merely the expression of a resentful peasant population. They operated within a larger network of relationships, which included peasant entrepreneurs, politicians, and state officials whose social positions enabled the outlaws to receive protection and assure their own impunity. State officials at the time designated the mutually beneficial and opportunistic collaboration between groups of bandits and powerful individuals as *manutengolismo,* or abetting, of the Mafia:

> The prominent citizen would shelter the bandit in his farms, he would provide him with information and supplies, or in any case ensure that his employees or leaseholders supplied information and supplies to him. In exchange, the bandit would refrain from hostile acts toward the family members, the clients, and the interests of the protected. Indeed, by performing hostile acts against the prominent citizens' adversaries, he would perform a welcome service to those prominent citizens (directly or indirectly). (Lupo 2009, 57)

If originally bandits were an expression of peasant resistance and rebellion, over time and due to *manutengolismo,* they turned—not unlike in Colombia—into armed self-defense groups representing the interests of their protectors and were integrated into the machinery that repressed the peasantry (Blok 1988, 99–102). Thus violence became not only a component of crime activities, but also part of a strategy to accumulate resources, power, and social mobility—and control over key political and economic sectors of Sicilian society (Pezzino 1990, 1999). As a result, robbery declined significantly and kidnappings ceased to occur. After the unification, incapable of imposing order from the center and confronted with resistance from the Sicilian elites, the Italian state did not hesitate to work in alliance with this network of *gabellotti* and private armed groups to enforce the law in Sicily. Blok noted that the Mafia was, on the one hand, the product of tensions among the central government, the *gabellotti,* and the peasants, and on the other, a conflict-management mechanism that developed within the entrails of the state (1988, 92–95). In other words, the Mafia "constituted a pragmatic dimension of the State," Blok concluded, putting the finger on the immanent character of the phenomenon (ibid., 96). The mafioso therefore emerged among the *gabellotti,* and from within the maze of interdependent relations enmeshing landlords, peasants, professionals, civil servants, and politicians, as a middleman and power broker.

This interlacement was recognized as a main feature of the Mafia phenomenon since its beginning. In 1876, two young Tuscan intellectuals, Leopoldo Franchetti and Sidney Sonnino, traveled to Sicily to conduct an independent study of the island's social and political conditions. Their report mirrored Northern Italians' perceptions of Sicily's elite as inadequate. Franchetti, who later became a member of the Italian parliament, focused his attention on political and administrative conditions, and though the emerging Mafia was not the object of his research, he recorded observations on the phenomenon that remain relevant to this day. He noticed, for example, that some individuals had tremendous power and enjoyed impunity for their crimes. "What are the causes of certain individuals' unheard-of power?" he asked himself ([1877] 2004, 2). It was difficult for him to grasp how the justice system could be oblivious to some of the criminals' whereabouts when they were a shared public secret:

What is more, it is publicly known that such and such an individual, a wealthy person, an owner, the renter of gardens, maybe even a councilman of his municipality, has established and increased his fortune interfering in private matters, imposing [his] will, and having those who do not submit be killed. . . . Violence is exercised openly, undisturbed, regularly; it is part of the normal course of things. (Ibid.)

Furthermore, Franchetti observed that the ruffians were "a rabble of rude evildoers" who "seem to be absolute masters of everything and everyone in the province" (ibid., 4) and enjoyed a certain sympathy among the wealthy:

In fact, one hears that such and such a person, who is influential in politics or in local administrations, has at his service such and such Mafia boss of Palermo or from a nearby town, and through him, a portion of that population of professional or occasional ruffians, who plague the city and its surroundings; which means that on one hand, he will take advantage of the terror inspired by these people; and on the other hand, he, whenever needed, will help and protect these clients of his. (Ibid., 5)

At about the same time as Franchetti and Sonnino's study trip to Sicily, Attorney General Vincenzo Calenda[2] compared the Mafia to a nervous system: "This large organization . . . like the nerves of a human organism, has entirely infiltrated in the social texture" (quoted in Pezzino 1999, 23).

In sum, the Mafia emerged in Sicily in the nineteenth century as part of Italy's state formation process and from the tensions arising among a variety of old and new forces. From its outset, the Mafia established itself as a hinge linking legal and illegal powers that extended into political, economic, and social domains. The Mafia did not exist as a separate entity from the state or contrary to the state. Rather, it was an organization and mechanism that presupposed the existence of the state. As Nando Dalla Chiesa (1976, 65) noted, the Mafia was the particular form of power by which the *gabellotti* enforced their class domination in Sicily after the unification of Italy. In other words, the Mafia was not a mere criminal organization but a system of domination. From the beginning, instead of fighting the Mafia, the state chose to negotiate with it in order to come to terms with it and acquire it as part of its entanglement in marginal areas constructed as backward and premodern.

The intertwinement of the Mafia with the state has been its defining characteristic not only at its origins, but also throughout its history. Rather than opposing and fighting this phenomenon, the state has relied on the Mafia for repression, control, and domination at the margins. Taussig's (2005) observation that states have no trouble in recruiting squads of killers and torturers when their backs are up against the wall accurately describes not only what has happened in Colombia and other Latin American countries, but also the intertwinement between the Italian state and the Mafia.

Thus, during the peasant revolts of the early 1890s, for example, Italy's national government used the Mafia to repress the peasant revolts known as the Fasci Siciliani. At the end of the nineteenth century, and encouraged by the establishment of the Socialist Party, peasants and workers in Sicily organized in leagues that demanded lower taxes and new rights from landowners protected by the Mafia. Strikes spread across the island after their demands were denied, and to prevent an insurrection, the Italian government declared a state of emergency: the protests were brutally repressed, and the Fasci, together with the Socialist Party, were disbanded (Schneider and Schneider 2003, 36).

Intertwinement between paramilitary death squads and the state's security apparatus is the most observable reality of the broader alliance between the paramilitaries and the state. During my Colombian fieldwork, I collected several examples of the association among police, military officers, and paramilitaries, some of which I have already described: the military checkpoint I encountered on my way to meet Doble Cero; Doble Cero's revelation that a retired army general had first introduced him to the Castaño brothers in Medellín; the indifference of the police when paramilitaries seized a truck driver one night in Bajo Cauca, Antioquia; the paramilitaries in civilian clothes chatting with a soldier on a street corner in an Eastern Antioquia village; and the constantly circulating rumors that the police were in cahoots with the paramilitaries.

I myself received confirmation of those rumors when, one day in Medellín, I walked through the Parque Bolívar with Óscar, a demobilized paramilitary in his midtwenties who had agreed to share his experience with me. I related to Óscar an experience in that square three years earlier, on the very first day of my first trip to Colombia: I had been mugged by a group of tough young men who tried to steal my thin gold chain by snatching it from my neck. I told Óscar how that episode left me trembling and that, as a consequence, until that very day, I had avoided Parque Bolívar.

"Now the place is clean," said Óscar, who often disguised his gaze behind dark sunglasses. He explained further: "Not long ago, while we were at the shelter [for demobilized paramilitaries], police officers looked for us and asked for our collaboration in cleaning the square of petty criminals. And we did. We didn't kill anyone. We just beat them up and told them to stay away." Óscar was proud of the results that he and his companions had achieved, and most likely felt satisfied that they were still useful despite the demobilization. Not only had Óscar confirmed the rumors circulating about policing conducted jointly by law enforcement and paramilitaries in Medellín; he also had highlighted that this interlacement was a distinguishing feature of the paramilitaries and the production of "ordered disorder." In wondering about intertwinement between police and paramilitaries, Taussig, in *Law in a Lawless Land: Diary of a* Limpieza *in Colombia,* noted that the criminal is unable to sense the nature of his actions since they mirror those of the state, such as spying, duping, bribing, and setting traps. "If Nietzsche puts us on the right track, is it surprising that the paras and the police are the same?" he asks (2005, 49).

Intertwinement among paramilitaries, police, and military has been amply documented in Colombia. In 2001, Human Rights Watch, for example, published a report entitled *The Sixth Division* about the ties between the paramilitaries and the army, presenting the Autodefensas Unidas de Colombia (AUC) as the sixth division of Colombia's armed forces. The report documented that the army, in several departments of the country, had looked the other way as paramilitaries penetrated a territory or had even provided logistical support to help them carry out their massacres (Human Rights Watch 2001).

In 2012, a judge sentenced General Rito Alejo del Río to twenty-five years in prison for the murder of Marino López Mena, a peasant whom paramilitaries killed and dismembered in the hamlet of Bijao—part of Urabá—in 1997. "Paramilitaries and militaries detained Marino López, tortured him, decapitated him with a machete, and cut him up in the presence of the community," reported the Inter-American Commission on Human Rights.[3] Following the killing of Marino López, several other members of his community were disappeared, and large parts of the local population were forced to leave the area and were displaced elsewhere. Marino López's killing happened during the Genesis Operation of February 1997,[4] headed by General Río, nicknamed the "Pacifier of Urabá," who at the time was the commander of the XVII Brigade. The operation was carried out in conjunction with the paramilitaries, as the paramilitary leader Hébert Veloza, whom I met in a detention center in New York, confirmed; he later stated, "At the time that Rito Alejo del Río was the commander of the XVII Brigade, I met with him at the brigade to coordinate operations in the rural area of Urabá" (Inter-American Commission on Human Rights 2011, 28). During the Genesis Operation, the Colombian air force indiscriminately bombarded communities to open the path for the penetration of the Bloque Calima paramilitary group, led by Fredy Rendón Herrera, who was nicknamed El Alemán.[5] The Inter-American Court established that the Genesis Operation was jointly carried out by the army and the paramilitaries and declared the Colombian state responsible for the violation of human rights.

The articulation or intertwinement between paramilitary groups and the state's security apparatus does not account, in and of itself, for the impunity, legitimacy, and even the broad sympathy that paramilitaries have enjoyed in Colombia. To comprehend the extent of the phenomenon, it is necessary to look beneath the tip of the iceberg and to analyze other forces that characterize the paramilitaries as a mechanism and form of domination. Only by including the totality of the intertwinements that constitute the paramilitaries is it possible to grasp this phenomenon and its complexity.

In fact, as in Sicily, the strength of Colombia's paramilitaries was not only its use of violence and the spectacle of that violence. Its strength also came from outside; that is, from its intertwinement or *intreccio* with emerging elites who make up the political and economic elites in departments across Colombia. These elites, like the *gabellotti,* did not hesitate to resort to violence and paramilitary death squads to advance their interests, accumulate land and resources, and win elections. Encouraged by a justificatory antiguerrilla discourse that emphasized the need for self-defense in a weak state incapable of providing security, the close relationship between paramilitary organizations and local political and economic elites had in fact existed since the genesis of the paramilitary phenomenon. As I mentioned in chapter 1, armed self-defense groups in the Middle Magdalena region, for example, were established with support and resources provided by local officials, the army, and a multinational oil corporation. The paramilitary project gained strength with the unlimited resources provided by drug cartels, which in turn transformed the paramilitaries into organizations where legal and illegal interests met and merged in a murky alliance with drug kingpins, private businesses, the military, and politicians.

Though at the outset of the 1980s, the paramilitaries were mainly local groups established by local elites for the purposes of self-defense, over the years the paramilitaries—as I briefly mentioned in the chapter 3—turned into armed groups that expanded beyond local boundaries and dedicated themselves to the accumulation of economic and political capital (Romero 2003; Ávila Martínez 2010). In other words, they occupied and controlled new territories; elected political officials not only at the municipal level, but also at the regional level; and killed political and opposition leaders, most notably members and representatives of the Unión Patriótica.[6] The synergy between the actions of the armed paramilitary groups and the interests of the regional elites that supported them is expressed in this passage from a document in which the founder of the AUC outlined the paramilitaries' political aims:

> The political thought of the AUC, embodied in the state's renovation and restructuring project, is expressed in the formulation of a glossary of proposals that aim to reconcile a democratic economy with a democratic politics to promote social equilibrium. In this sense, we take [a] part from the socialist stance of the insurgency, which aims at the hypothetical conquest of equity suppressing liberty through the random discourse of the proletariat's dictatorship, which is nothing more than the military tyranny of a workers' political aristocracy, which represents the interests of the party's leadership and not those of the people. (Quoted in Ávila Martínez 2010, 120)

In the summer of 2001, thirty-two social and political leaders met in Santa Fe de Ralito (see chapter 6), in the department of Córdoba, with four commanders of major paramilitary groups in order to sign an agreement, the intention of which was to "refund the fatherland" and "sign a new social contract" (Cepeda and Rojas 2008, 85). The meeting was called by Salvatore Mancuso, a rancher from Córdoba turned paramilitary leader, and the agreement was also signed by Diego Fernando Murillo Bejarano (alias Don Berna), Edward Cobos Téllez (alias Diego Vecino), and Rodrigo Tovar Pupo (alias Jorge 40).[7] In addition, there were a dozen members of congress, two governors, three mayors, and several council members and public administration officials. When the agreement was revealed to the public, the Colombian magazine *Semana* wrote, "part of the Colombian state joined its own destiny with one of the most fearsome criminal organizations in the recent history of the country." It defined the agreement as a pact with the devil, a Faustian agreement:

> Only two months ago, 150 men of the Special Forces and 40 of the prosecutor's office had begun the largest offensive on the heart of the AUC in Monteria. They were after Carlos Castaño and Salvatore Mancuso. At that time, they were the two most wanted men in Colombia. They were wanted for extradition on drug trafficking, and the Colombian justice system chased after them for crimes against humanity.

Mancuso and Castaño were at the head of a war machine at its military peak and were rooted in the fight against the guerrillas and the extermination of the civilian population. The trail of blood preceding the meeting could not have been more chilling. Over the past five years, according to figures by the authorities, the paramilitaries had committed more than 250 massacres that left more than 1,700 dead. Since the killing in Mapiripán—where [paramilitaries] demonstrated that they could reach any corner of the country to spread terror—to the massacre of El Aro and La Granja—where there was a systematic plan to exterminate the civilian population—to the killings in El Salado and Chengue, which revealed that the degree of brutality and cruelty had no boundaries. In the latest massacre, the men of the AUC brought death to its most degrading state: to make torture and death into a public spectacle. This macabre backdrop of the meeting did not seem to matter to politicians.[8]

The extent of the intertwinement came to light during the so-called *parapolítica* between 2008 and 2010, when prosecutors indicted about four hundred politicians for having ties with the AUC's paramilitary umbrella organization. As discussed by Claudia Nayibe López Hernández (2010, 41–43), democratic reforms aimed at broadening political representation and participation, such as the direct and popular elections of mayors since 1986 and the 1991 Constitution, were turned by political and economic interests into an opportunity, using paramilitaries' violence and capacity for intimidation to influence access to the political process and condition the results of elections. López argued, for example, that the constitutional reforms resulted in an increase of senators supported by paramilitaries being elected in departments where paramilitary groups had established domination. About 35 percent of the senators elected in 2002, the year when President Uribe began his administration, had ties with, and enjoyed the support of, the paramilitaries (ibid., 43). Moreover, López highlighted that the expansion of the paramilitaries favored the rise of a hybrid elite group who represented and defended the interests of traditional local barons and the illegal interests of drug kingpins. In other words, the paramilitaries' political representatives became the power brokers and the mediators of both legal and illegal interests and activities (ibid., 56). Local and national politicians had formed a society of mutual aid with members of the paramilitaries.

Not only political leaders have been part of this mutual aid association, this broad gray area; business leaders and multinational corporations have participated as well. Recent investigations have brought to light the direct involvement of both large national and multinational corporations in financing paramilitary groups in several departments of Colombia, showing that the corporations have relied on paramilitaries not only to protect private property from guerrillas and guard their employees from kidnappings, but to also dispossess peasants from their land, which has been increasingly concentrated to the advantage of agroindustrial businesses and mining companies (Reyes Posada 2009). Paramilitary death squads have played a fundamental role in the repression of workers' organizations and the selective killings of union leaders. The Medellín-based Escuela Nacional Sindical (2007) reported that between 1986 and 2006—that is, during the twenty years when paramilitary terror spread throughout the country—over twenty-five hundred union members were killed in Colombia. During the same period, according to official data provided by the Ministry of Agriculture, nearly 8.3 million hectares (20.5 million acres) were dispossessed or abandoned due to violence (Grupo Memoria Histórica 2013, 76).

Businesses have been the accomplices of paramilitary groups, or at the very least have tolerated and shown tacit sympathy to their presence and actions. A great number of businesses that paid protection money declared themselves victims rather than associates of the paramilitaries. This, for example, was the defense put forward in the years after the AUC's demobilization by one of Colombia's biggest banana plantation owners, an influential member of the Antioquia elite whose family controls a popular newspaper in the region and whose sons have held offices at the departmental and municipal levels. After the demobilization of the paramilitaries, a mass grave containing the remains of paramilitary victims was found on one of the owner's properties in Urabá. The businessman, who admitted to paying protection money to paramilitary groups, dismissed the finding of the grave on his property, declined any responsibility for it, and in an interview declared that one is not responsible if a shooting happens in front of one's own house.

Important multinational companies, such as Chiquita Brands, Drummond, and Coca-Cola (Gill 2004), have also relied on paramilitary groups to provide security. Chiquita financed paramilitaries in Urabá and Santa Marta between 1997 and 2004; that is, during the time when violence intensified in that region and paramilitary death squads carried out sixty-two massacres, killing over three thousand people and displacing about sixty thousand people. Chiquita admitted the financing of paramilitaries groups, which executives of the company defined as "sensitive payments," and in exchange for legal immunity paid a fee of US$25 million to the U.S. Department of Justice (Romero et al. 2011, 155). "Banana companies, not just Chiquita Brands, supported us," declared the leader of the Bananero paramilitary group, Hébert Veloza, in a 2008 statement to Colombian prosecutors. "All banana companies contributed because we were present in the entire banana area and everyone paid."[9] He declared:

> When as a commandant I penetrated [Urabá], the instruction that I received in 1995 was to establish our presence in the entire banana area and to totally prohibit strikes. . . . What is clear is that the Castaño brothers made arrangements with the banana plantation owners to send the group that I belonged to into the area of Urabá . . . and as I repeatedly said, we pressured banana workers to work, I prohibited strikes, and I went to the estates to have meetings. In other words, since 1995, banana plantations owners have financed the self-defense groups. (Voluntary statement, Hébert Veloza, September 2008)

Multinational and national companies made their "sensitive payments" to the paramilitaries through private vigilante groups, known as Convivir, which President Ernesto Samper[10] promoted in 1996 and that three years later were disbanded due to political pressure. Established with the goal of providing logistic support and intelligence to the army, Convivir employed almost ten thousand men belonging to more than five hundred private vigilante groups. Chiquita Brands, together with other banana companies in Urabá, for example, deposited its protection money into the accounts of the Convivir Papagayo. As Veloza confirmed in a deposition to Colombian prosecutors, Convivir provided legal cover for paramilitary organizations: "The Convivir were legal organizations, and we used them like we used members of the law enforcement. Here we mentioned militaries, police officers, mayors, senators. . . . The Convivir was a legal organization basically established by the state. We used it for illegal activities" (informal transcript, June 10 and July 9, 2008).

Medellín is not only the capital of the department of Antioquia, but also one of the Colombian cities where the intertwinement of paramilitaries with the state has been most tightly woven. Indeed, the city produced the paramilitaries as an embodiment of the paramilitary-state articulation, and Medellín remains an allegory of the desires, fantasies, and interests that have shaped the history of Colombia.

In this next part of this chapter, building on the concepts and analysis above, I present a portrait of Medellín that is in part a collage of its history and is in part drawn from my own ethnographic encounters and observations. In particular, to further explore the notion of intertwinement, I focus on the development of a network of gangs in the late 1970s and 1980s; the hunting and the killing of the legendary drug kingpin Pablo Escobar, which resulted in the establishment of Los Pepes, whose legal and illegal forces cooperated to take down the founder of the Medellín cartel; the pacification of Comuna 13; and finally the rise of the Cacique Nutibara paramilitary group.

Mary Roldán described Medellín as the city "where paternalism, civic duty, a tradition of nonpartisan public service, and ascent based on merit have always coexisted with exclusion, discrimination, parochialism and selective repression" (2003, 129). Founded in 1675 by aristocratic families, Medellín soon became Colombia's engine of business and commerce. Between the 1960s and the 1970s, in the wake of a major decline in textile manufacturing, criminality and violence spread throughout the city. Powerful smugglers of cigarettes, whisky, and household appliances, such as Alfredo Gómez, from the suburb of Envigado, became role models for individuals such as Pablo Escobar, who at the time was in his early twenties and only at the beginning of his criminal career. Those were the years when marijuana, and later cocaine, paved the way to quick and easy wealth and rapid social ascent. Regions such as Antioquia, wrote Alonso Salazar in his biography of Pablo Escobar, are areas "where [people] pray ceaselessly, but where also agile, and at the time illegal, forms of enrichment are practiced without shame; where one dreams exaggeratedly about money, about the ignoble metal" (2001, 45). Those were the years when Griselda Blanco, nicknamed the "Queen of Cocaine," developed her trade in the Santísima Trinidad neighborhood, which at the time was a sort of tolerance zone that the police dared not enter.

It was Blanco who eventually introduced young Pablo Escobar to the secrets of cocaine trafficking and its routes. Referring to increasing cocaine demand from the United States, Escobar and his comrades would say that, as a means to accumulate wealth and as compared to marijuana, cocaine was even better than gold (ibid., 50). Those were also the years when cocaine encouraged the interlacement of future powerful drug kingpins, such as Pablo Escobar, the Ochoa family, and the paramilitary leader Fidel Castaño.

At the beginning of the 1980s, and to the beat of metal and punk music, teenagers in Medellín begun to form groups that eventually turned into mighty gangs. Youth from working-class neighborhoods, such as Santander and Florencia in the northwestern part of the city, first formed small gangs, which committed robberies against women, children, and the elderly. They assaulted buses to pay for fashionable clothes, marijuana, and alcohol.

Because they dressed in black, wore boots with metal toes, and listened to punk music, they called themselves Los Punkeros.

Discovering drugs as a source of ready wealth, these groups of teens eventually turned into death squads. The gangs had affinities with Los Monjes, "the monks," in the town of Bello north of Medellín, who were known for their initiation rituals, tattoos, and pacts of blood, and with Los Priscos, named after a family from Aranjuez, a densely populated barrio in the northern part of the city. They became acquainted with Escobar, who in this barrio promoted social initiatives and provided lighting for the soccer field, paved streets, and organized soccer tournaments. Furthermore, the northeastern part of the city was controlled by the criminal band of Los Nachos.

In the mid-1980s, tired of being harassed and terrorized by gangs, the city's population organized self-defense groups; responding to violence with violence, their intention was to cleanse their neighborhoods of crime. Squads of hooded men killed gang members and junkies, known in Medellín as *pillos*. This is when guerrilla militias, especially the ELN and the M-19, made the strategic decision to penetrate urban areas. As the paramilitaries would do in subsequent years, the militias first sowed terror and fear and later made use of persuasion, negotiating with gangs and incorporating them into their own ranks.

The shantytowns in the northeastern part of the city, perched on the slopes surrounding Medellín, were the main theater of violence in these years. Medellín-born writer Fernando Vallejo, now living in Mexico, wrote about the disorder of his city in the novel *La virgen de los sicarios*. Describing how the city is divided between the shantytown suburbs in the hills and the well-to-do homes spreading at the bottom of the valley, Vallejo wrote:

> The city below never goes up to the city above, but vice versa, sure: those from above come down, to prowl around, to steal, to stick people up, to murder. The ones who are still alive come down, I should say, because the majority of them up there, up there so very close to the clouds and to heaven, are killed before they can make it down to do their own killing. (2001, 88–89)

During my fieldwork in Medellín, I often went to the "city above," which I reached by riding on the modern cableway, smoothly sailing over the jam of tin-roofed or unfinished structures and terraces exposed to the sun. Closer to the hilltops, the homes were wooden shanties resting on precarious ground.

One day I rode the cableway with Lucas, a former ELN guerrilla, to the upper end of the barrio of Santo Domingo. Lucas drew imaginary boundaries with his index finger as we traveled, marking the front lines of the urban warfare in which he had first-hand experience. Medellín had long been crossed by these invisible but powerful boundaries, and transgression could trigger a death sentence from a rival armed group. These lines have shifted constantly, and residents have learned which streets to travel on, which ones to avoid, and which boundaries not to cross. Walking on the wrong side of a street can get you killed. In several of the city's barrios, survival has been a matter of such cartographic knowledge.

The alleys down there, Lucas pointed out, marked the border between two territories controlled by two rival armed groups. Militias dominated the side closer to the hills, while gangs had a grip on the other side. Checkpoints were set up at the gate of each territory. Armed young men stopped buses and cars and frisked passengers. They executed, on the spot, those suspected of being enemies or snitches and those who were on their death lists. At sunset, around six o'clock, the gunfights began. Young thugs, who took positions in the hills or in forcibly occupied houses transformed into fortresses, opened fire on rival groups. The civilian population was caught in the middle. Stray bullets occasionally penetrated the defenseless shanties, injuring or killing innocent bystanders.

When I had first met Lucas, who wore jeans and a T-shirt covering his muscular frame, he was about forty years old and considered himself a lucky survivor of the violence of these years. At the time of our meeting, in the summer of 2006, he was working as a security guard, doing night shifts watching over a construction site. He dreamed of finding a job in a nongovernmental organization to serve the needy living in his neighborhood, as he had used to do back in the days when he was a local commander of the ELN militias. Lucas and his wife—who, he told me, had been the girlfriend of a drug trafficker in her youth—and their three children still lived in the small and humble home where he had grown up. Small round holes marked the external walls of his home, the marks of bullets fired from the hills. Once he told me that it must have been La Virgen, Our Lady, who protected him, since many times he had had near-death experiences. Lucas also confessed that in order to save his life, he had allied at one point with the police special forces to hand over some of his enemies, whom he called *culebras,* or poisonous snakes.[11]

On a terrace overlooking the city, and under a billboard advertising the construction of a new public library, Lucas shared his story, telling me how violent the city had been in his childhood and why, eventually, he had decided to join the militias:

I was born here. My childhood was normal. I went to the daycare center. When I was in primary school, there were gangs, [such as] Los Nachos. Each block had its own gang. They arrived from all sides to monopolize their domination. They robbed stores; they assaulted soda and beer trucks that provisioned the stores. When the trucks stopped driving up to our neighborhood, the shopkeepers had to go to downtown Medellín. In my own neighborhood, we never had gangs, but they came from elsewhere. I grew up observing these conflicts. They killed people merely to steal a pair of sneakers. When you saw people wearing fancy sneakers and riding powerful motorbikes, you knew they were members of a gang. I witnessed all of this while I was still a child. For this reason, eventually militias were created. These were the Popular Militias of the Aburrá Valley. This was in 1988.

I joined the militias in 1992. My idea to join the fight came about because I wanted to defend my neighborhood. One couldn't cope with [the harassment] anymore. When they gave us the opportunity to use arms, I really thought about it. There was a man living in our neighborhood, a good man, and he had good ideals. He was a community leader. He was the one who invited us. He called me as well. "What are we going to do to face this problem?" he would ask. "Are we just going to stand by while all these people come and attack us? What are we going to do? I can offer you this: I can bring someone to you who can organize you, who can guide you and arm you." This is how we met Commander Rafa. He armed us, and he collaborated with other people to build a meaningful presence [of the militias]. Later they gave us [money] to support ourselves and to buy clothes.

The leftist [armed groups] had recruited educated people who could teach us. We would meet every three or four days [to be trained]. They were talking a lot about Lenin and Che Guevara. Especially about Che Guevara. It was for this reason that one joins them: because one realizes many things. They open your mind. I really liked those lectures because I did not know anything. They were explaining reality. . . .

To enter the militia was not a big deal. I was not frightened. We defended the neighborhood fiercely. We covered our faces and we patrolled the streets. People who came to fuck things up soon found out that there were scary people here [guarding the barrio]. We attacked each other and got furious. [W]e got to the point that nobody could enter the area [under our control] without our consent.

Since I had served in the military, I knew how to use weapons, and I liked it. I had very happy moments. It satisfied me to see the community doing well, to see people grateful and happy and without problems, [to see them happy] when we organized activities for the children and their mothers. I enjoyed all these activities very much.

The aim was to get to the point where people could relax because you had a good and solid organization. You can relax because there are people collaborating with you. They will report to you everything that happens in the neighborhood. Before someone comes to hurt you, he has to breach the security cordons made up of these people. An intelligence security cordon is the solid base of support. When you enter a militia area, you find security cordons; you run into people who will speak to you, with no need for you to know if he or she is part of the militia. They will investigate you. A shopkeeper listens to something; the bus driver listens to something else. And they report it to the militia.

At first, the population backed the militias, but over time, the order they established only deepened the sense of chaos and disorder. In the 1990s, after the death of Pablo Escobar, fragmentation and violent competition spread among gangs who were regulating the illicit market in Medellín, and the militias increasingly turned into violent criminal groups that harassed the population. This is when the paramilitaries begun to penetrate peripheral neighborhoods of the city. It thus happened that some young people, growing up in Medellín, from time to time shifted and changed masters, belonging first to a gang, then to a militia group, and finally to the paramilitaries: to Doble Cero's Bloque Metro at first and later to Don Berna's Cacique Nutibara and Héroes de Granada.

In August 2006, in one of the most populated neighborhoods of Medellín, a battleground since the times when the first gangs were established, I met Alejandro, who at the time of our encounter was the president of the Junta de Acción Comunal, a community action committee. His neighborhood was a large shantytown, occupied mainly by thousands of people the violence had displaced from rural areas over the years. It was a microcosm of the regions and people making up the heterogeneous cultural reality of Colombia. Alejandro was elected along with a small team of people, and he was responsible for organizing social and recreational activities for the residents of his barrio. His career, like Lucas's, had started as a member of the popular militias. In more recent years, he had belonged first to Doble Cero's paramilitary group and then to the Cacique Nutibara group until its demobilization in the fall of 2003.

His small and humble office bustled with people asking Alejandro for favors and advice. At one point, a woman entered his office and interrupted our conversation. She complained that someone had stolen some clothing she had hung to dry. Alejandro explained that he was no longer in charge of solving such problems, as he had been when he was with the paramilitaries. He said he could not send the *muchachos* anymore, and that she had to call the communitarian police. The woman gave him a disappointed look and left. When our conversation resumed, Alejandro provided an overview of the complex dynamics that regulated Medellín's urban conflict:

In the past here we had severe public order problems. We lacked electricity and water. It was a slum area, and because of the fear of evacuation there were many confrontations between the community and law enforcement. Stones were thrown. When there were evacuation orders, the reaction was spontaneous. The police were seen as the enemy of those slums, and it was only natural to see the police as the enemy. There weren't any good schools, either. I came here with my parents because we'd had a problem with a neighbor in a different barrio. Ours was a voluntary displacement. At that time, banditry wasn't seen yet. When the M-19 guerrillas demobilized, the anarchy of the youth began, and it was a disaster. . . .

Later, gangs such as Los Calvos and La Salida began to form. They operated in different areas of the neighborhood, stealing and kidnapping, until they put themselves at the service of the drug trade in 1990. They wouldn't allow any cars to enter the barrio. There were robberies, kidnappings, rapes, and murders. This was an off-limit zone for law enforcement.

At the time, I was thirteen or fourteen years old, and seeing this empire of evil, young people of my own age with guns, I asked myself, "What is the role of law enforcement?" There was disregard toward the police force because of corruption and because of the relationship between the gangs and the police. So I asked myself, "How can we solve this?" These gangs were against the community, and they stunted the development of the community. There was no inclusion. I imagined that there had to be a solution, that the state had to intervene and control [the situation]. But I didn't see how these people were going to do anything for the town.

That's when the militia intervened and started eliminating the gangs. This was in 1991, and the change was absolute. Initially they did a good job. There was temporary peace. . . . Commerce increased and so did the involvement of the city government. Later, when the militias demobilized, . . . the neighborhood was left on standby, and the people started wondering what would come next.

There was banditry again and new criminal gangs. Many of them were youth who liked the world of weapons. They continued being militias, but not in the true sense, because they didn't endorse any particular ideology. The years between 1994 and 1998 were chaos, and that's what created the need for a self-defense force. At that time, Carlos Castaño threatened to come in and take over the neighborhood. There was tremendous fear because the neighborhood was full of graffiti, and this was seen as an indication of militia activities. We were worried about how they were going to act toward us.

Our hope was to prevent this incursion through negotiations, and we explained [to Castaño] that it wasn't necessary to eliminate the leaders [of the gangs], only for them to understand that [the kids] weren't militias, just delinquents. There were negotiations with the commander of the Bloque Metro. At the time, my work was political as well as social. My role was to explain to the people why it was necessary to work with the community. Also, when I was with the militias, I mostly did political work, promoting sports and culture and trying to minimize the effects of the violence. My role with the militia was to oversee a transition phase, promoting participation and education. It was social service for the community. My job was to gain the trust of the people so that the community would not be left in poverty—so that there wouldn't be scoundrels and junkies, because those were unhealthy things.

At the time of Castaño's threat, there was fear because the neighborhood was stigmatized as a militia neighborhood due to its history. So we looked for a different solution that wouldn't induce the incursion of the self-defense forces. In that way, we were able to explain to the people in the community that now the Bloque Metro was going to be present. This way there were no massacres, and if there were some security flaws, we could talk about it. We went from the use of weapons to dialogue, and we talked to people. We'd meet with the gangs and talk to them. We'd tell them that it was stupid to keep fighting, and we looked for other opportunities for them, like professional training and inclusion in decisions affecting the community. At that time, it was possible to work with the Bloque Metro.

At the same time, the young people who previously worked with us [in the militia] continued to be with us. These were the ones that were in charge of security. They became members of the self-defense forces and developed the political-military school in the Oriente.

Both the commanders and leaders doing political work for the Bloque Metro came to our neighborhood. The political leaders [los políticos] of the group came to check on our work, meet with the people to explain what the organization was doing, and carry out social work. They did this to better the community, to ease fear over the presence of the self-defense forces. There had been no public consumption of drugs in this neighborhood since 1991. Drugs could not be consumed in public view, before people and children. The murder rate dropped significantly after 1994.

At the end of 2001 and the beginning of 2002, there was a confrontation between the Bloque Metro and the Cacique Nutibara [paramilitary groups]. Movement of armed people began, people appeared in the middle of the night, and there were threats and explosions. Something was happening. My reaction was to look for a solution to this problem, and it had to be done quickly. We contacted the people of the Cacique Nutibara; they gave their reasons, and we asked them what the solution could be. Through the radio and newspapers, I learned that the Bloque Metro was in trouble and that fighting was going on among defense groups. I thought that none of this was our concern, as we didn't know Doble Cero's intentions, and we weren't [there] to defend any particular interest. Thus we decided to join the Cacique

Nutibara at the beginning of 2002. We heard that there were disagreements [with the Bloque Metro], and we sensed that we had become a military target. That's why we decided to support the Cacique Nutibara, and that's why we went to talk to them.

The way we operated changed radically. The social and political work increased, and so did the participation of the people in providing solutions to the problems. The Bloque Metro wasn't as community-based [as the Cacique Nutibara], . . . but in the Cacique Nutibara, there was more interaction with the community. The line of action was to work with the community. The discipline was stricter, and the interaction [with the community] more regular.

My role today is the same, though now I do it from an institutional position. Before I was doing this work with the self-defense groups. The Community Action Committee is a not-for-profit and community-based organization made up of a group of people who are community leaders and who work for the development of a community through a democratic, participatory process. The funding comes from the city of Medellín, the national government, the office for social development, and donations. We [the members of the Community Action Committee] take care of education, health, housing, culture, and sport. We were selected through a democratic process. I presented to the assembly of the community a group of individuals who were going to work with me. Among them, I was the only demobilized member [of the paramilitaries]. We were elected in 2004, and we'll stay in power until 2008. Of course, the demobilize youth helped me out; about sixty-five demobilized youth assisted me with the latest recreational activities we organized.

A watershed moment in the history of violence in Medellín came in 1984, when Pablo Escobar declared war against the state. This was in response to Justice Minister Rodrigo Lara Bonilla's determination to go after Escobar's "hot money" and to stem his increasing political influence. Looking for legitimacy from Colombia's traditional elites and attempting to fight the policy of extradition, Escobar had decided to run for the national congress as a candidate of a wing of the Liberal party. To associates who cautioned him about the perils of such a move, Escobar had responded, "We already have the economic power, now we go after the political power" (quoted in Salazar 2001, 92).

The 1982 political campaign was the first in Colombia to be marked by public debate about elections financed by drug money. Eventually, Escobar was indeed elected to the national congress as a substitute for the Envigado representative Jairo Ortega. Yet the political victory turned into a curse for the drug lord. Prosecutors went after the sources of his wealth, and in January 1984, Escobar was forced to surrender his congressional seat. Three months later, Justice Minister Lara was murdered. The killing marked the beginning of the long chain of terrorist attacks beginning in 1984, in which police officers, prosecutors, journalists, and presidential candidates were assassinated by Escobar and the Medellín drug cartel.[12]

At the beginning of the 1990s, in response to Escobar's acts against the state, the Colombian government, under President Carlos Gaviria Díaz and with the backing of the United States, created a special search unit to bring Escobar to justice. In parallel, a murky pact to kill Medellín's drug kingpin was sealed among the Colombian police, business leaders, drug traffickers of the Cali and North Valley cartels, and emerging paramilitary leaders. They all joined forces to form Los Pepes (from "Perseguidos por Pablo Escobar," or the People Persecuted by Pablo Escobar) (Bowden 2001).

Los Pepes are an example of the workings of intertwinement in Colombia: a loose network, and a flexible, ambiguous, fluid, opportunistic, and transitory arrangement. Both a product and an expression of the space of exception, Los Pepes contributed to a new wave of terror, killings, and retaliations.

Commandant Rodrigo Doble Cero, the leader of Bloque Metro and a former army official, was a leading figure among Los Pepes. When we met, he shared with me a memo he had written about the history of violence in Medellín (Civico 2006, 2012; Sanford and Angel-Ajani 2006). Describing the hunt for Escobar, he highlighted the pivotal role played by Diego Fernando Murillo Bejarano, alias Don Berna, a former bodyguard of drug lord Fernando Galeano.[13] Don Berna was a power broker, shuttling between the legal and illegal worlds, weaving the threads of interlacement, and embodying the convergence of interests and intentions among representatives of the state and the underworld of organized crime. After the death of Escobar in 1993, Don Berna acquired a prominent role in Medellín's organized crime underworld, inheriting and expanding Escobar's domination and monopoly of the entirety of the illicit markets (La Rotta and Morales 2009). At the end of the 1990s, Don Berna became a member of the AUC leadership. In the memo, Doble Cero addressed Don Berna's alliance with the command of the Colombian National Police in Medellín. It is a detailed description of the elements of the intertwinement and its mode of operation. As Agamben states, in the space of exception, "everything is possible" (1998, 170). Doble Cero wrote in the memo:

The Search Bloc was formed. To "recuperate" [Pablo Escobar], Don Berna . . . made contact with the North Valley Cartel and explained the situation to them. They put [Don Berna] in touch with the associates of the Cali Cartel.

After a few days, Don Berna was coordinating operatives against the Medellín Cartel with the police and the DAS [the Departamento Administrativo de Seguridad, the Colombian version of the U.S. FBI]. . . . Later, the so-called Los Pepes were formed, which represented a combination of the Cali Cartel, the North Valley Cartel, the remains of the Medellín Cartel headed by Don Berna, the police of Medellín, and the counterguerrilla organization of Fidel Castaño.[14] This ad hoc organization, using completely irregular war tactics, achieved the destruction of Pablo's terror machine and killed him. Don Berna remained as Escobar's heir. (Autodefensas Campesinas Bloque Metro 2003, 3)

The leaders of Los Pepes were later among the founders of the AUC and were at the head of the Bloque Metro and the Cacique Nutibara paramilitary groups. Carlos Castaño, founder of the AUC, referring to the experience of Los Pepes, mentioned the permanent state of exception in which Colombia found itself: "The public prosecutor's office, the police, the army, and the DAS all tolerated us. Even President César Gaviria Trujillo never ordered our prosecution. The journalists applauded us. And rightly so! The state protects itself with the Constitution, and acts outside of it when it feels threatened by a monster like Pablo Escobar" (Aranguren Molina 2001, 142).

This experimental configuration had several important consequences, including the atomization of drug cartels, which today represent a significant part of Colombia's cocaine trade; the consolidation of the so-called *oficinas,* or Mafia-like[15] power centers, which regulate the illicit market in Medellín and beyond; the establishment of an alliance between Medellín drug baron Don Berna and the Castaño brothers in establishing the AUC; the expansion of powerful and autonomous gangs, such as La Terraza and Los Triana; and the establishment of links among law enforcement, Mafia, and paramilitary groups in Medellín and throughout Colombia (Espinal, Alonso, Giraldo, and Sierra 2007, 91–92).

Pablo Escobar was killed in 1993, but the Cacique Nutibara paramilitary group, founded by Don Berna almost ten years afterward, had its roots in the experience of Los Pepes. In fact, the Cacique Nutibara, rather than a hierarchical organization, was a network linking various criminal nodes throughout and beyond Medellín. It brought together the experiences of the self-defense groups established in the 1980s, the private armies of drug kingpins, and well-organized independent gangs, such as La Banda Frank, La Terraza, Los Triana, and the remains of Doble Cero's Bloque Metro. The Cacique Nutibara's mission was the extraction of revenues from the illicit market as well as social and territorial control (ibid., 100).

Fabio Acevedo, an associate of Don Berna since the time of Pablo Escobar and a Medellín-based paramilitary leader, justified the establishment of the Cacique Nutibara in a conversation I had with him at the headquarters of the Corporación Democracia[16] in downtown Medellín. He posited the rise of his group as an independent initiative promoted by concerned citizens who were really drug traffickers preoccupied with consolidating the monopoly of their illicit business and strengthening their political influence:

> The Cacique Nutibara was basically born by the petition of the community itself, in the sense that we are part of the Medellín community, and we are people who have lived and continue to live in the different *comunas* of Medellín. We saw that Medellín was sinking and in a condition of an unbearable conflict. So different people started to think about what we could do to bring peace back to Medellín. In the first six months of 2000, we conducted a study to see what was really going on in Medellín. We realized that the gangs and the combos were different. The gangs were [made up of people] who came together to commit crimes with [the ultimate] goal of making money. They sold themselves to the highest bidder. The combos, on the other hand, were [made up of] boys who hung out on street corners. You have to look at the sociological reality. During our youth, we had constructed our vision at home, in church, and in school. But when we did [our] study, we realized that young people had changed, and that they had created their life vision on street corners. Here, because of the drug trade, there was a mentality of easy money, that life wasn't worth much, and that the only thing that mattered was giving your mom a house and leaving her [economically] stable if you died at age fourteen, fifteen, sixteen, seventeen, or eighteen. So it was the parents who buried the children, when it should've been the opposite. When the war with Pablo Escobar was over, young people were left with that mindset of easy money, and they killed one another. There was a horrible attitude about war and death. Life didn't mean anything. Life was worth a pair of sneakers.
>
> Then came the militias, with their even more radical politics. First of all, anyone who smoked marijuana or used any kind of hallucinogenic drug was declared a military target and had to be assassinated, even though the widespread use of drugs, especially marijuana, was a reality in the *comunas* of Medellín. So imagine how many people fell into the hands of the militias. The militias also reached out to the kids who were part of the combos. They created [the combos] because the militia told them: "You join us, you arm yourselves to fight against us, or you leave the neighborhood." The youth armed themselves, and it can be said, almost objectively, that the first self-defense groups that existed in the *comunas* of Medellín to protect themselves from the militias were these combos. There are [invisible] frontiers because of that in Medellín. That was something that Don Adolfo Paz [that is, Don

Berna] always saw . . . that one could not walk around in peace, and just by being a resident of a neighborhood or moving to another [neighborhood], you were declared a military target. Here, every sector [was controlled by a different group]. Often, you couldn't even move from one sector to the other of a neighborhood. A person had to walk with detours, going around and avoiding a particular sector, in order to reach a given place.

That's why some sort of self-defense was needed. At a critical moment, Don Adolfo Paz worried a lot about the city. From the start, Alfonso Paz had a very clear political and social vision for the self-defense groups. When he summoned us, we went, and it was during a meeting with him that the real process of studying Medellín began, of rethinking and meditating about the city. If we had to take military action, [we also had to] put emphasis on the social, on policies that weren't militarily [oriented]. Of course, without disregarding the fact that we had to have the ability to take military action, because sadly, in the [real world], nothing is taken seriously without the use of force; but lots of emphasis was still placed on the social aspect.

We [the associates of Don Berna] have always said that the self-defense groups of Cacique Nutibara and Los Héroes de Granada didn't extinguish the militias and the guerrillas in Medellín, but the community did. We showed the community a different political agenda, and despite the fact that we were illegal factions, perhaps we showed them a different option. [We showed them that we were] providing more peace since we'd get rid of the invisible boundaries and remove guns from the neighborhoods. So lots of [political actions were taken] that animated and socialized the conflict.

We were illegal, but honestly, it was because of the inefficiency of the state, its inability to protect the maximum well-being of every citizen and its lack of presence in these communes, that the self-defense groups were established. Because we have to be really clear here: Paramilitaries don't exist in Colombia, because paramilitaries are armed groups at the edge of the law. They are like the government's and state's dark or secret forces. Neither the Cacique Nutibara nor the Héroes de Granada nor any other Colombian self-defense group has been managed, manipulated, or financed by the military or the state. They've simply had their own self-regulation, their own self-imposed [structures for] conformity, and their financing has been autonomous. Because of this, we can't talk about paramilitarism, which is a stigma placed on us by detractors of the process who come from the outside to misrepresent and legitimize the true [*verdaderas*] self-defenses.

So what were we to do? We convened the community leaders: "Come, we want to join you, we want to make you a proposition of peaceful coexistence." We also wanted the gangs to change their criminal conduct, for them to become closer to the communities. That was our work. We started sending written communiqués to those armed groups who were generating a lot of confusion, lots of extortion, and lots of deaths in the city of Medellín. We invited them to begin lowering the extortion, homicide rate, and hostility toward the community. The response was mostly positive. Of course, it was gradual because breaking the traditional cycle of violence was not an easy thing. We didn't intervene directly with the gangs; they simply started understanding and comprehending. In other words, they started self-regulating, and they themselves started communicating with us. We talked to them specifically regarding some norms of social behavior, and that was definitely a very important complement to the serious necessity of realizing the process. There were some who responded and accepted, but there were other organizations that didn't want to do it, as in the case of Frank's organization.

Ours was a discourse of peace, of peaceful coexistence, of the rehumanization [of the conflict]. From the start, Don Adolfo [Paz] told us that you have to look at the conflict from the social point of view, the human point of view. And when he said we had to begin lowering the intensity of the conflict, we immediately knew that was the solution—to start to listen to the people, start solving their problems and their issues. More or less, that was the first thing we did. That gave us an extraordinary result.

The language of war generates much terror and fear. We didn't spread a message of war. We talked a social language. We spoke a conceptual language—a language of dialogue. So [the community] started to understand, comprehend, and look at us from a completely different point of view. In a very short period of time, we really gained a lot of credit—lots of social credibility—precisely in the way we planted our ideas and our model of a true self-defense. When one speaks of the social and emphasizes it, this is when room for debate and agreement is created, when room for dialogue with the community to talk about new social and political propositions is created.

The narrative of this paramilitary leader draws on the justificatory discourse of a weak state and a disorder that needed to be regulated. This was an explanation that accounted for the need to establish the paramilitaries' presence in marginal areas of Medellín and that legitimized their violence and philanthropic initiatives. The paramilitaries, he said, filled the void left by an inefficient and absent state. When I asked Fabio Acevedo why, instead of creating an armed group, they did not promote a new political party—to transform reality using legal and democratic institutions—he spoke of the Colombian state as one that had not respected the social contract, that did not allow new forces to organize in a legal and legitimate way. In his words, one heard the echo of a disenfranchised group of people who, empowered by the unheard-of resources made available by drug trafficking and the violence of the paramilitary groups, presented itself, not unlike the *gabellotti* in Sicily, as a new and emerging class willing to redefine the social contract and found anew the homeland. This idea was expressed in a secret pact, known as the

Pacto de Ralito, signed in 2001 by AUC leaders and a group of local and national politicians. Acevedo explained further:

> The state has always been possessive of its social, political, and economic platform. That's to say, the state has its tool, and it's not going to permit anyone [to appropriate it]. . . . The problem was definitely the absence or the inefficiency of the state against the great threat of the guerrillas' army. This is because the self-defense [groups] were first created in response to the absence or inefficiency of the state, and second because of the continuous guerrilla-hostage situation. We worked in the social and political sector, supporting the state; [we did] what the state didn't do.
>
> In Medellín, the state was missing a commitment to a social contract. The state has a duty to protect the properties of a society that pays taxes. [If] the state doesn't do it the way it should, [if] the state doesn't act, be it in the city or in the rural areas, precisely there is a void that needs to be filled. And generally, when the state isn't there, the community finds an alternative resource. If all of us Colombians had the protection and insurance of the state, there definitely wouldn't have been war between the self-defense groups and the guerrillas. What happens is that the state has been too weak and inefficient with regard to its social duties. If there's no state, a state of necessity is created and the self-defense groups surge. If the state doesn't respond to me, then I need to defend my own, I need to defend my property, and I need to defend my life. So I look for an alternative security, and that alternative security is the self-defense groups.
>
> When the self-defense groups at the national level saw what we wanted [here in Medellín], they supported us militarily. There were some gangs here that were dedicated to the business of kidnapping. They were not only gangs, but also part of the conflict because they sold [their] kidnapping victims to the militias and guerrillas. They violated with *las vacunas* and all of that. The Cacique Nutibara wasn't born with a great military structure, but we did find support from different groups on that end. We had to confront Frank's gang, which supported itself particularly with Rodrigo or Doble Cero to continue its criminal activity and [to continue] growing and [using] extortion. We had to confront militias; that was very clear. We can't say that we were nuns dedicated to charity, because [that would make us] liars. We came in with military capabilities, but right away we didn't need them. We decreased the violence and started social work aimed at awareness for better living.
>
> We weren't legal, but we were legitimate in the sense that we were doing something for the well-being of the community, for the well-being of the people. That discourse was very important in the shift in mentality of the people who had other ideas of a Communist left. In our speeches, we always talked about supporting institutions, about the respect that there should be toward the state. Even if the state was weak and imperfect, it deserved respect.

We didn't defend the rich. The state defended the rich. [What we offered] was not simply protection but a social project with which we wanted to tell the state, "Go and fulfill your responsibilities, fulfill your duties." There was a big misunderstanding abroad regarding the self-defense groups, or what they called the paramilitaries.

The opportunistic, transitory, and flexible nature of the country's Mafia-like intertwinement is further illustrated by the infamous case of Comuna 13, a large subdivision of Medellín. In even less subtle ways than in previous ethnographic examples, the state acquired the paramilitary "war machine" to subdue this area of the city, which for several years had been an impregnable fortress of guerrilla militias. The army, the national police, and the Cacique Nutibara joined forces to cleanse and pacify this neighborhood, and their alliance represented an upgraded version of the one established at the time of Los Pepes. Ultimately, it consolidated the presence and the domination of the Cacique Nutibara in Medellín.

On October 16, 2002, at the order of President Uribe, thousands of uniformed soldiers, police, and members of other security forces arrived in several sectors of Comuna 13, riding in black SUVs and accompanied by hooded informants. It was the beginning of an unprecedented massive military intervention. Launching urban warfare against the FARC and the ELN, law enforcement used machine guns, rifles, and Blackhawk helicopters. While the media presented the operation as a success, human rights groups documented and denounced indiscriminate violence against the civilian population. According to the Center for Investigation and Popular Education (CINEP), a human rights organization led by Jesuits, one civilian was killed and thirty-eight were wounded, including several minors. Eight civilians were disappeared by members of the army and the paramilitary. Three hundred and fifty-five residents were detained, 185 arbitrarily. Others were threatened and their homes destroyed. There was massive forced displacement from the inner city. After two months of fighting, the so-called Orión Operation ended at the beginning of December. While the government declared full control of the neighborhood, a detective in the prosecutor's office admitted, "Declaring that there are no self-defense groups in Comuna 13 is like denying [the existence of] one's own mother." After the military returned to their barracks, the paramilitaries remained to police the neighborhood (Rozema 2008).

In the memo Doble Cero gave me, he wrote:

With all this information, Fabio Orión [an associate of Don Berna] made contact with his friends in the Metropolitan Police, making an extensive presentation on the situation to them, and [suggesting] how a coordinated operation might allow them to penetrate, dominate the situation, and evict the guerrillas. [He suggested] the Cacique Nutibara would take over control little by little, which is what ultimately happened. (Autodefensas Campesinas Bloque Metro 2003, 10)

Doble Cero's account is confirmed by Don Berna, who, on February 25, 2009, declared the following to a federal judge of the Southern District of New York in a written testimonial: "The forces of the Cacique Nutibara arrived in the Comuna 13 as part of an alliance with the army's Fourth Brigade, including generals Mario Montoya of the army and Leonardo Gallego of the police" (Verdad Abierta 2009).[17] In addition, Don Berna asserted that the domination of this sector of Medellín "by the police, the army, and the paramilitary had as its political aim eliminating the guerrillas and making an effort to help the community" (ibid.).

In recent years, prosecutors looking into the alliances and agreements between paramilitary groups and political leaders in Antioquia have shed some light on the system of protections and alliances that the Cacique Nutibara and other groups enjoyed, thus allowing them to spread and dominate across Medellín and Antioquia. In a scrupulous study of electoral behavior in the department of Antioquia, Claudia Nayibe López Hernández (2007) demonstrated not only that death squads linked to the paramilitaries and drug cartels were responsible for annihilating the leftist Unión Patriótica, but also that since the end of the 1990s, when the AUC was formed, the paramilitaries had influenced the outcomes of elections in favor of their own interests. López recorded atypical electoral behavior in municipalities across Antioquia with a strong military presence of the paramilitaries. In these areas, candidates who often had no history or presence in the district that elected them gained more than 70 percent of the vote. This is a tendency that was consolidated during the early years of the 2000s so that in Antioquia, as in other areas of the country, the expansion of the paramilitaries through massacres and forced massive displacement of people coincided with the consolidation of political power of parties, often newly formed, and political leaders in cahoots with the paramilitaries. During their voluntary rendition in courts, several paramilitary leaders declared that political leaders had actively sought their support, fearing that a successful peace process between the government of President Pastrana and the FARC might have harmed their interests (ibid., 227). To get a sense of the expansion achieved by the paramilitaries during those years, it is enough to consider that ten major paramilitary groups demobilized in Antioquia only after 2003, as I will illustrate in the next chapter. As López wrote:

> Without economic, political, and military support, the government's blindness and the large social and judicial impunity, the paramilitaries would have never achieved the magnitude they did. With nothing stopping them for years, the soul and the social, economic and political profile of Antioquia and the country changed. (Ibid., 232)

As I have tried to show throughout this chapter, the intertwinement of the paramilitaries with the state is a defining characteristic in Colombia. The spectacular violence carried out by paramilitary death squads, and their ties to drug trafficking, does not exhaust this criminal phenomenon. Neither does the AUC exhaust the entirety of the paramilitaries as a reality. It is equally important to focus on the generalized impunity that these armed groups have enjoyed, one guaranteed by a convergence of interests that have bound together criminal interests and the economic and political interests of emerging regional elites, owners of large estates, and even multinational corporations. The paramilitaries could have not prospered to the extent they did without this complicit convergence. I therefore suggest that paramilitaries in Colombia are a historical and social phenomenon analogous to that of the Sicilian Mafia.

Nethertheless, the convergence of interests among armed, political, and economic actors is not the only aspect of the intertwinement. With regard to the Mafia, the Italian sociologist Nando Dalla Chiesa (2010) suggested that one also reflect on a different kind of convergence that accounts for the links between the Mafia and the larger society. This form of convergence is not an agreement to undertake a crime, or a conscious understanding to satisfy shared interests, but instead a convergence that, given its political and intellectual qualities, cannot be brought in front of a jury. Yet it has an effect on the laws that are made and on behaviors and values that create a more favorable and sympathetic environment for the Mafia. This is a more subtle form of convergence, one that focuses on the predisposition of a society to tolerate or even to sympathize with the Mafia.

This form of convergence is present in Colombia, since it has allowed a silent majority to remain indifferent and oblivious as paramilitaries massacred and disappeared thousands of people and violently uprooted millions of peasants from their land. It is a convergence that left large sectors of Colombian society with eyes wide open to the violence and the horrors committed by the guerrillas yet looking the other way when confronted with the paramilitaries' bloodbath.

"Seguimos bailando al lado del muerto" (We keep dancing at the side of death), a former guerrilla leader once told me to emphasize the numbness and the sleep of reason into which Colombia has fallen. As I related in the introduction, it was the notion of the paramilitaries as a lesser and necessary evil that characterized the rationalization of a mining company owner from Urabá whom I met in the apartment of a U.S. Embassy official. If it weren't for the paramilitaries, he said, there would be no more banana fields or banana companies in Colombia.

"How do you explain the decline in homicides?" I once asked a taxi driver in Medellín.

"It was the work of the president," he responded, referring to then-President Álvaro Uribe.

"How did he do it?" I pressed the taxi driver further.

"The magic words are 'the paramilitaries,'" he told me with a large smile. When the militias occupied the peripheral neighborhoods of the city, he said, he would not venture there in his taxi. They were too dangerous and too frightening. "Now it is different," he emphasized, "because the paramilitaries brought security." He was grateful for their service.

Almost five million people went into the streets in July 2007 to protest the FARC's killings of eleven members of the department assembly of Valle del Cauca in Cali, whom the guerrillas had kidnapped almost a decade earlier. There has been no major and massive national outpouring of indignation to protest the massacres and the disappearances perpetuated by the paramilitaries across the country over three decades. While national political leaders, including presidents, have always been very vocal in denouncing the guerrillas and in portraying them as evil, this has not been the case for the paramilitaries. These are all examples of what Dalla Chiesa defined as "innocent complicities," since they cannot be brought in front of a jury: "The attitudes, cultural trends, collective feelings, the mental dispositions that nourish the daily life of the country and that entangle it in a network of conditionings, obstructing its parts toward legality and, in a particular way, the fight against organized crime" (2010, 256).

The intertwinement between paramilitaries and entities representing the state, or the convergence of interests between paramilitaries and individuals or groups that are external to its organization, designate the paramilitaries as a Mafia phenomenon. But there is also the "innocent convergence" that in Colombia rests on a discourse that presents the state as inefficient, weak, and incapable of confronting the security threat embodied by the guerrillas and their intertwinement with social movements, human rights organizations, teachers' unions, and other groups.

It is with this understanding of the paramilitaries as the product of complex and large convergences that one needs to interpret the disarmament, demobilization, and reintegration process of AUC combatants between 2003 and 2006 in Colombia. What did this demobilization represent? Was it a caesura of convergences, the breaking of the ties linking paramilitaries to the state? Or did it represent a further attempt to legitimize their domination? What was masked in this unmasking of the paramilitaries?

SIX

Demobilization and the Unmasking of the State

In Miami, in April 2006, I was waiting for a connecting flight to Medellín when a black-and-white photo in the international section of the *Diario Las Américas* caught my attention. The photo portrayed a large group of people, for the most part men, wearing white T-shirts and holding up signs. The image brought to my mind similar images of marches and protests from other corners of the world where victims occupied and reclaimed the public sphere, as in the case of Argentina's mothers demanding truth and justice for the disappearance of thousands of their sons and daughters; or images from Eastern Europe when masses had assembled following the fall of the Berlin Wall; or, in recent times, angry multitudes rising in the Arab world, Latin America, and Europe. The people who caught my attention in the newspaper's photo were marching in protest through the streets of Medellín. The article explained that the demonstrators' signs, written in both Spanish and English, called for the international community to monitor the disarmament and demobilization process of the paramilitaries. One young man held a sign expressing solidarity with the victims of the Madrid bombing of March 11, 2004.

But what was wrong with this picture? Those marching were not victims of abuse or violence, but victimizers: they were members of Medellín-based paramilitary death squads that had demobilized just a few months earlier. Five thousand of them and their families, friends, and supporters marched that day, making demands and occupying the public sphere. They were borrowing and redefining the modes of counterdiscourse and resistance that are conventionally employed by victims and the oppressed. Marching through city streets, holding signs, and chanting slogans are all marks of protest, and often acts of resistance, of disobedience, of transgression. In his interpretation of the Argentinian mothers assembling in the Plaza de Mayo in Buenos

Aires, Taussig wrote that their protest relocated memory in the contested public sphere and that by "courageously naming the names and holding the photographic image of the dead and disappeared, the mothers create the specific image necessary to reverse public and State memory" (1992, 28).

Juxtaposing, as in a collage, the black-and-white photo of marching demobilized paramilitaries with Taussig's notion of protest and disobedience, one perceives the chilling and strident contrast between the two, which in turn sparks questions about the meaning and practice of paramilitaries occupying the public sphere. What, then, did the demobilization and the reintegration of paramilitaries across Colombia mean? What did they undo; what did they unmask? What did they cover, and what did they perpetuate?

In mid-2000, the leader and founder of the AUC, Carlos Castaño, in a few interviews broadcast nationally and overall well received by the general public, exposed the paramilitaries' political ambitions. At the time, Colombia was experiencing deep frustration with the inconclusive peace negotiations between the government of President Andrés Pastrana and the FARC guerrillas. During my first visit to Medellín, in April 2001, several people expressed their disillusionment and even suggested a United States–led military intervention. Presidential candidate Álvaro Uribe Vélez leveraged the deep collective disappointment and frustration, and in May 2002, he won the elections by a landslide on his vow to defeat the leftist rebels militarily and to establish order.

As Rafael Pardo (2007) has observed, Carlos Castaño's interviews represented the paramilitaries' reaction and response to a report presented by the Pastrana administration on paramilitary groups' presence and increasing influence throughout the country. The report was written granting demands that the FARC had advanced during the peace negotiations. In fact, the guerrillas had accused the government of turning a blind eye to the formation of paramilitary groups, which, at the outset of the peace talks with the guerrillas, had organized within the AUC (see chapter 1). In addition, mimicking modes of social protest, the AUC had mobilized a large number of peasants to protest against the peace talks between the government and the FARC. Paramilitaries had kidnapped several members of congress and demanded political recognition to acquire the same status the guerrillas enjoyed at the time. While refusing to recognize the paramilitaries as political actors, President Pastrana authorized the Catholic Church to open back channels with the AUC leadership. After Uribe's election in October 2002, the AUC communicated to the envoys of the Catholic Church its intention to declare a unilateral ceasefire to create favorable conditions for direct negotiations with the government. This ceasefire eventually started on December 1, 2002, during the first months of Uribe's administration. Only the paramilitary group of Commandant Doble Cero refused to participate in the negotiations, protesting the presence at the table of major drug kingpins who were also paramilitary leaders, such as Don Berna.

One of Uribe's first presidential acts was to ask congress to change the Public Order Law as it was enforced at the time. Laws enacted since 1993 had given the government authorization to enter negotiations with guerrilla groups, thus recognizing the political status of the insurgents. The law that President Uribe had congress pass in 2002 authorized government officials to negotiate with all armed groups, including paramilitaries. The law equalized the guerrillas and the paramilitaries, erasing the difference between insurgent groups, who aimed to subvert the state order and paramilitaries, who often represented an articulation and an ally of the state. One of the drafters of the law was Rafael Pardo, defense minister during the search for Pablo Escobar and the persecution of the Medellín cartel and a longtime senator of the Liberal party. In a speech to the senate, he defended the need to equalize the guerrillas and the paramilitaries: "The Colombian conflict has two autonomous elements that act against or at the margin of the State: the guerrillas and the paramilitaries. . . . Both combine politics and weapons, and in this sense they are political-military projects" (2007, 47).

An ad hoc commission was established, which engaged in preliminary talks with AUC representatives in regions across Colombia and eventually drafted a memorandum advising Uribe's government to move forward with direct negotiations. The commission's final report suggested, among other measures, the demobilization and reintegration of AUC combatants, the cessation of all illegal activities including drug trafficking and kidnapping, and the crafting of a legal solution allowing the negotiations to move forward. While the commission was engaged in pre-talks during the last months of 2002, the leaders of the AUC actively lobbied the Colombian Congress to pass laws that were favorable to them:

> In parallel with the first meetings [with the government], [paramilitary leader] Mancuso pulled the strings of high politics. In an exclusive club in northern Bogotá, the military chief of the self-defense met with his friends in congress. In broad daylight, as if it were an ordinary business lunch and not a

meeting with one of the most wanted people by justice, Mancuso started to explain why Castaño—and himself—had decided not to surrender to American justice. Afterward, he asked the lawmakers for their support to find a legal structure to forgive their criminal acts without having to recognize their political status. (Ibid., 56)

The meeting took place in the same exclusive club that only a few months later would be bombed, allegedly by the FARC. On July 15, 2003, the government and the AUC signed the Pacto de Ralito, which ratified the unilateral ceasefire of the AUC and established the disarmament and demobilization of the AUC paramilitary groups. The same summer, Carlos Castaño granted a televised interview from his compound, immersed in tropical vegetation and surrounded by young and heavily armed paramilitary members. In a dry tone, as if dispatching orders, Castaño affirmed: "The end of the Autodefensas is a reality. We are taking gradual steps toward the demobilization, which will end at the very latest on December 31, 2005, but I think it will be complete even before."[1] A month later, in August 2003, the government presented a bill in congress on alternative punishments to facilitate the demobilization and reintegration of former combatants. One of the most controversial benefits the bill foresaw was no prison time for the perpetrators of gross human rights violations, which sparked strong debate and uproar. Eventually, giving in to the critics and the pressures expressed domestically as well as internationally, the government drafted the Law for Truth, Justice, and Reconciliation. The alternative punishment foresaw a prison sentence between five and ten years for crimes committed by AUC leaders and members. Eventually, in 2005, the Colombian Congress approved the Justice and Peace Law. "The approved penal procedure favors those who submitted [to law], in this case the paramilitaries, and leaves the State in a condition of total inferiority," wrote Rafael Pardo (ibid., 104). The *New York Times* defined the law as a law of impunity and wrote that Colombia had capitulated (ibid., 105).

On July 29, 2004, three senior AUC leaders traveled to Bogotá to address congress: Salvatore Mancuso, Ernesto Báez, and Ramón Isaza.[2] Wearing new suits and ties, they spoke for about an hour and a half to 60 members (out of 268) of congress, highlighting the historical weakness of the state in its peripheries and the heroism of the self-defense groups. "This was something immense . . . an immense triumph," Don Berna declared from his prison in Miami to Colombian judges (quoted in *El Espectador*, 2013).

By the end of 2003, the paramilitaries of the Cacique Nutibara, the Oficina de Envigado's de facto army, had established their domination over

Medellín. Not only did they establish their military presence in all the populous neighborhoods of the city, but they also held the monopoly on illegal markets, from drug trafficking to revenues from games of chance. When Medellín was chosen as the first city to experiment with large-scale disarmament, demobilization, and reintegration of paramilitary combatants, the Cacique Nutibara had already either eliminated or subjugated all rival armed groups. Broadcast live on national TV on November 25, 2003, 860 members of the Cacique Nutibara handed over their weapons and demobilized. The former combatants were concentrated in the town of La Ceja, not far from Medellín, and they received an intense three-week reintegration course. They were granted social, psychological, and legal assistance. Some underwent community leadership and security training. At the same time, judicial authorities checked their criminal records.

As highlighted by Amnesty International (2005) before the demobilization, the Cacique Nutibara had an estimated two thousand combatants, and fewer than half had disarmed and demobilized. In fact, the remaining contingent of the Cacique Nutibara established the Héroes of Granada paramilitary bloc, which operated mainly in Eastern Antioquia and Medellín. This group was also owned and led by Don Berna or Adolfo Paz, and its main commander was known as Danielito, a longtime confidante and partner of Don Berna in the Oficina de Envigado. As asserted by several of the former combatants I interviewed, the new paramilitary group joined the AUC's war against the Bloque Metro of Commandant Doble Cero. As reported by Amnesty International (ibid.), despite the demobilization of Medellín's major paramilitary group, selective killing by paramilitaries continued in the capital of Antioquia.

Luna, the paramilitary who had shared his life history with me, also told me about the time when the Cacique Nutibara demobilized. In the months leading up to the AUC's disarmament and demobilization, Luna had been the field commander of the group in a northwestern neighborhood of Medellín:

> After the Cacique [Nutibara] demobilized, we started working as Héroes of Granada.... We continued with the same ideology. The only thing we changed was the name. We threw away the armband we had. The majority of us surrendered with the armbands, and those who remained became the Héroes of Granada.
>
> This happened when the Cacique died, when the Cacique Nutibara demobilized. We continued working in the same area. We didn't change the area;

we just continued operating in the same area, just with different names. We didn't even change personnel. We had twenty people [in our group] who demobilized. Those who wanted to go back home demobilized. Those who wanted to continue stayed on with the [Héroes of Granada] group....

The majority of the demobilization was all just a big lie. As I see things, the demobilization was not a serious thing. At least, what we did with the Cacique Nutibara, this was a big scam. The demobilization of the group was a big lie because we trained people and I cleaned most of the weapons that were handed over. They were old weapons that were not useful at all—the worst the bloc possessed. We recruited people on the street, and we recruited them to demobilize them as Cacique Nutibara—to surrender. We gave them a special training during a period of a month, teaching them the prayers and the hymn of the self-defense groups.... So now, when I hear that a paramilitary group is demobilizing, I doubt it.... They didn't ask us anything. Our own boss told us, "As of today, you are the Héroes of Granada."... The demobilization was a farce. That's what I believe, because I was there.

Most of my fieldwork in Medellín was conducted at the time of the paramilitaries' disarmament and demobilization. Medellín had been chosen to experiment with the process, and Mayor Luís Perez had signed an agreement with the national government. But it was the administration of the reformist Sergio Fajardo that had to implement that agreement after he took office on January 1, 2004. Fajardo, as he told me in numerous conversations, was skeptical about the process but had decided to respect the agreement signed by his predecessor just a short time before the mayoral election. The demobilization of the Cacique Nutibara, then, was the context in which I collected most of the interviews and long narratives from paramilitaries presented in this book. I visited the peripheral neighborhoods of the city, where violence had been most intense, and I observed the local government's work in leading the challenging and unprecedented process.

Often the overly optimistic picture presented by the local government, which was aimed at attracting international donors and building civic support for the disarmament and demobilization process, contrasted with conversations I had and direct observations I made while walking around Medellín. The optimistic language of the government did not match the skepticism and cynicism that I often heard among residents of the barrios where the paramilitaries had been operating. "This is a time bomb" or "They are just reorganizing" or "This is a farce" were comments I often heard.

What I heard from residents also matched what I observed: small groups of paramilitaries that in several areas of the city had not demobilized continued to conduct business as usual; paramilitaries who were no longer carrying guns concealed under their shorts were still enforcing order; others "demobilized" during the day and rearmed at night; and some paramilitaries were displaced to other areas of Colombia, into the centers of cocaine production and trade. Yet I also met several *paras* who took advantage of the process, turning it into an opportunity to restart their own lives, and those of their families. In other words, a complex, contradictory, and sometimes confusing picture emerged from my own fieldwork.

What follows are ethnographic vignettes lifted from the demobilization and reintegration process as I experienced and observed it in Colombia. These are fragments from a fractured reality and, patched together, they interrupt the often overly positive state narrative that presents the demobilization and reintegration process of the AUC combatants as largely a great success and a model for the international community to imitate.

In March 2004, only a few months after the Disarmament, Demobilization, and Reintegration (DDR) process, as it was officially known, had begun, I flew to Medellín. At the time, the DDR office was on the third floor of City Hall. The morning I arrived, five demobilized paramilitaries were sitting in the hallway before the office. They all wore fancy jeans, colorful shirts, and trendy sneakers. They all had cop mustaches. In small backpacks, they held radios. Two handsome young female program officers shuttled between the hallway and the office with lists in their hands and asked questions of the demobilized combatants. Hiring beautiful women to be at the front desk, I learned later, was a strategy intended to lure former paramilitaries to the program's office.

In a small office, I met with a young government official, the representative of the High Commissioner for Peace. Sitting behind his desk, wearing a red shirt and black jeans, he held two cell phones in front of him, which at times interrupted our hour-long conversation. Speaking in the dry language of a bureaucrat, he chose his words carefully, preoccupied with the task of making the national government look good and efficient. I asked him questions about the demobilization process in Medellín. The official's reply was neat and ordered. In his sanitized language, everything was logical, organized, and clean, with no contradictions, no ambiguity, no uncertainties, and no doubts—everything was under control and in strong, secure hands.

At first, the official summarized the steps of the demobilization process: he emphasized that it was "supported by civil society, the church, and the

High Commissioner for Peace." In the narrative of the official, the paramilitaries were not bloodthirsty murderers or the dangerous perpetrators of gross human rights violations. He did not mention the cruel deeds that they had carried out in Medellín or their relationship with narcotrafficking and other profitable illicit activities. Rather, the official chose to emphasize what he had discovered during the initial phase of the demobilization process: the sort of social work that the Cacique Nutibara group had been carrying out in the marginal barrios of the city. He described them as social workers and benefactors of Medellín more than as assassins. The paramilitaries were people who brought order and even provided forms of justice, he said. The image of the paramilitaries as masters of terror was washed away and substituted with the production of a "truth" that portrayed them as benevolent. This representative of the national government drew a picture as confusing as the black-and-white photo that had caught my attention in the Miami newspaper.

In the account provided by this official, the Cacique Nutibara was a paramilitary group of a particular kind. It was an urban organization and not a rural one, which led them to engage in social work that conferred a "certain degree of credibility in their interlocutors." "We trust them," he said at one point.

As I was listening to these words, I tried to keep a poker face, but the official must have guessed my uneasiness with such a benevolent description of people who had systematically killed and tortured and whose deeds were presented now to me as social work. Thus he told me of one Cacique Nutibara leader who "did political work in the barrios of Medellín" and who "has enjoyed huge support among the population."

"What do you mean by 'social work'?" I asked.

"In the different neighborhoods of Medellín, they developed economic, educational, and artistic projects. They committed themselves to providing effective solutions for the population, also administering justice. This is why they have a strong support among the population. They do valuable social work," he added. I was stunned by this benevolent description of the paramilitaries, which reflected the convergence of interests that mark the articulation of the state with the paramilitaries.

The official provided other details of the process. Between July and November 2003, forty meetings were called for the demobilization of the Cacique Nutibara. The disarmament and reinsertion of the ex-combatants had happened over a period of three weeks, when the AUC combatants were concentrated in a center in La Ceja, a town in Eastern Antioquia, not far from Medellín. Identity documents were provided to the demobilizing para-militaries so that they could look for jobs and apply to schools. A group of prosecutors determined possible penal responsibilities. Social-psychological tests were administered to the ex-combatants to identify their educational, working, and leadership skills. On December 16, 2004, the former paramilitaries were allowed to return to the neighborhoods they came from, to their homes and families. In the truth produced by the state official, Medellín was now a secure city.

At the office of the Peace and Reconciliation Program at City Hall, I also ran into the coordinator of a team of psychologists whose responsibility it was to facilitate weekly workshops and one-on-one sessions to rehabilitate former combatants. On a computer screen, he showed me figures and per-centages describing the demobilization process. Since the beginning of the process, data had been collected on the identity, needs, education, skills, and expectations of the more than eight hundred people who demobilized. Those data were then summarized and analyzed, producing a variety of colorful graphs.

The chief psychologist also showed me the structure set up to support the paramilitaries' reintegration into society. The state intervention was aimed at the individual, his family, and the community where the paramilitaries once operated and where they continued to live, now disarmed and demobilized. In every neighborhood where paramilitaries have been present was a team coordinated by a professional psychologist and a demobilized paramilitary (called a field supervisor). There were a total of forty supervisors, who in most cases were themselves former paramilitary field commanders, and each one coordinated a group of twenty demobilized paramilitaries. The psychologist also told me that there is a fluctuation of people from barrio to barrio, and thus the groups around the supervisors needed to be trained again and again.

During our conversation, the psychologist used the verb *to support* many times when describing the methodology of the demobilization and reintegra-tion program: the designed intervention was intended to support the reinte-gration into society of the former combatants and to support their new life projects. At one point, though, his tongue slipped, and he used the verb *to control*. He corrected himself immediately, but he revealed to me in a wink what all the efforts of the program were intended to do: to monitor and control.

The language that government officials employed was one of order. Expressions were generally positive, and words were sanitized, as if a *limpieza* of the language accompanied the paramilitaries' social cleansing. The reality was confined within clear-cut boundaries. There was little or no complexity in the descriptions. Simplification was preferred over complexity. The paramilitaries were not labeled as combatants, assassins, killers, or perpetrators, but simply as *muchachos,* or "guys." They were described as individuals whose needs were now to be met. The *muchachos* were analyzed, studied, and described; only the fact that the government could do so with statistics and graphs afforded a sense of control, of being in command. Order came together with a new set of words and labels. It came with graphs and figures. When a reality can be translated into charts and graphs, one is then in control.[3]

A few days later, the chief psychologist invited me to visit a barrio in the northwestern hills of Medellín. An additional psychologist and a social worker who were going to facilitate a workshop for demobilized paramilitaries took the ride with us.

This particular barrio was one of the city's strategic gates. The paramilitary had built a security belt around the northern periphery of the city, occupying and dominating the neighborhoods that form an arc linking the eastern and western sides of Medellín. By controlling access to the city, the paramilitaries wanted to prevent the infiltration of guerrilla groups and to control the cocaine corridor that reaches from Medellín to the northern coast of Colombia (see chapter 4).

As we drove up the hills, the psychologist hinted at some of the challenges of the demobilization process. Paramilitaries had subjugated the gangs, who now were operating under the command of the paramilitaries. Because they were classified as gangs, their members were not allowed to join the disarmament and demobilization process. Over time, members of the paramilitaries and gangs intertwined, and their members shared comradeship. Currently they continue to hang out together, and despite the demobilization process, some still join friends in the gangs to commit crimes. Because of that, people in these communities, the psychologist admitted, still feel that the paramilitaries continue to dominate.

To my question concerning who had filled the power vacuum left by the paramilitaries, the psychologist responded that the state did. But this might have been more his vision and hope than the reality. As Gustavo Villegas, the director of the Peace and Reconciliation Program, told me repeatedly, the initial effort of the local government was to gain respect and trust from former paramilitary leaders. Only then, the theory went, would it be possible for the state to gain space and authority within territory once dominated by paramilitaries. The state and the paramilitaries were now competing for control and domination of the same spaces. The competition itself was a novelty and a sign that a process had started, he said. It was as if the state now wanted to dispose of this particular ally that it had tolerated and even nourished in previous years.

This was the explanation provided to me in 2004, at the outset of the demobilization and reintegration process. Time would show that the criminal world in which the paramilitaries were rooted still rules in Medellín.

The van climbed the hill to the neighborhood in northeastern Medellín. Many houses looked unfinished, but this was not one of the poorest barrios of the city, the psychologist explained to me. We drove through small alleys where kids were playing until we reached a humble one-store building hosting an elementary school. A group of fourteen boys and girls was waiting for the team of the city administration to conduct an educational workshop. "¡Llegó la alcaldía!" (The city administration has arrived!), one of the boys screamed, as if someone foreign, an outsider, had arrived as a guest in an unrelated territory. His expression in itself mirrored the thin and fragile presence of the local government in these marginal areas of Medellín.

The schoolroom was large and poor. A portrait of Jesus hung on the wall. The benches were small and old, and blue and red backpacks hung on the chairs. One city official explained to the children that though she was a psychologist, she was not there to treat crazy people.

The sudden noise of a motorbike reached us through the window, and after a few seconds a young man walked in with a secure stride and greeted the chief psychologist. It was Pablo, a former member of the Cacique Nutibara bloc, now acting as a field supervisor of the reintegration program. He was wearing jeans, a blue T-shirt, and sunglasses and had a cop mustache and very short hair. He greeted us and sat down, curious about my presence. Right away, he spoke highly of the social work the demobilized paramilitary were doing in the barrio, organizing events for children and the elderly. Pablo had the attitude of a leader and spoke like someone used to being in command. "In the past two years, we carried out social work," he explained, "because we wanted the community to be attached to us." He used the verb *pegar*, which translates as "to stick," "to glue," or "to attach." His choice of words suggested that the paramilitary promoted social activities as part of their strategy to gain the sympathy and loyalty of the barrios' residents.

As Rodrigo Doble Cero had already taught me, the paramilitaries had used terror as their primary means to impose subjugation. But in this second stage, employing a strategy they borrowed from guerrilla militias, they attached themselves to the community by promoting soft power through social and political work. Showing magnanimity was part of their policing.

In interacting with demobilized paramilitaries, the chief psychologist tried to be at ease with them. His attitude was that of a companion, a partner, or a friend. Talking to Pablo, he praised the work of the demobilized combatants and their presence in the neighborhood. This was a way to encourage in them what he described as positive leadership carried out within a legal framework and no longer as an expression of criminal activity.

And yet what one could observe and perceive was that the one in charge in that barrio was not the state, but the (demobilized) paramilitaries. While negotiations between the state and the paramilitaries contributed to the reduction of violence and the unveiling of paramilitaries' domination in the city's neighborhoods, the *paras'* domination continued. In Medellín, they existed in an interface between the state and the underworld, the legal and the illegal. They continued to be part of the state's function of capture, the hinge linking the exterior with the interior, the uncivilized with the civilized.

During our conversation, Pablo offered to arrange a meeting with other demobilized paramilitaries. He got on his motorbike, and we followed him in the official city government van. We stopped before another school building, and two demobilized paramilitaries joined us. The guy who did most of the talking was short and fat and wore a rosary around his neck. Between his index finger and the thumb of his right hand, he had a tattoo of a small swastika. He sniffed continuously and often brought his fingers to his nostrils. "Today we closed the street to traffic," he explained, "so that children can bike freely."

A few months later, I returned to the same neighborhood, this time to meet with Jorge Andrés, the first demobilized paramilitary to share his life history with me (see chapter 2). He had moved to this barrio with his young wife and their newborn baby. They were living in a small wooden shack. Jorge Andrés was diligently going to the workshops and meetings organized by the city's Peace and Reconciliation Program. We took a walk, and he brought me to a green clearing overlooking the city and the neighborhood.

"This is our zone of tolerance," Jorge Andrés told me. "Here's where junkies can come and smoke."

"What happens if someone uses drugs outside this area?" I asked him.

"Then we punish them," he declared.

"I thought you disarmed," I said.

"To have a gun is not the only way to do harm when needed," he replied, and he told me about a man who had stolen a television set from a house. The owner, a woman, came to the demobilized paramilitaries for aid. Far more efficient than the police, they investigated the facts, identified the thief, and harshly beat him, intimidating him to abandon the neighborhood. The demobilized paramilitaries in that neighborhood continued to be the agency of policing.

As we continued to walk, a curious kid came toward us, fascinated by the camera I had in my hands, and asked questions about who I was. Jorge Andrés changed his expression, staring at the kid with a vicious and menacing gaze I had never before see in him. The kid froze, stopped asking questions, and walked away. A year later (as I noted earlier), I learned that Jorge Andrés's wife had left him and moved to a different town due to his domestic violence.

May 2006: With Juan Pablo, a psychologist of the Peace and Reconciliation Program, I went to observe a workshop for demobilized paramilitaries. Orlando, a demobilized paramilitary and the field supervisor of the sector, was waiting for us at a small café. Heavy-set, he wore fake Gucci glasses and an orange shirt. He spoke very little. From his accent, I presumed he was from the northern coast of Colombia.

Little by little, other demobilized paramilitaries joined us, and we entered a humble room used for community meetings. By the time the meeting started, they numbered about ten, and judging from their age (around twenty-five), they must have been senior members in the organization.

Opening the meeting, Juan Pablo explained that in a few days there would be a soccer tournament among the groups of demobilized paramilitaries. He spoke with enthusiasm and tried to animate the *muchachos,* but he met with little response. Juan Pablo said that for those who had demobilized first, the eighteen months of the program were almost over, but that for those who showed commitment and attendance, they still had the opportunity to prolong their participation in the program and therefore to receive benefits such as the monthly subsidy of about US$300 for an additional six months. Juan

Pablo invited everyone to participate actively, to stick to the program, and to encourage everyone else to do likewise so that they could enjoy the benefits for another six months.

He then explained that the theme for the day's workshop: "conflict resolution." He asked, "What does conflict resolution mean?" and called on some of the participants. They were not very responsive.

Eventually Orlando came to the aid of Juan Pablo and provided an answer to the question: conflict resolution, he said, saying what Juan Pablo wanted to hear, meant using words and conversation instead of violence to solve problems.

Next was a practice exercise. The demobilized paramilitaries were separated into pairs, and they tied each other's wrists with cords. They had to find a way to free each other without cutting the cords or cheating in any way. Yet almost everyone cheated. A discussion followed, revealing the anxiety and tensions that demobilized paramilitaries were experiencing at that time.

Orlando was the first to talk. He complained that many things were not working out in the program. He had had problems with some documents and concluded by saying that if he had been Don Berna, the famous narcotrafficker and leader of the Cacique Nutibara, he would have "given up" his people only once all the state's guarantees were met. Someone else complained about the money, saying that some got paid more than others. But then the real reason for the simmering tension emerged. Orlando and another companion expressed fear that a recent decision by the Constitutional Court about the law regulating demobilization could affect them by revoking the benefits that had been promised. Another former paramilitary asked Juan Pablo what would happen if presidential candidate Carlos Gaviria (from the leftist Polo Democrático coalition, referred to during the meeting as a "guerrilla guy") won elections this upcoming Sunday. A third man claimed that even the communitarian police would not vote for Uribe, because they believed that demobilized paramilitaries enjoyed more guarantees then the police did. Another man, who mentioned that he had been part of the Bloque Minero[4] operating in Bajo Cauca and had been indicted for attempted extortion, complained that now, when something bad happened in the community, the residents did not call the paramilitaries anymore but instead called the police directly, who responded. "We are nobody no more," he said with resentment and frustration.

The conversation was again picked up by Orlando's companion. He spoke in a very sarcastic and aggressive manner, dismissing the process and its credibility. "We are ready to go back to the previous mode of living," he said.

Juan Pablo remained apparently calm, though his right foot trembled nervously. He tried to help the guys to remain focused. He invited them to read the newspapers more carefully. He assured them that in meetings with Don Effe and Don Daniel, the leaders of the demobilized paramilitaries, the decision had been made to continue the program. All in the room had doubtful looks. Finally, the *muchachos* signed the attendance form, and one after another left the room.

I rode back to the city on a Vespa with Juan Pablo. He told me that in the office, they had foreseen anxiety among the demobilized members of the paramilitary. Other colleagues had collected similar comments and said that overall attendance had gone down this week. He judged it as positive that they openly voiced criticism of Don Berna. He saw it as a step forward because it might signal that the drug lord's leadership was beginning to be questioned. Yet Juan Pablo excused himself to me because only a few *paras* had shown up. I sensed the fragility of the process.

Behind the hillside of the Comuna 13, in a squatter district in the western part of Medellín, like other marginal areas largely populated with internally displaced people, there was a group of paramilitary who had not demobilized. They continued to control the area, a strategic corridor for drugs and arms trafficking from the northern region of Urabá to the city, patrolling the neighborhood on motorbikes or on foot. I visited the neighborhood several times in 2005 and 2006, when both the Cacique Nutibara and the Héroes of Granada had already demobilized, to meet with Carlos, a former soldier and a paramilitary commander, before he demobilized and moves to this squatter district to live with his nineteen-year-old wife and two small children. Every time I visited, his wife would prepare and serve rice and fried meat to her husband and me while we sat talking at the table under a big framed photo of a slender Carlos, still in his teen years, wearing the uniform of the Colombian army and embracing a semiautomatic rifle.

As part of his reintegration process, Carlos had taken some training in tailoring, hoping one day to set up a clothing shop. In the meantime, the paramilitary of his shantytown, trusting him as one of their own, put him in charge of the neighborhood's club, where young people, especially on weekends, could get together, get drunk, and dance. The club was a rundown, small, naked room, with a few plastic tables and chairs, some red-and-green light bulbs, and a couple of speakers blasting the beats of salsa and *vallenato*.

When I went to visit Carlos one Saturday afternoon, I heard music booming from the club from far away. I soon learned that the local paramilitaries had asked Carlos to open the club just for them on that particular day. They had been there since dawn, dancing and drinking. When I arrived in the company of a couple of friends, Carlos introduced me to everyone in the room, including Jairo, the paramilitary field commander. One paramilitary, intoxicated and shirtless, took out his cell phone and showed me pictures of his small daughters. "I take good care of them," he said, looking at me with watering eyes. The table in front of him was occupied with empty bottles of beer and rum, while another man, the field commander of a neighboring area, was dancing *vallenato* with Jairo's woman.

One of my friends imprudently asked the drunken paramilitary a question about area paramilitaries, and the room filled with tension. The other paramilitaries reacted by thinking that we were members of military intelligence. "I know who you are," the drunk man said in an increasingly menacing tone. "And you are their boss," he said, pointing an accusatory index finger at me. Jairo came over and tried to calm things down. Carlos intervened as well, and said to Jairo that he doesn't like it when his *muchachos* terrorize his guests.

"I recognize you. I saw you already," insisted the drunken, paranoid paramilitary. My friend who had asked the question turned pale, and I grew anxious.

At some point, Carlos decided to close down the club and send everyone home before the situation got out of control. "The barrio has been tense these days," Carlos said once we got to his small apartment, just around the corner from the club. "The *muchachos* have felt under pressure," he continued, without giving specifics. He took me to his small bedroom and showed me that he had hidden a Smith & Wesson under a pile of clothes. "In case I need to defend myself and my family," he commented.

This all happened in Medellín, at a time when the local administration and the national media were presenting the city as a successful model of the paramilitaries' demobilization and reintegration process.

My appointment with Milton, the spokesperson of Los Triana gang in Medellín, was at a bakery in front of the subway station Acevedo, the entry point to the Popular One and Two barrios.[5] He wore shiny new Nike sneakers, jeans, and an olive-green shirt with a white abstract graphic design. He came accompanied by a taxi driver, who would be our driver for the afternoon.

Drinking tropical juice, we had a brief initial chat. Milton was euphoric and saw our meeting as an opportunity to tell the world that the members of the Triana gang are not bad people or criminals. Yes, of course, they had to do bad things here and there, he admitted, but it was for a good reason and a legitimate goal: to achieve peace.

Milton had grown up with his family in this barrio. In this area of Medellín, the northeastern side, the conflict had been intense, violent, and unbearable. Gangs and militias had been harassing the community. There was violence—a lot of violence. Terror reigned, and everyone lived in fear. Self-defense was necessary, Milton told me, reinforcing a refrain I had heard many times.

Young people had organized, led by the three Triana brothers, who had decided not to stay on the sidelines and passively watch what was happening to their barrio. During robberies, gang members had killed the Trianas' mother and other relatives. Thus they organized revenge, taking justice into their own hands and imposing order in their barrio. Though lacking training or preparation, the kids took up arms. They learned how to shoot and how to occupy a barrio. "We wanted peace, not power" was Milton's motto.

We toured the barrio. There were homes abandoned in debris and destroyed by grenades. Bullet holes marked the still-standing walls, reminders of an intense urban war in which houses had been turned into trenches. There had been insane shooting from house to house, from street corner to street corner, and the shots would echo throughout the barrio, forcing residents to lock themselves in their apartments, frozen in terror. During my tour with Milton, a resident pointed to a phone booth at the top of a hill from which snipers had fired bullets into the houses. Many residents of this barrio were given a few hours, or even just a few moments, to collect their modest belongings and flee their houses and their neighborhoods, looking for refuge in another part of the city. Gangs would then occupy their homes and turn them into trenches or bases for drug dealers.

David, a young law student who had once lived here, was displaced from the barrio with his family. The fighting had become too intense, and his parents felt insecure. When he was a child, his dream was to work as a crime scene investigator because he was fascinated by the action around a murder scene. One afternoon, David's family decided to leave the barrio for another section of the city where they felt more secure. He told me:

You could hear grenades day and night. One day in November 2001, the fighting was particularly intense, and my family decided to abandon the barrio. When we moved, someone followed us on a motorbike. At one point, they stopped and interrogated us. Initially they accused us of being collaborators of the [guerrilla] militias, and they had their guns pointed at my father and myself. They were determined to kill us. Then they called a witness, someone who knew us and who affirmed we were good people. Thus they let us go.

I asked David why he thought the paramilitary and gangs such as the Triana, which had been working in partnership with the paramilitary groups, had succeeded in their strategy to become attached to the communities while the guerrillas had not. David listed two main reasons:

> The *paras* got involved in the private life of the families. They regulated the private relationships between wives and husbands, for example. They did so according to their rules, at the barrel of the gun.
>
> Second, young people started seeing their peers going around the barrio with great motorbikes, in luxury cars, picking up the most beautiful women of the barrio. This ostentatious luxury didn't apply to the militias. In this way, the *paras* conquered the minds of the community, or at least many of them. There were many places where one could buy drugs. In addition, the Triana demanded a sort of weekly tax, the *vacuna,* of every shop, bus, or taxi owner and for every apartment. This is how they financed themselves, and how they still do. My family pays a thousand pesos every week, the shops five thousand, and the buses between ten and fifteen thousand.

Milton told me that the Triana are currently a *combo,* which is a gang of about eight hundred members, mostly kids. They had been imitating paramilitary techniques of waging urban war, dominating a community, and shoring up a form of hegemony. They often did so in close collaboration with the paramilitaries. Now the Triana also wanted to imitate them in demobilization to have access to the judiciary and social benefits the state guaranteed: free health insurance, free education, job training, and a monthly payment of about US$300. Milton did not talk about giving up control and domination. Rather, he spoke of a transformation and a shift from overt violence to magnanimity.

In Colombia, there is currently no judicial framework that allows gang members to demobilize, and therefore there are no legal tools for the state to negotiate and formalize agreements with lower-level criminal organizations. Gang members, who looked up to the paramilitaries, were disappointed and did not understand why they had been left without the benefits of the demobilization and reintegration process championed by the city administration. Milton at one point took his wallet out of his pocket and showed me his photo ID, identifying him as a demobilized paramilitary of the Bloque Minero. Attributing to him the status of a paramilitary was the strategy the state employed to be able to hold talks with key members of the Triana gang.

During our tour, Milton introduced me to many members and leaders of the gang. They all talked about building *convivencia* (coexistence), and they repeated it as a refrain they had memorized. Today their strategy is to show magnanimity to gain benefits for themselves and for their boss, Elkin Triana, who is currently locked up in the high-security prison Itagüí, near Medellín. They want him to be perceived not as a leader of terror but as a leader of peace. Thus, Milton told me about microcredit programs that the Triana gang wants to set up to benefit the barrio population, with the help and the blessing of drug kingpin Don Berna and the nonprofit organization Corporación Democrácia, which was founded by demobilized leaders of the Cacique Nutibara.

Magnanimity is also about transforming physical space. Showing me the remains of houses destroyed by intense fighting, Milton told me about the hope he had that the city administration would turn the area into a park and a soccer field for children. Here, on Sundays, the members of the Triana gang would cook *sancocho*—the traditional peasant soup of Antioquia, prepared with chicken, potatoes, carrots, and other vegetables—for the entire town.

An older woman, sitting under a poster calling for a ban on the use of weapons, told me that now there was peace in the barrio. Now she was able to sit on the outdoor steps of her small apartment, enjoying the passersby and the kiss of the sun. Why did things change? "The *muchachos* are now just very different," she said. As if through divine intervention, the hearts and minds of these young people had changed. She attributed the peace now surrounding her to a miraculous transformation. She was happy to be back in the barrio where she had lived in fear a few years earlier.

Will the guerrillas ever come back? I asked Milton.

Now the kids are organized, he responded, and there is order and no power vacuum. It was his definition of peace. But this is a peace imposed by the Triana and not freely chosen by the residents of the Popular One and Two barrios. Despite their discourse of benefiting the community by creating conditions for coexistence, the Triana are still the law in town.

I had a small taste of this while touring the barrio. When Milton saw a construction worker dump a wheelbarrow filled with debris on sod near a demolished house, he did not like what he saw and said he wanted to talk to the worker's boss. While I was listening to the woman sitting on the steps of her house, Milton went looking for the boss in order to complain and enforce the rule. It was a show of power and an affirmation of who was is charge. Public space was dominated and controlled by the Triana. It continued to be a despotic space.

More than excitement, there was curiosity. People pressed against the security fences while others sat on the top of walls or watched the scene from the windows of their houses. Security was tight. Soldiers patrolled the streets leading to the Popular One barrio, where a highly publicized event was about to take place.

The main street crossing the barrio was closed, and a stage had been erected. The event was to mark a symbolic act of magnanimity by the Triana gang: the restitution of previously seized houses to their legitimate owners, who were allowed to come back and live again in their barrio. Among the beneficiaries of this act of reparation was an couple in their eighties. They had been evicted by a local gang, who had taken over their humble house and turned it into a "plaza"; that is, a location where they sold drugs and hid weapons.

When I met the couple the following day, they were excited and grateful to the members of the Triana gang who now were giving back their home. "They are good *muchachos,* they are good kids," they repeated, sitting on their bed next to a small green bird chirping happily from his cage. I thought of Nietzsche, who wrote that not only harming but also benefiting others was a way to exercise power over them. Actually, Nietzsche wrote that magnanimity benefits those who are already dependent on a given source of power. While the pain resulting from hurt always raises the question of the origin of that suffering, the pleasure resulting from benevolence stops with itself, and one therefore does not question its origin (1974, 86–87). I wondered if the paramilitaries, with their unilateral decision to disarm and demobilize at the peak of their domination, had decided to relinquish some of their power or if they wanted to consolidate what they had captured through the magnanimous act of demobilization and acts of reparation like the one I was witnessing that afternoon. For Milton, rather than an act of reconciliation, as the media portrayed that event, the act of restitution was about gaining the sympathy of the state.

In the first four rows in front of the stage, demobilized paramilitary leaders mingled with city officials and members of the National Commission for

Reparation and Reconciliation,[6] which had been established to protect the rights of paramilitary violence's victims. At that time, it was headed by Eduardo Pizarro, whose brother Carlos was the charismatic leader of the demobilized M-19 guerrilla group killed by the paramilitaries during his presidential campaign.[7]

Pizarro sat on the stage, at the far right corner of a table, sharing the panel with state officials who sat next to paramilitary leaders and representatives of the Triana gang. Among the speakers was Daniel Mejia, alias Danielito, for many years considered Don Berna's second-in-command in the business of drug trafficking in Medellín. At the time of the event, he was also the president of the Corporación Democracia. When, during the ceremony, he spotted an empty seat next to Vice President Santos, he immediately went to occupy it. It was quite a picture to see the two of them sitting next to each other. I wondered how a resident of this barrio, harassed over the years by militias, paramilitaries, and gangs, would interpret this scene. Would he see an example of peace and reconciliation, as the discourse of the day implied, or would he believe that the event represented the legitimization of paramilitary and gang domination? And what were Daniel and the vice president thinking while sitting next to each other? Did Daniel feel more powerful and legitimized? Did the vice president feel finally satisfied to be able to set his feet in this barrio, where the state had been banned and where hitmen had been rewarded with US$500 apiece for killing police officers? To me, that table, where state officials sat shoulder to shoulder with paramilitary leaders, was an allegory of the state's intertwinement with criminal groups such as the paramilitaries.

People did not seem to pay much attention to the words pronounced by the speakers. The only applause arrived during Milton's speech when he spoke of Don Berna, or "Adolfo Paz," as a leader for peace and a man of hope:

> Today we thank the friendly hand of peace leader Diego Fernando Murillo, who, as a demobilized [leader] and a promoter of peace stretched his hand to us and invited us to stay in favor of overcoming fear and looking at life with hope. Today I tell you that we have shown that there is hope only when the people around us have hope. We feel more hope when we can give, when we can make up for the damages we have caused. . . .
>
> We, the young men and women united under the name of the Triana, with the leadership of our friends Elkin Triana and Mario Triana, who are behind bars in the prison of Itagüí, and with the support of our friend and leader for peace Diego Fernando Murillo, want to have an active part in the reconciliation processes that are underway in the municipalities of Medellín and Bello.

The impression of an outside observer was that the Triana people and their paramilitary friends and allies were still very much in control of this territory. The event and the handing over of the houses to their legitimate owners were presented as the results of a facilitation led by the Corporación Democracia. "These are concrete acts of peace," Don Fabio Acevedo, one of the main leaders of the organization, commented happily when I greeted him at the end of the ceremony.

One final observation: Milton was nervous when he read his speech. His presentation was bumpy, and he had difficulties in reading his prepared remarks with fluency. And yet, I thought, he must have been proud of himself, up there on the stage addressing local and national government authorities. It was a scene that certainly had not been in his mind when he had left the seminary, joined the Triana, and put a gun under his shirt. Was it thanks to the terror that he had disseminated in this barrio that he had gained this opportunity? But why did none of the victims talk in public, speaking truth to power?

In the public sphere of contemporary Colombia, paramilitaries show their smiling faces as they shake hands with authorities. They promote gestures of peace and reconciliation. They are committed to social work in barrios. They like to repeat the refrain "We are working for peace in Colombia." It is a discourse that gives them legitimacy; it allows them to say that something is changing for the better, and it allows the state to give the impression that it is capturing, deterritorializing, and reterritorializing spaces of externality.

Meanwhile, in the murky shadows, the dirty business of drug trafficking and its derivatives of violence and corruption continue. There is a double game going on here, and it prompts the question of why the paramilitaries unilaterally decided to demobilize.

The paramilitaries announced their demobilization at the peak of their power, after the victory of a president they considered sympathetic. Was it ever their intention to disarm and to disband? Was it ever their intention to give up their immense assets, their uncountable amounts of money and land, and their equally incalculable influence and power?

I returned to Medellín in December 2012. In the past few years, especially since 2007, the city had experienced a resurgence of violence, for the most part due to the settling of accounts among rival factions of the Oficina de Envigado and a more recent and upcoming criminal group, the so-called Urabeños,[8] who have been increasingly penetrating the illegal market in Antioquia and its capital. The war that has ensued from these rivalries and competition for domination has once again left in Medellín a long trail of blood among members of opposing camps in the criminal world.

The settling of accounts had already begun during the demobilization process in Medellín. On July 3, 2006, a squad of hitmen killed Gustavo Adolfo Upegui López on his farm near Medellín: López was a former right-hand man of Pablo Escobar who later, with Don Berna, became a primary leader of the Oficina de Envigado. At the same time, Upegui was one of the largest shareholders in the professional soccer team of Envigado. In following years, other leaders were either killed or extradited to the United States. Daniel Alberto Mejía, alias Danielito, was tortured and killed. In an upper-class restaurant in Medellín, a hitman killed Job, a leader of the Cacique Nutibara and of the Oficina de Envigado, who in his youth had served in the ELN guerrillas. He was a major spokesperson for the demobilized paramilitaries, who had regular meetings with the mayor of Medellín and city officials, as well as with close advisers of President Álvaro Uribe in the Casa de Nariño, the presidential palace. In turn, Don Berna was first arrested for being the instigator of the killing of a congress member and later extradited to the United States in May 2008, together with thirteen leaders of the AUC. Another leader of the Oficina de Envigado, Rogelio,[9] who had replaced Don Berna in the leadership and was rumored to be the instigator of Danielito's execution, was extradited to the United States. The erosion of the historical leadership of the Oficina de Envigado and of the paramilitaries in Medellín soon paved the way for a bloody rivalry for control of the organization between two men, known as Sebastián y Valenciano,[10] who since their early teen years had worked as hitmen under the wing of Don Berna.

At the end of 2012, violence had picked up again in Medellín. When I arrived there, I wanted to see for myself what was going on. With the help of some of my contacts, I reached out to Gabriel, a demobilized paramilitary field commander who had served with the Cacique Nutibara and continued to live in the neighborhood where he had grown up. A few reliable sources also told me that Gabriel was the representative of Sebastián's faction within the Oficina de Envigado in that neighborhood. Gabriel agreed to meet, and so one morning I drove up to his neighborhood. Our meeting point was not far from a soccer field, which marked a still existing but invisible boundary between the neighborhood where Gabriel lived and the one controlled by a rival armed group. A few months previously, I was told, a couple of teenagers had been tortured and assassinated on that soccer field.

It was a sunny and warm morning. A few people were busy assembling a nativity scene. The person accompanying me, who had arranged the meeting, sent a text message, and after a few minutes, I saw Gabriel, a tall, athletic man in his late thirties, walking up a steep street surrounded by a few other men, who, I guessed, acted as his bodyguards. When we greeted each other, he was affable and invited me to the home of the president of the local action committee, a woman. We sat down in the living room next to a Christmas tree. We were served soda and started talking.

The previous day at a public official ceremony, I had seen Gabriel parade along with other demobilized paramilitaries, who, after almost a decade, were graduating from the reintegration program. I spotted him entering the large hall filled with public officials and journalists, walking in line with other comrades and holding a fake plastic flower in his right hand. The scene was awkward, not only because of the line of a few dozen former paramilitary combatants holding fake flowers, but also because Gabriel was part of a graduation ceremony that celebrated the successful reintegration of former combatants into civil life while he continued to be an important leader of the criminal world in his neighborhood. I wondered how many like Gabriel had graduated that afternoon.

I was not the only one who was aware of Gabriel's double life on that afternoon. Senior officials of the city administration knew, and had confirmed to me, Gabriel's links to Sebastián and the Oficina de Envigado. Thus Gabriel's was not the sole ambiguity. The state, too, by holding up the fiction of Gabriel's demobilization and reintegration, continued to perpetuate and reconfigure that shifting entanglement, that public secret that makes up the Mafia phenomenon.

During our conversation in his neighborhood, Gabriel did not openly admit his relationship with the Oficina de Envigado, but rather presented himself as a recognized and valued community leader dedicated to the wellbeing of his neighborhood. He was running a small bodega, he told me, and wanted to continue serving his community. This is why, he explained, he and his friends, a few months ago, had collaborated with the police to apprehend a drug dealer who was operating from an adjoining neighborhood. This individual was abusing the community, Gabriel told me, using excessive violence and collecting protection money from small shops, buses, and taxi drivers. "I convinced someone to go to the police and declare against this man so that he could be charged," he told me in a proud voice.

If I hadn't been aware of his ongoing involvement with the Oficina de Envigado, Gabriel would have sounded like a committed and responsible citizen. Yet Gabriel's enemy, the drug dealer he had helped to capture, was his primary enemy and adversary: the local leader for Valenciano, who headed the wing of the Oficina de Envigado competing against Sebastián. Listening to Gabriel's account and learning from him about the role he and his associates had in helping the police to capture Valenciano's associate, I wondered about a public secret circulating at that time in Medellín: that the police were siding with Sebastián's group and against Valenciano's. A year earlier, in a different neighborhood of the city, a member of Valenciano's gang had told me that the police often captured some of his people only to set them free in a territory controlled by Sebastián, where they could be caught and killed by their enemies.

As I drove out of the neighborhood, I passed by the area where Gabriel's rival had engaged in a firefight with the police, killing two officers before being arrested. I wondered how Gabriel, instead of directly confronting his enemy and thus jeopardizing his position as a leader of the demobilized paramilitaries as well as the tranquility of his neighborhood, had used the police to get rid of his enemy. When I related this experience to a senior official of the national government as an example of the shortcomings of the demobilization and reintegration program, he told me that if I gave him Gabriel's name, he was going to make sure Gabriel was arrested. Then he paused and said, "Well, then again, he probably doesn't have any charges against him." And thus Gabriel continues to be another hinge connecting the state to the underworld of crime.

What was this whole disarmament and demobilization process about, then? What was its meaning? In explaining and justifying the process, the discourse of the state has generously borrowed from the peacemaking and postconflict lexicon. Words such as *negotiations, disarmament, demobilization, reintegration,* and *reparation* have become part of a recurrent vocabulary used to construct the fiction of the peace process with the paramilitaries. Not only interest groups within Colombia, but also foreign governments, multilateral agencies, and the community of donors, have bought into this language and perpetuated it, amplifying and celebrating the boldness and innovative character of the large-scale process.

This language, rather than exposing and unmasking the public secret and the truth about the relationship between the paramilitaries and the state, has allowed the forgetting and deflection of the truth that the paramilitaries were not an enemy adverse to the state and were not motivated by the intention to subvert order, but rather were instrumental in consolidating order, in refounding it, as paramilitary and political leaders affirmed in a document they have signed together. The paramilitaries, in fact, have been an essential component of the pacification process in Colombia.

The paramilitaries, as I have claimed throughout this book, are at the same time within and outside the state. While transgressing the law, they affirm the state's right to capture. While operating in spaces where constitutional order is suspended, they preserve and affirm the necessity and legitimacy of that order.

Rather than the break or an interruption that a peace process with an enemy entails, the state, like an illusionist, has perpetuated its fiction of legitimacy. If, as Taussig (1999) wrote, unmasking is the process of making the invisible even more believable, and strengthening rather than weakening an illusion, then one might understand the demobilization of former paramilitary combatants as the state's sleight of hand, which has included the legitimacy the state claims for itself as it intertwines with paramilitary death squads.

Conclusion

On an afternoon in late August 2005, a long line of buses entered the parking area of the sports hall in Envigado, a town neighboring Medellín that is known for harboring the residences of several drug kingpins. It is the town where Pablo Escobar grew up and that gave its name to the Oficina de Envigado. It was also the home of Gustavo Adolfo Upegui López, the owner of the town soccer club and also one of the principals of the criminal organization and a long-time associate of Don Berna. Upegui was killed in the summer of 2006.

Hundreds of young men, all demobilized members of the Cacique Nutibara and the Héroes de Granada paramilitary groups, got off the buses, formed orderly lines, and slowly entered the sports hall, filling the stadium bleachers. The event that was about to begin that afternoon had been presented as an important one, as a milestone in the demobilization and reintegration process of Medellín. The Héroes de Granada paramilitary group had formed only in 2003, just a few weeks before the Cacique Nutibara had disarmed in early November.

In this official ceremony, the new board of the Corporación Democracia organization, an NGO, was announced, which from then onward would be headed by former leaders of the Cacique Nutibara and the Héroes de Granada. What these leaders all had in common were their links to Don Berna, who headed both paramilitary groups, and their affiliation to the Oficina de Envigado.

On the floor of the sports hall was a long table, behind which the leaders of the demobilized groups sat with a senior official of the city of Medellín and a representative of the Organization of American States, which was responsible for monitoring the demobilization and reintegration of former combatants in Colombia. Among the leaders, I distinguished Job, a heavyset man and the spokesperson of the demobilized paramilitaries. He had a long history of crime. In the 1970s, he was a member of the ELN guerrillas, and only in the 1990s did he join the paramilitaries. He was a senior member of the Oficina de Envigado and one of Don Berna's closest confidants. Three years later, in July 2008, Job would be killed while having lunch with his assistant in an upper-class Medellín restaurant owned by another drug kingpin and paramilitary leader known as Macaco.[1]

Next to Job sat Don Effe, or Fabio Acevedo, also a man of Don Berna and among the founders of the Cacique Nutibara. I also distinguished Danielito, who I would see again a year later during the victims' reparation event that I describe in chapter 6. Danielito was the leader of the Héroes de Granada and Don Berna's right arm in the Oficina de Envigado. According to investigators, he would be responsible for the assassination next year of Upegui. Danielito himself was later disappeared and presumably killed when a war among leaders of the Oficina de Envigado to inherit control of the organization and its illicit market was sparked after Don Berna's arrest and subsequent extradition to the United States in May 2008. Those I saw before me were not only the general staff of the paramilitaries that had dominated Medellín, but also the *capos* of the Medellín "Mafia," whose ascendancy could be traced back to the time of Pablo Escobar.

The ceremony began with the notes of Colombia's national anthem blasting from the speakers. About a thousand former paramilitaries got to their feet, put their right hands on their hearts, and sang the hymn at the top of their lungs. While the last note reverberated in the hall, one paramilitary leader went to the microphone. "Let's have a minute of silence for all those who died for our homeland and are no longer with us," he proposed. Silence descended on the arena.

I was disturbed by the scene. "I am angry," I hastily scribbled in my small notebook. This request implied the *paras* had been heroes, soldiers in a legitimate war who fought alongside the state. None of the state officials present distanced himself from what had been said. Even in these words uttered and the approving silence, one could perceive the long shadow of the intertwinement that has shaped the fate of Colombia. And I felt that the victims had been squeezed out, left in the cold.

The same paramilitary leader, after the minute of silence, took to the floor again. "An applause for peace!" he screamed into the microphone, and thunderous applause erupted from all corners of the sports hall. "We complied!

We complied!" the paramilitary leader screamed excitedly. Then he gave a little speech in which he even quoted Bertrand Russell's *Freedom in Society*. "Long live Colombia!" he said at the end, inspiring another deafening round of applause.

As the attendants left the sports hall, I lingered, observing as the former paramilitaries—now the board members of their own legitimate NGO— had small chats. Some laughed, while others greeted each other with pats on the shoulder. There was a sense of accomplishment. A man came toward me and introduced himself. He was tall and slim and had a white beard, short white hair, and light-framed glasses. He told me that he was the former political leader of the Cacique Nutibara. For a long time, he had been a recognized leader of the Conservative party in Medellín and had even served as a deputy minister of labor in the mid-1990s. In recent times, he had grown disillusioned with the Conservative party because he sensed it had lost its way. A long-time friend of Don Berna and of Job, he saw in the paramilitaries' project a viable and better alternative, and he willingly provided ideological discourse to the Cacique Nutibara. In greeting me, he mentioned he had a son who had studied in the United States and was now finishing his law degree in a Catholic university in Medellín.

I met this son of the Cacique Nutibara political leader a few years later, in New York, where he introduced himself as a lawyer for Don Berna. It was not until our conversation, in a fancy downtown Manhattan hotel, did I realize that he was indeed the son of the man I had encountered at the demobilized paramilitary event in Envigado. When I told him I had met his father and that he had spoken to me about him, I was able to connect with him, and gain his trust. Together with his father, I learned, he was a founding member of the Corporación Democracia, and he had also been a member of the Cacique Nutibara paramilitary group.

In 2013, a couple of years after our first meeting, I had the chance to again meet this son, Don Berna's lawyer, in Medellín. We chatted and had a coffee, and then the lawyer invited me to assist at a meeting he had planned in a nearby restaurant. "It's for someone who is in trouble with a gang in his neighborhood," he told me.

At the restaurant, we joined two men sitting at a table. The lawyer introduced me to one of the men, a demobilized paramilitary. "We were together in San Ralito," he said. He inflated my bio while presenting me: "He is a columnist for the *New York Times*."

"For the Colombian newspaper *El Espectador*," I corrected.

The second man at the table was in his late twenties, pale, wearing jeans and a white T-shirt. He looked intimidated, almost scared, as he started to share his situation. He and the demobilized paramilitary who had arranged the meeting had met at a private security firm where they were both employed. He was living in a marginal area of the city, in an apartment he shared with his wife and their children. A neighbor had told him that a local gang had decided to kill him and advised him to leave the neighborhood immediately. Apparently, the spur for the deadly threat was the fact that his brother, who lived in a different neighborhood, up in the hills of the city, belonged to a rival gang. Because the man visited that neighborhood to see his mother, the gang where he resided believed he was affiliated with his brother's gang. "That's why they want to kill me," he said.

The lawyer inquired further into why the brother had become involved with a gang.

"It's because of a dispute around a woman. My brother felt harassed and looked for protection from a gang," the threatened man said.

"I see the situation is complicated," said the lawyer.

"He is an honest and serious guy. He has nothing to do with any of the gangs," the ex-paramilitary assured the lawyer.

The lawyer asked more questions, inquiring about the name of the gang that was threatening the man and the name of its commander. "They call him 'the condemned,'" the man responded.

"Things are not like they were in the past," the lawyer explained, adding a layer of complexity to the threatened man's situation. "No longer is there just one leader who controls everything. Now they don't listen to you, they don't follow orders. Each one goes his own way. I cannot promise you anything. This is not something one can resolve overnight. One has to inquiry carefully." It sounded like the lawyer could not do much, or was not willing to do much. "What's important is to save one's life, because life is what matters most. And it's better not to involve the police because that makes things even more complicated."

The threatened man sat in silence for a while. "That means I am not going back to my home today," he said, with deep sadness.

This encounter reflected the shifting dynamics in Medellín at the time of our meeting, in early 2013. While I was in town, several leaders of the Oficina de Envigado, who were also demobilized from the Cacique Nutibara, had been killed in a villa at the end of a party. The Urabeños were penetrating the city, taking control of neighborhoods by paying gangs that earlier had been loyal to Valenciano, one of the leaders of the Oficina, who was disputing the control of Medellín's illicit market with Sebastián, the head of a rival wing of the Oficina.

As I was jotting down notes for this conclusion, the lawyer contacted me again by email. He confirmed that the Oficina de Envigado and the Urabeños had in the past few months reached a ceasefire agreement and had agreed on some labor division in Medellín. Additionally, he mentioned that they were willing to negotiate a submission to justice with the government. With a peace process underway with the guerrillas, the lawyer explained, the leaders of organized crime organizations were willing to negotiate with the government as well. A few days later, a scandal broke out in the Colombian media when it was revealed that a close adviser to the president of the republic had worked in 2011 with heads of the Colombian Mafia to draft a document proposing a negotiation with the government.

The events leading to the demobilization of the Héroes de Granada paramilitaries, headed by historic leaders of the Oficina de Envigado; the meeting with the lawyer, himself a demobilized paramilitary; and the new initiatives of negotiations between the state and organized crime groups that were an offspring of the paramilitaries' demobilization process brought me to ask myself what these recent developments suggested about the nature of the relationship between the state and illegal groups.

As I mulled over the emails from the lawyer and news clips about the scandal involving the president's office, I wondered if the negotiation between the state and organized crime was just another facet of the intertwinement I have analyzed throughout this book. Colombia, in fact, has a long history of negotiations between the state and its Mafia.

The first negotiation goes back to the time when Pablo Escobar was expanding his cocaine empire. He deeply resented that a very few political leaders and a very few journalists had dared to denounce his crimes publicly. He had started a direct attack against his enemies, having representatives of the institutions, journalists, police officers, and prosecutors killed. When, at Escobar's order, Justice Minister Rodrigo Lara Bonilla was killed in 1984, President Betancur ratified an extradition agreement with the United States, which generated deep fear and anxiety among the heads of drug cartels. "We prefer a grave in Colombia to a prison cell in the United States," they used to say at the time. In an attempt to avoid extradition, Escobar and his associates met in Panama with a former president of Colombia, Alfonso López Michelsen, and Colombia's past attorney general. The drug lord used the good offices of the two men to send a message to President Betancur that they were ready to give up drug trafficking if extradition was going to be upheld. The proposal was rejected by the United States and by some sectors of Colombian society, and thus the negotiation died.

In the subsequent years, other negotiation attempts followed. During the administration of President Virgilio Barco Vargas, an attempt to reach an agreement was made when family members of the president's chief of staff were kidnapped. At the end of the 1980s, when Escobar and his associates started to kidnap members of the Bogotá-based elite, President César Gaviria, in an attempt to halt the spread of terror and violence, proposed lenient punishment for drug lords who submitted to, and collaborated with, justice.

The Constituent Assembly also became an opportunity for negotiation with the drug cartels on the issue of extradition. When in 1991 the assembly passed Article 35, which prohibited the extradition of Colombian citizens to the United States, Pablo Escobar gave himself up and was locked up in a prison built on a piece of land that Escobar owned and from which the leader of the Medellín Cartel continued to commit crimes. Escobar also hosted lavish parties there for his associates, and he eventually escaped without meeting any resistance.

At the end of the 1990s, as I have written in previous chapters, the drug lords became the owners and the leaders of the AUC paramilitary umbrella. The government of Álvaro Uribe sat down with them to negotiate the disarmament, demobilization, and reintegration of paramilitary combatants. Later, information about new negotiations between the state and drug kingpins emerged under President Juan Manuel Santos Calderón.

As I highlighted in chapter 6, negotiation between the state and the paramilitaries is an expression of the complex intertwinement that the state is permanently engaged in reconfiguring, adapting, masking, and unmasking; it is constantly reaffirming its legitimacy, both when it allies with machines such as the paramilitaries and when it renegotiates those alliances through formal and secretive negotiations. El Doctor, the drug trafficker and paramilitary supporter about whom I wrote in chapter 1, told me that the elites in Colombia have always been ready to arm and disarm illegal armed groups according to their own needs and interests. "When these groups become too powerful," he told me, "they dismantle them." Whether the elites are assembling or dissembling their murky alliance with illegal armed groups, they are expressing the state's legitimacy and its expenditure of power.

Whether the state works in cahoots with paramilitary groups, which are often simultaneously the private armies of drug kingpins, to carry out social "cleansings" of rural areas and towns, or whether it negotiates the disarmament or submission to justice of these same groups, these two modes of relations are part of a continuum, one in which the state and criminal groups interpenetrate. I have defined this intertwinement as a distinguishing feature of the Mafia, and as one that contra-distinguishes the Mafia from other social phenomena. And not only is the relationship with the state a defining feature of the Mafia, but it is also a defining feature of the state itself. I thus suggest that the negotiations that the state at times undertakes with groups such as the paramilitaries are the recalibration of correlated forces.

In other words, my own observations in the field, combined with the historical record, suggest that in the case of Colombia, a direct confrontation between the state and organized crime, such as the paramilitaries and the related drug-trafficking cartels, has been the exception—as when the state declared a war against Pablo Escobar and the Medellín cartel—but the norm has been either alliance or negotiation between the state and the illegal groups.

The notion of a continuum, characterized by moments in which the state allies with illegal groups and others in which it negotiates its disarmament or submission to justice, becomes clearer if I once again compare Colombia to Italy. During a visit to Palermo in June 2012, I had the opportunity to interview the prosecutor Antonio Ingroia, who in his youth had worked closely with the prosecutors Giovanni Falcone and Paolo Borsellino, both of whom were killed by the Mafia in 1992. At the time, Ingroia was investigating a criminal negotiation allegedly conducted by the government of Italy with the head of the Cosa Nostra. The negotiation was intended to diffuse the wave of violence and terror that the Sicilian Mafia had undertaken in reaction to the final ruling of Italy's high courts, which confirmed the life sentences of Cosa Nostra's bosses. Bombs went off not only in Sicily, but also in Rome and Florence. According to the prosecutors, the state agreed to change the Mafia bosses' detention regime of isolation in exchange for a halt to terrorist attacks. In addition, the prosecutors advanced the thesis that Falcone and Borsellino were killed because they had learned about the ongoing negotiation and opposed it.

Sitting behind a desk covered with stacks of folders, Ingroia lectured me on the nature of the Sicilian Mafia and its relationship with the state. The mafiosi, the prosecutor told me, do not relate themselves to legitimate power in order to augment their wealth, but primarily in order to accumulate power. The Mafia is a power system that aligns itself with other powers to concentrate more power. The control over a given territory, Ingroia specified, allows the Mafia to accumulate resources, shape the economy, control the movement of people, and influence political participation. This is why every unit of the Mafia is linked to a specific territory. "If the Mafia is a power system that administers power, then its aim is to have relationship with other systems of power, including the legal ones," Ingroia explained.

The prosecutor added that at times, a Mafia organization might be in competition with, but not in opposition to, the state. That reminded me of what a paramilitary leader once told me in Medellin: "We are not with the government, but we are not against the state."

When the Mafia attacks with spectacular violence, Ingroia continued, it is because it is breaking a given equilibrium in order to establish a new one. In the case of Italy, the Cosa Nostra's terror attack at the beginning of the 1990s reflected the deep changes in Italy's political system, which until then had rested on the hegemony of the Democrazia Cristiana party. According to Ingroia, the wave of violence mirrored the Sicilian Mafia's attempts to establish a new pact, a new agreement with the new political and post–Cold War arrangement that had begun to govern the country. This new equilibrium, the prosecutor explained, was at the root of the negotiation between the Italian state and the Cosa Nostra. "With a few exceptions, the strategy of the state has been to contain the power of the Mafia, but never to annihilate it."

In their recent volume on democracy and violence in Latin America, Enrique Desmond Arias and Daniel Goldstein emphasized that throughout the continent today, states considered viable coexist and engage with a variety of armed actors: "They often strengthen their position working *with* rather than *against* armed groups" (2010, 9), since violence continues to shape political practice and remains an instrument for political rule. Colombia, as I have tried to demonstrate in this book, is a case in point: it is the country with the region's oldest democratic institutions, but at the same time it has violence as a foundation and key element of its contentious political and democratic life. Arias and Goldstein concluded that "violence stems from the structure and the activities that support existing social relations and from the way state power is exercised" (ibid., 13). In Colombia, this has taken the form of an intertwinement between the state and the paramilitaries that expresses the state's function of capture. As an articulation of power, this intertwinement allows the accumulation of still more power and legitimizes its violent and spectacular expenditure. Thus the paramilitaries represent the war machine that the state acquired to deterritorialize and reterritorialize spaces across the country produced as an externalities. These are spaces of exception, as I suggested in chapter 3, that are also spaces of despo-capitalism, since the desires that are unchained by capitalism are controlled, channeled, and constrained by the rule and the violence imposed by the despot. The expenditure that characterizes capitalism is linked to and depends on the use of violence and repression and the maintenance of disorder in the marginal spaces of despo-capitalism. Therefore, not only have these spaces engendered the intertwinement between the Colombian state and the paramilitaries, but the intertwinement has also engendered spaces that are conceived as marginal and as an externality that needs to be tamed and brought into order. It is in these spaces that the lives of young men who join the paramilitaries, like the *muchachos de confianza* whose stories I share in this book, are shaped—and almost frozen—in patterns of violence and death, with little chance for a dignified and dignifying escape.

The intertwinement between the state and paramilitaries has subdued the possibility of a vibrant and deliberative democracy in Colombia. The chances that the cultural norms that engender a radical democracy will develop and deepen depend on the state's willingness and capacity to sever its entanglement with the Mafia. This requires an effort to reimagine the state and democratic life in Colombia. I witnessed the seeds of such a possibility in the very spaces marked by violence and marginalization, where young people in particular have not given up their hope and their commitment to engender a different and alternate reality. They are a war machine in themselves, a creative machine that in a rhizomatic way creates spaces that, though often small and fragile, are marked by participation and deliberation. These are spaces of resilience, and they resist and transcend the capture attempted by the state and its entanglement with the Mafia.

NOTES

INTRODUCTION

1. Note that paramilitary violence remains an ongoing phenomenon in Colombia, though under different names than the ones I use in this book. Thus both past- and present-tense descriptions are used in this text.

2. The Fuerzas Armadas Revolucionarias de Colombia (FARC) is a peasant Marxist-Leninist guerrilla group established in 1964. Its origins are tracked to Operation Marquetalia, when the Colombian armed forces bombed the town of Marquetalia, a Communist enclave, during the counterinsurgency operation known as Plan Lazo in May of that year. Several FARC founders had been members and leaders of the Liberal guerrillas, who had fought against the Conservatives during the sectarian upheaval of La Violencia in the 1950s. By 1997, when the administration of President Andrés Pastrana initiated peace talks with the FARC, it was estimated that guerrillas were present in 30 percent of the national territory. When peace talks broke down, the counterinsurgency efforts led by President Álvaro Uribe Vélez significantly reduced the number of FARC combatants, and guerrillas were forced to retreat toward the border of the country. In 2012, the guerrillas agreed to peace talks with administration of President Juan Manuel Santos in Cuba.

3. Álvaro Uribe Vélez was president of Colombia from 2002 to 2010. He was elected in a landslide by an electorate frustrated with the failures of peace talks. President Uribe adopted a warrior's approach, intensifying counterinsurgency efforts against the guerrillas. When Uribe had served as a governor of Antioquia for two years in the 1990s, he was a fierce advocate for the legalization of antiguerrilla militias, known as Convivir. At the time, Fabio Valencia Cossio a Conservative who later served as Uribe's minister of the interior, accused Uribe himself, when he served as governor of Antioquia, of "sponsoring the paramilitaries" (Hylton 2006, 93).

4. Urabá, a subregion on the northern coast of Colombia, is part of the department of Antioquia. Because of its geostrategic position, it was raided, beginning during La Violencia (the 1950s-era period of sectarian violence), by several armed

groups. In the 1990s, paramilitaries penetrated this region, which had a significant presence of guerrillas, and repressed peasants and workers' movements. Chapter 5 describes and analyzes more in depth the intertwinement among paramilitaries, the armed forces, and business owners in Urabá.

5. Within their work, anthropologists have privileged the accounts, memories, and truths produced by the subalterns and the victims on whose bodies the effects of violence are inscribed (e.g., Green 1999; Malkki 1995; Sanford 2004; Scheper-Hughes 1992; Theidon 2012). Lending an ear to the victims has been the primary tactic that anthropologists have employed to unravel strategies of domination and hegemony and to further the understanding of how violence has been inscribed into historical memory and political ideologies (Das and Poole 1994). Writing about the U.S.-trained Salvadoran army's massacre in El Mozote, Leigh Binford emphasized the importance of the witness: "I believe that every member of an oppressed group has a story to tell" (1996, 10). Putting the silenced, forgotten, excluded, and vilified at the center of anthropological inquiry has been a merit of the discipline and an important contribution to the study of political violence. Nancy Scheper-Hughes defined the seeing, listening, and recording done with care and sensitivity by the ethnographer as "acts of fraternity and sisterhood, acts of solidarity" (1992, 28). This is an ethics that I sympathize with.

In recent years, several anthropologists have argued that in addition to the study of victims, attention also has to be paid to perpetrators to further the understanding of violence and violent actors. Neil L. Whitehead wrote emphatically about the importance of anthropology to balance the study of violence between victims and perpetrators:

> Any study we make must clearly reach beyond the political and economic conditions under which violence is triggered, or indeed the suffering of victims and the psychology of its interpersonal dynamics. We also now need to focus on the role of perpetrators, their motivations and the social conditions under which they are able to operate. We need to redress any imbalance, in terms of focus, between victims and perpetrators. (2004, 2)

The study of violent perpetrators has therefore become an additional strategy that anthropologists have employed to study the powerful and their practices of domination and hegemony. Most of these researchers have conducted their work among agents engaged in wars of resistance or self-determination. Armed actors and political activists in Northern Ireland, for example, were the emphasis of Jeffrey A. Sluka (1989), Allen Feldman (1991), Begoña Aretxaga (1997), and Begoña Aretxaga and Joseba Zulaika (2005). Zulaika (1988) provided a cultural interpretation of Basque resistance, focusing on the worldviews, the resentments, and the militancy of Euskadi Ta Askatasunam (ETA) members. In the attempt to go beyond labels such as "fundamentalism" and "terrorism," Cynthia Keppley Mahmood (1996) concentrated on the human experience of Sikh militants. David M. Rosen (2005) wrote about child soldiers, problematizing the view of them as simply passive victims, and demonstrated how children can make a rational choice in joining an armed resistance. Similarly, Margaret Trawick (2007) has written an insightful account of youth in Sri Lanka who joined the Tamil Tigers.

A smaller number of anthropologists have directly engaged with members of death squads, gangs, and organized crime in order to understand their motivation and their cultural worlds. Philippe Bourgois (1995), for example, explored inner-city crime, doing fieldwork among crack dealers in Spanish Harlem. In analyzing Argentina's Dirty War, Antonius C. G. M. Robben (2007) included the voices of the generals, as did Jennifer Schirmer (1998) while documenting the Guatemalan military's role in suppressing its own citizens. Martha Knisely Huggins et al. (2002), in their ethnography of Brazilian policemen defined as violence workers, highlighted the continuation of authoritarian practices after Brazil's transition to democracy. Alexander Laban Hinton and Robert Jay Lifton (2004) focused on encounters and interviews with a perpetrator in order to provide a cultural account of Cambodia's genocide. More recently, Danny Hoffman (2011) provided a study of young combatants in Sierra Leone and Liberia who are made available for violent labor in a world that increasingly outsources warfare and security.

In the attempt to provide an analysis of violent actors, some anthropological work has emphasized the relationship between violence and masculinity. Huggins and her colleagues (2002) considered that a sense of group masculinity underpinned forms of power emphasizing competitions, dominance, and control—all considered to be qualities of the masculine. In her study of the military in Bolivia, Lesley Gill (1997)—in an attempt to understand why young men belonging to impoverished ethnic groups and working classes are eager to serve as foot soldiers in the army—emphasized how the Cold War's legacy, populist nationalism, and conditions of marginality have supported the large-scale militarization of masculinity in Bolivia.

Other anthropologists have instead suggested moving away from an anthropology of identity, with its emphasis on political, economic, and social dynamics, and instead shifting toward an anthropology of experience that focuses on violence as a cultural expression and performance, since the "performance of violence cannot . . . be amputated from that wider body of cultural performance" (Whitehead 2004, 10). This is the approach that several anthropologists have embraced in studying political violence, civil wars, and political violence from Africa (e.g., Finnström 2008; Malkki 1995; Taylor 1999) to South America (Das and Poole 2004; Taussig 1987; Warren 1993) to South and Southeast Asia (Daniel 1996; Hinton et al. 2004; Finnström 2008; Skidmore 2004).

A handful of anthropologists have provided accounts of Colombia's political violence (see Gill 2004; Sanford 2004; Taussig 1991, 2004, 2005, 2012; Theidon 2003, 2009; Sanford 2004; Tate 2007). In general, these studies fall between the two analytical approaches that I mention above. In his pioneering work on the terror linked to rubber production in Southern Colombia, for example, Michael Taussig (1987) introduced the notion of the "space of death" as an area of mimesis in which the civilized mimics the violence imputed to the savage. In the 1980s, he wrote about the spreading culture of terror at the beginning of the nineteenth century in the Putumayo region; during the years of escalating paramilitary violence in Colombia and Central America; and at the time that the testimonies of the Dirty War emerged in Argentina. More recently, Taussig (2005) has suggested parallels between the terror spread by the Spaniards in their search for gold and the present-day violence perpetuated by the private armies that drug kingpins, ranchers, and landowners mobilized for the accumulation of capital and the selling of private protection. Kimberly Theidon's (2003) analysis of demobilized paramilitaries explored the notion of militarized masculinity, including its production and performance, highlighting how the link among weapons, masculinities, and violence are essential to the maintenance of militarism. While issues of masculinity clearly emerged in the conversations that I had with members of the paramilitaries and are reflected in the narratives that I recorded, the emphasis of my present analysis is on the meanings and practices that the paramilitaries I met attributed to their experience, and how their experience shed light on the larger forces that have mobilized them.

6. Giovanni Falcone and Paolo Borsellino were two prosecutors who used innovative investigation methods to fight the Cosa Nostra in Sicily. In the 1980s, their investigations led to the first comprehensive trial against the leadership of the Sicilian Mafia. Both prosecutors were killed, together with their bodyguards, in two separate terror attacks in 1992.

CHAPTER 1. "EVERYTHING I DID IN THE NAME OF PEACE"

1. Pablo Escobar, the drug kingpin who founded the Medellín Cartel, began his carrier as a drug trafficker crossing the border of Colombia into Ecuador, where he would acquire cocaine base and resell it in Colombia.

2. Colombia is a republic formed of thirty-two departments, and Antioquia is one of them. The city of Medellín is the capital of Antioquia.

3. In Colombia, "Conservative" and "Liberal" refer to the political identities with which Colombians ally themselves as adherents of the country's two traditional political parties, the Conservatives and the Liberals.

4. http://2001–2009.state.gov/p/inl/narc/rewards/39429.htm.

5. The North Valley Cartel was formed in the Valle del Cauca department in the late 1990s and operated until 2012. After the fragmentation of the Medellín Cartel and the Cali Cartel, the North Valley Cartel became the hegemonic drug organization in Colombia.

6. Tuluá is today a major industrial and commercial center in the Valle del Cauca department in Colombia. It continues to be an epicenter of violence.

7. Julio Alberto Hoyos, quoted in Guzmán Campos, Orlando Fals Borda, and Eduardo Umaña Luna, *La Violencia en Colombia: Estudio de un proceso social* (Tomo I), 186–87.

8. The ELN was established in 1964. It was inspired by the Cuban Revolution and by liberation theology. It is today the second-largest guerrilla group in Colom-

bia, with about three thousand armed fighters and a larger network of supporters among union leaders, teachers, intellectuals, and others.

9. The ranch Las Tangas was a farm in the northern department of Córdoba owned by the Castaño brothers. It became the headquarters of the paramilitaries.

10. In 1978, President Julio César Turbay Ayala introduced the Security Statute, increasing the freedom of the military to arrest, interrogate, and detain individuals who were suspected of being collaborators or members of the guerrillas. Soon afterward, in 1981, Colombian writer Gabriel García Márquez, informed of the possibility of his imminent arrest, left Colombia for Mexico, where he lived with his wife until his death in 2014.

11. On January 18, 1989, a paramilitary death squad in La Rochela, a town in the department of Santander, killed twelve judicial officials. Drug traffickers as well as members of the military were involved in the assassination.

12. The Oficina de Envigado (Envigado Office) refers to the Medellín drug cartel and its illegal affairs after the death of Pablo Escobar. Envigado itself is a municipality at the outskirt of Medellín. After Escobar died, the leader of the Oficina de Envigado was Diego Murillo Bejarano, known as Don Berna or Adolfo Paz. Don Berna played a key role in the hunt and killing of Escobar and in the late 1990s became a leader of the paramilitaries.

CHAPTER 2. FRAGMENTS FROM THE SHADOWS OF WAR

1. In 2003, Medellín was selected as the first city to begin the nationwide disarmament, demobilization, and reintegration (DDR) of former members of paramilitary groups. The Peace and Reconciliation Program was responsible for the implementation of the DDR program. Over a few years, about five thousand former combatants came to reside in Medellín.

2. The Cacique Nutibara paramilitary group was the first such organization to demobilize in Colombia. It was also the main paramilitary organization in Medellín. Its leader was Diego Murillo Bejarano, known also as Don Berna, a drug kingpin who played a key role in the persecution of Pablo Escobar and inherited the illicit business linked to the Medellín Cartel. The other two paramilitary organizations that operated in Medellín were the Bloque Metro, whose leader was Doble Cero, and the Héroes de Granada, which formed after the demobilization of the Cacique Nutibara and whose leader, called Danielito, was a lieutenant of Don Berna.

3. These are small towns in the department of Antioquia.

4. Comuna 13 is one of the sixteen administrative areas into which the city of Medellín, the capital of Antioquia, is divided. It is also one of the poorest areas of the city and is known as a major epicenter of violence as well as of state intervention.

5. The Elmer Cárdenas paramilitary group operated in Urabá, a subregion in northern Antioquia department on the Atlantic coast. It was founded in 1995 and led by Freddy Rendón, known as El Alemán. It is also the paramilitary group that expropriated most land from peasants through violence.

6. Dabeiba is a municipality in the department of Antioquia.

7. *Panela* is concentrated raw sugar packed into small rectangular loaves.

8. I write in more detail about the Orión Operation in chapter 5.

9. The Bloque Metro was the paramilitary group led by Doble Cero. More information on the war between the Cacique Nutibara and the Bloque Metro can be found in the prologue and chapter 5.

10. The Ejército Popular de Liberación (EPL) was established in 1967 as an offshoot of the Communist Party. It demobilized in 1991. Afterward, some of its former members joined the paramilitaries in Urabá, Antioquia. Former leaders of the EPL are today accused of being the leaders of the Urabeños, a recent criminal group that emerged from the demobilization of the AUC paramilitaries in 2003.

11. The Caucana is a subregion of Antioquia. I write more about this area and the Minero paramilitary group in chapter 4.

12. This is a municipality in northeastern Antioquia.

13. Don Berna is the alias of Diego Murillo Bejarano, the drug kingpin who led the Cacique Nutibara paramilitary bloc. He is one of the fourteen AUC leaders who were extradited to the United States in 2008. I write more about him in chapters 5 and 6.

14. Belén is a neighborhood in Medellín.

15. On the Héroes of Granada, see chapter 6.

16. This is a municipality in Antioquia, two hours' drive north of Medellín.

17. The Thousand Days' War (1899–1902) was a civil war fought between the Liberal and the Conservative parties from the end of the nineteenth century to the beginning of the twentieth century. It left one hundred thousand dead. Its end marked the beginning the Conservative Party's three decades of political hegemony.

18. Rafael Uribe Uribe was a general in the Liberal Party's rebel army and participated in the War of a Thousand Days.

19. *El Colombiano* is still Medellín's major newspaper.

20. On November 6, 1985, the M-19 occupied the justice palace in Bogotá and held the magistrates of the Supreme Court of Colombia hostage. The army reacted forcefully; and after a military raid, eleven of the twenty-five judges were killed by the army. The M-19 was established in 1974 as a mainly urban guerrilla group after the presidential election was stolen from Gustavo Rojas Pinilla. The aim of this group was not the overthrow of the state, but the opening up of the democratic system. The M-19 signed a peace agreement with the government of Colombia in 1990, and its leaders participated in the Constituent Assembly of 1991.

21. Puerto Berrío is a municipality in the Middle Magdalena region that saw the rise of the paramilitaries. See chapter 1.

22. Amalfi is a municipality of the department of Antioquia, and the home of the Castaño family.

23. San Carlos is a municipality in Eastern Antioquia and has been an epicenter of violence. See more in chapter 4.

24. Chocó is a region in Eastern Colombia, on the Pacific Coast, mostly inhabited by an Afro-Colombian population.

25. Drug kingpin Pablo Escobar surrendered to Colombian justice in 1991, agreeing to serve time in a prison that he himself had built and that was known as La Catedral (the Cathedral). Escobar escaped from the prison in July 1992.

26. Doble Cero refers here to the Cali Cartel.

CHAPTER 3. *LIMPIEZA:* THE EXPENDITURE OF SPECTACULAR VIOLENCE

1. The Spanish word *limpieza* translates in English as "cleaning," "cleanup," "purification," "ablution," or "immaculacy."

2. José Vicente Castaño, the brother of Fidel and Carlos Castaño and a drug trafficker, was known as El Profe, the Professor. Vicente played a key role in the establishment of the paramilitaries in the departments of Córdoba and Urabá in the 1990s and later in the founding of the AUC. He demobilized in 2006, but he refused to submit to justice and disappeared.

3. In his study of the Nuer, Evans-Pritchard (1940) presented the notion of time as a cultural construct.

4. As Foucault highlighted in his analysis of torture, "a whole economy of power is invested" in its excesses (1977, 35).

5. I further develop this point in chapter 5.

6. I write more about the history and the role of Cuco Vanoy in relationship to the paramilitaries and drug trafficking in chapter 4.

CHAPTER 4. AN ETHNOGRAPHY OF COCAINE

1. The democratic security campaign, designed and implemented during the Uribe administration, aimed to deny sanctuary to guerrillas by establishing a military presence in the FARC's rearguard.

2. Yarumal is a municipality in the Antioquia department.

3. See Karl Marx and Friedrich Engels, *The German Ideology* (Prometheus, [1845–46] 1998).

4. Gilberto Rodríguez Orejuela was a drug kingpin and one of the main leaders of the Cali Cartel. Established in the 1970s, the Cali Cartel was the principal

competitor to the cocaine business of Pablo Escobar and the Medellín Cartel. Rodríguez Orejuela was arrested in 1995 and extradited to the United States in 2004.

José Gonzalo Rodríguez Gacha was known as El Mejicano, "the Mexican." A drug lord, he was a partner of Pablo Escobar in the Medellín Cartel. Along with Escobar, he was implicated in the assassination of presidential candidate Luís Carlos Galán.

The Ochoa family, from Medellín, and especially the brothers Jorge Luís, Juan David, and Fabio, were Pablo Escobar's primary partners in the establishment of the Medellín Cartel.

Carlos Lehder, a pioneer of drug trafficking in Colombia, was a partner of Pablo Escobar and a member of the Cali Cartel. To facilitate transport of cocaine from Colombia to the United States, Lehder bought the Caribbean island of Norman's Cay and ran it as a transshipment base from 1978 to 1982.

5. The Bloque Centauro paramilitary group was affiliated with the AUC. It operated in the regions of Meta and Guaviare, in southeastern Colombia, both former FARC sanctuaries. The paramilitary group is accused of carrying out the massacre of Mapiripán in 1997 (see chapter 3), which marked the beginning of the paramilitaries' expansion through the national territory.

6. Jader, transcript of interview with author, July 29, 2006.

7. Ibid.

8. *Vereda* refers to a small, rural territorial administrative area.

CHAPTER 5. THE INTERTWINEMENT

1. Giovanni Falcone was an anti-Mafia prosecutors who, in the 1980s, led the prosecution against the *cupola* of the Cosa Nostra, the Sicilian Mafia. He was killed in Palermo by the Corleonesi Mafia near Capaci, Sicily, in 1992.

2. Vincenzo Calenda was also a senator of the Kingdom of Italy in 1886.

3. See Inter-American Commission on Human Rights, "Marino López et al. (Operation Genesis), Colombia," report no. 64/111 (Washington, DC: Organization of American States, 2011), www.oas.org/en/iachr/decisions/court /12.573FondoEng.pdf.

4. The Genesis Operation was carried out by Colombian army special forces belonging to XVII Brigade. Their target was Front 57 of the FARC. The operation lasted four days in February 1997.

5. Herrera, or El Alemán, was born in 1974 in Amalfi, the hometown of the Castaño brothers. He was living in Urabá when he joined the paramilitaries at twenty-two. In 1998, he became the leader of the Élmer Cárdenas paramilitary group.

6. The Unión Patriótica (UP) is a leftist political party founded in 1985 by the FARC and the Communist Party as a result of ceasefire talks between the guerrillas

and the government of Belisario Betancur. Within a few years, its leadership was exterminated by the paramilitaries. Among those killed, in 1987, was Jaime Pardo Leal, the UP's presidential candidate in 1986.

7. Edward Cobos Téllez, alias Diego Vecino, is a drug lord and a paramilitary leader who operated initially in the region of Sucre and later in Bolívar, both in Northern Colombia. Rodrigo Tovar Pupo, known as Jorge 40, was the leader of the Northern Bloc of the paramilitaries, in the departments of Cesar, La Guajira, Magdalena, and Atlántico. He joined the paramilitaries in 1996 and was extradited to the United States in 2008.

8. "Pacto con el diablo," *Semana* (Bogotá), February 16, 2008.

9. Transcript of declaration by Hébert Veloza, head of the Bananero paramilitary group, to Colombian prosecutors on September 9, 2008.

10. The self-defense groups known as Convivir, which later would turn into several different paramilitary groups, were established during the government of president César Gaviria (1991–94) but developed further under president Ernesto Samper (1994–98). A Liberal, Samper was later accused of having accepted drug money to finance his presidential campaign, and as a result the United States withdrew his visa.

11. See chapter 1 on the notion of an enemy as a snake.

12. Besides Rodrigo Lara Bonilla, minister of justice (murdered in 1984), those killed by the Medellín Cartel included Supreme Court Justice Hernando Baquero Borda (1986); police colonel Jaime Ramírez (1986); Jaime Pardo Leal, the Unión Patriótica's presidential candidate (1987); Luís Carlos Galán, the Liberal party's presidential candidate (1989); and journalist Diana Turbay (1991).

13. In July 1992, Escobar killed Galeano at La Catedral, the luxurious prison in which Escobar was imprisoned after negotiating his surrender to the state.

14. Fidel Castaño, Carlos Castaño's brother, had founded self-defense groups in the regions of Urabá and Cordoba in the mid-1990s. They constituted a pilot project for the later formation of the AUC. Fidel was presumably killed in 1994 in a fight with EPL guerrillas, but his body was never found.

15. Expanding on the definition of *Mafia* used by Italian prosecutors and scholars to designate the Cosa Nostra, I refer here to "the Mafia" as the social phenomenon in which a criminal organization has a strategic alliance with legal institutions, as is the case in Colombia.

16. The Corporación Democracia was a nongovernmental organization established in Medellín in 2004 by the leaders of the demobilized Cacique Nutibara as a result of negotiation with the Colombian government under President Álvaro Uribe Vélez. Members of the Corporación Democracia were former Cacique Nutibara combatants. Eventually the NGO was closed following the accusation that it was operating as the political wing of Don Berna's Oficina de Envigado drug network.

17. Along with other thirteen leaders of the paramilitaries, Don Berna was extradited to the United States in May 2008.

CHAPTER 6. DEMOBILIZATION AND THE
UNMASKING OF THE STATE

1. Transcript of interview with Carlos Castaño, broadcast July 22, 2003, by Canal Caracol.

2. Iván Roberto Duque, alias Ernesto Báez, was among the early supporters of the self-defense groups in the Middle Magdalena region, where he was active as a politician. Later he became the leader of the Central Bolívar bloc of the AUC. Ramón Isaza grew up in the Middle Magdalena region, near the town of Puerto Triunfo. He was a pioneer in the establishment of armed self-defense groups. In the 1990s, he was among the enemies of Pablo Escobar and contributed to his persecution. Several of his sons became paramilitary commanders.

3. Regarding numbers and statistics, Taussig wrote, "In the end, the numbers numb, burning themselves up as soon as they appear in the dark firmament of our ignorance. They evade our grasp, eager to control reality through quantifying it. Worse still, numbers drain the meaning ouf of the stuff being numbered . . . numbers flatten our understanding of the social world and the imagination that sustains it" (2003, 88).

4. This is a paramilitary group that operated in the old mining area of Colombia and was therefore called *los mineros*. The Bloque Mineros emerged from a criminal alliance among merchants, cattle ranchers, gold-mine owners, the police, and the armed forces. Its leader was Ramiro "Cuco" Vanoy.

5. Los Triana, a powerful gang that operates in the northeastern neighborhoods of Medellín, served as a mercenary association of paramilitary groups as well as of the Oficina de Envigado.

6. This commission was set up by the Colombian government to provide reparations to victims of the paramilitary.

7. Carlos Pizarro, among the main leaders of the M-19 guerrillas, was one of the negotiators of the peace agreement between the M-19 and the Colombian government. He was assassinated on a plane on April 26, 1990, while he was running as a presidential candidate for the M-19.

8. Los Urabeños is a criminal and drug-trafficking group that emerged after the demobilization of the AUC paramilitaries. Its leaders comprise former heads of the EPL guerrillas.

9. Carlos Mario Aguilar Echeverri, alias Rogelio, was one of the mightiest leaders of the Oficina de Envigado. He was in charge of "public relations" for the criminal organization of Don Berna, the police, and several politicians. He was extradited to the United States, where he accused, among others, a former governor of Antioquia of relationships with paramilitaries.

10. Ericson Vargas Cardona, alias Sebastián, started his career as a hitman and became one Don Berna's trusted men. Sebastián became a head of the Oficina de Envigado after Don Berna's extradition to the United States in 2008.

Maximiliano Bonilla Orozco, or Valenciano, was also one of Don Berna's teenage hitmen. He expanded the Oficina de Envigado's business toward the Urabá region and led an internal war against Sebastián for leadership of the Oficina de Envigado after Don Berna's the extradition.

CONCLUSION

1. Carlos Mario Jiménez, alias Macaco, was a drug dealer and a member of the North Valley Cartel. He became a paramilitary leader in 1998 and became the leader of the Bloque Central Bolívar, which operated in several departments and areas of Colombia: Putumayo, Caquetá, Nariño, Valle, Sur de Bolívar, Eje Cafetero, Magdalena Medio, and Santander. He demobilized in 2006 and was extradited to the United States in 2008.

REFERENCES

Abrams, Phillip. 1988. "Notes on the Difficulty of Studying the State." *Journal of Historical Sociology* 1, no. 1:58–89.

Agamben, Giorgio. 1998. *Homo Sacer: Sovereign Power and Bare Life.* Stanford University Press.

Amnesty International. 2005. *The Paramilitaries in Medellín: Demobilization or Legalization?* Amnesty International.

Angel-Ajani, Asale, and Victoria Sanford. 2006. *Engaged Observer: Anthropology, Advocacy, and Activism.* Rutgers University Press.

Appadurai, Arjun. 1996. *Modernity at Large: Cultural Dimensions of Globalization.* University of Minnesota Press.

Aranguren Molina, Mauricio. 2005. *Mi confesión: Carlos Castaño revela sus secretos.* Editorial Oveja Negra.

Aretxaga, Begoña. 1997. *Shattering Silence.* Princeton University Press.

———. 1999. "A Fictional Reality: Paramilitary Death Squads and the Construction of State Terror in Spain." In Jeffrey A. Sluka, ed., *Death Squad: The Anthropology of State Terror.* 46–69. University of Pennsylvania Press.

———. 2003. "Maddening States." *Annual Review of Anthropology,* Vol. 32 393–410.

Aretxaga, Begoña, and Joseba Zulaika. 2005. *States of Terror: Begoña Aretxaga's Essays.* Center for Basque Studies, University of Nevada.

Arias, Enrique Desmond, and Daniel M. Goldstein, eds. 2010. *Violent Democracies in Latin America.* Cultures and Practice of Violence. Duke University Press.

Autodefensas Campesinas Bloque Metro. 2003. *El conflicto en Medellín.* Unpublished document.

Ávila Martínez, Ariel Fernando. 2010. "Injerencia política de los grupos armados ilegales." In Claudia López Hernández, ed., *Y refundaron la patria: De cómo mafiosos y políticos reconfiguraron el estado colombiano,* 79–214. Random House Mondadori.

Bataille, Georges. 1991a. *The Accursed Share: An Essay on General Economy,* Vol. 1: *Consumption.* Zone Books.

———. 1991b. *The Trial of Gilles de Rai*. Trans. Richard Robinson. Amok Books.

———. 2004. *The Trial of Gilles de Rais*. Amok Books.

Benjamin, Walter. 1968. *Illuminations: Essays and Reflection*. Schocken Books.

———. 1986. *Reflections: Essays, Aphorisms, Autobiographical Writings*. Schocken Books.

Berlant, Lauren. 2011. *Cruel Optimism*. Duke University Press.

Binford, Leigh. 1996. *The El Mozote Massacre: Anthropology and Human Rights*. Hegemony and Experience. University of Arizona Press.

Blok, Anton. 1988. *The Mafia of a Sicilian Village, 1860–1960: A Study of Violent Peasant Entrepreneurs*. Waveland Press.

Bourgois, Philippe. 1995. *In Search of Respect: Selling Crack in El Barrio*. Cambridge University Press.

Bowden, Michael. 2001. *Killing Pablo: The Hunt for the World's Greatest Outlaw*. Atlantic Monthly Press.

Burroughs, William. 1973. *Exterminator! A novel*. Viking Press

Canetti, Elias. 1984. *Crowds and Power*. Farrar, Straus and Giroux.

Capote, Truman. [1966] 1994. *In Cold Blood*. Vintage.

Cepeda, Iván, and Jorge Rojas. 2008. *A las puertas de El Ubérrimo*. Ed Random House Mondadori.

Civico, Aldo. 2006. "Portrait of a Paramilitary: Putting a Human Face on the Colombian Conflict." In Victoria Sanford and A. Angel-Ajani, eds., *Engaged Observer: Anthropology, Advocacy, and Activism*, 131–46. Rutgers University Press.

———. 2009. *No divulgar hasta que los implicados estén muertos: Las guerras de "doblecero."* Intermedio Editores.

———. 2012. "'We Are Illegal, but Not Illegitimate': Modes of Policing in Medellín, Colombia." *Political and Legal Anthropology Review* 35, no. 1 (May): 77–93.

Clastres, Pierre. 1989. *Society against the State: Essays in Political Anthropology*. Zone Books.

Comaroff, Jean Comaroff. 2011. "Anthropology, Theology, Critical Pedagogy: Conversation with Jean Comaroff and David Kuyman Kim." Interview with David Kyuman. *Cultural Anthropology* 26, no. 2: 158–78.

Coronil, Fernando. 1997. *The Magical State: Nature, Money and Modernity in Venezuela*. University of Chicago Press.

Dalla Chiesa, Nando. 1976. *Il potere mafioso: Economia e ideologia*. G. Mazzotta.

———. 2010. *La convergenza: Mafia e politica nella seconda Repubblica*. Melampo.

Daniel, E. Valentine. 1996. *Charred Lullabies*. Princeton University Press.

Das, Veena, and Deborah Poole. 2004. *Anthropology in the Margins of the State*. School of American Research Press.

Deleuze, Gilles. 1983. *Nietzsche and Philosophy*. Columbia Classics in Philosophy. Columbia University Press.

Deleuze, Gilles, and Felix Guattari. 1983. *Anti-Oedipus: Capitalism and Schizophrenia*. University of Minnesota Press.

———. 1987. *A Thousand Plateaus: Capitalism and Schizophrenia*. University of Minnesota Press.

Duncan, Gustavo. 2006. *Los señores de la guerra: De paramilitares, mafiosos y autodefensas en Colombia*. Editorial Planeta.

Durkheim, Émile. 1995. *The Elementary Forms of Religious Life*. Trans. Karen E. Fields. Free Press.

Escuela Nacional Sindical. 2007. Informe annual.

Espinal, Manuel Alonso, Jorge Giraldo, and Diego Jorge Sierra. 2007. "Medellín: El complejo camino de la competencia armada." In Mauricio Romero, ed., *Parapolítica: La ruta de la expansión paramilitar y los acuerdos políticos*, 83–122. Intermedio Editores.

Evans-Pritchard, E.E.. 1940. E. E. Evans-Pritchard, eds., *African Political Systems*. Oxford University Press.

Feldman, Allen. 1991. *Formations of Violence: The Narrative of the Body and Political Terror in Northern Ireland*. University of Chicago Press.

Ferguson, James. 2006. *Global Shadows: Africa in the Neoliberal World Order*. Duke University Press.

Finnström, Sverker. 2008. *El Bajo cauca antioqueño: Cómo ver las regiones*. Cultures and Practice of Violence. Duke University Press.

Foucault, Michel. [1977.] 1995. *Discipline and Punish: The Birth of the Prison*. Vintage Books.

———. 1994. *Essential Works of Foucault 1954–1984*. Vol. 1: *Ethics, Subjectivity and Truth*. New Press.

Franchetti, Leopoldo, and Sidney Sonnino. [1877] 2004. *L'inchiesta in Sicilia di Franchetti e Sonnino: La Sicilia nel 1876*. Kalós.

Gambetta, Diego. 1993. *The Sicilian Mafia: The Business of Private Protection*. Harvard University Press.

García, Clara Inés. 1993. *El Bajo cauca antioqueño: Cómo ver las regiones*. Cinep.

Gill, Lesley. 1997. "Creating Citizens, Making Men: The Military and Masculinity in Bolivia." *Cultural Anthropology* 12, no. 4: 527–50.

———. 2004. *The School of the Americas: Military Training and Political Violence in the Americas*. Duke University Press.

Goldstein, Daniel. 2010. "Towards a Critical Anthropology of Security." *Current Anthropology* 51, no. 4: 487–517.

———. 2012. *Outlawed: Between Security and Rights in a Bolivian City*. Duke University Press.

Gootenberg, Paul. 2008. *Andean Cocaine: The Making of a Global Drug*. University of North Carolina Press.

Green, Linda. 1999. *Fear as a Way of Life*. Columbia University Press.

Grupo de Memoria Histórica. 2011. *San Carlos: Memorias del éxodo en la guerra*. Imprenta Nacional.

———. 2013. *¡Basta ya! Colombia: Memorias de guerra y dignidad*. Imprenta Nacional.

Gupta, Akhil. 1995. "Blurred Boundaries: The Discourse of Corruption, the Culture of Politics, and the Imagined State." *American Ethnologist* 22, no. 2:375–402.

Guzmán Campos, Germán, Orlando Fals Borda, and Eduardo Umaña Luna. 1962. *La Violencia en Colombia: Estudio de un proceso social*. Vol. I. Ediciones Tercer Mundo.

Hardt, Michael, and Antonio Negri. 2001. *Empire*. Harvard University Press.

———. 2005. *Multitude: War and Democracy in the Age of Empire*. Penguin Books.

Hinton, Alexander Laban, and Robert Jay Lifton. 2004. *Why Did They Kill?: Cambodia in the Shadow of Genocide*. University of California Press.

Hoffman, Danny. 2011. *The War Machines: Young Men and Violence in Sierra Leone and Liberia*. Duke University Press.

Holland, Eugene W. 1999. *Deleuze and Guattari's Anti-Oedipus: Introduction to Schizoanalysis*. Routledge.

Huggins, Martha Knisely, Mika Haritos-Fatouros, and Philip G. Zimbardo. 2002. *Violence Workers: Police Torturers and Murderers Reconstruct Brazilian Atrocities*. University of California Press.

Human Rights Watch. 2001. *The Sixth Division: Military-Paramilitary Ties and US Policy in Colombia*. Human Rights Watch.

Hylton, Forrest. 2006. *Evil Hour in Colombia*. Verso.

Inter-American Commission on Human Rights. 2011. "Marino López et al. (Operation Genesis), Colombia." Report no. 64/111. Washington, DC: Organization of American States, March 31.

Jaffe, Rivke. 2013. "The Hybrid State: Crime and Citizenship in Urban Jamaica." *American Ethnologist* 40, no. 4: 734–48.

Kosmatopoulos, Nikolas. 2011. "Toward an Anthropology of 'State Failure': Lebanon's Leviathan and Peace Expertise." *Social Analysis* 55, no. 3: 115–42.

Lacan Jacques, 1977. *Escrits: A Selection*. Translated by Alan Sheridan. Norton, 1977.

Léon, Pedro de Cieza de. 2001. *The Travels of Pedro de Cieza de Léon, a.d. 1532–50, Contained in the First Part of His Chronicle of Peru*. Adamant Media Corporation.

Levi, Primo. 1989. *The Drowned and the Saved*. Vintage.

López, Andrés. 2008. *El Cartel de los Sapos*. Planeta.

López Hernández, Claudia Nayibe. 2010. *Y refundaron la patria? De cómo mafiosos y políticos reconfiguraron el estado colombiano*. Random House Mondadori.

López Hernández, Claudia Nayibe, and Gustavo Duncan. 2007. *Retos electorales, riesgos y recomendaciones: Elecciones Colombia, Octubre 28 de 2007*. Misión de Observación Electoral.

Lupo, Salvatore. 2009. *Storia della Mafia: dalle origini ai nostril giorni*. Donzelli Editore.

———. 2011. *History of the Mafia*. Columbia University Press.

Mahmood, Cynthia Keppley. 1996. *Fighting for Faith and Nation: Dialogues with Sikh Militants*. University of Pennsylvania Press.

Malinowski, Bronisław. [1922] 1984. *Argonauts of the Western Pacific*. Waveland.

Malkki, Liisa H. 1995. *Purity and Exile: Violence, Memory, and National Cosmology among Hutu Refugees in Tanzania*. University of Chicago Press.

Marx, Karl. 1992. *Early Writings*. Penguin Classics.

Marx, Karl, and Friedrich Engels. [1845–46] 1998. *The German Ideology.*

Mauss, Marcel. 2000. *The Gift: The Form and Reason for Exchange in Archaic Societies.* W. W. Norton & Company.

Medina Gallego, Carlos. 1990. *Autodefensas, paramilitares y narcotráfico en Colombia: Origen, desarrollo y consolidación: El caso "Puerto Boyacá."* Editorial Documentos Periodísticos.

Ministerio de Defensa (Colombia). 2000. Estudio sobre los paramilitares. Gobierno de Colombia.

Mitchell, Timothy. 1999. Society, Economy and the State Effect. *In State/Culture: State Formation after the Cultural Turn.* 76–97. Cornell University Press.

Nagengast, Carole. 1994. Violence, Terror, and the Crisis of the State. *In Annual Review of Anthropology* 23, no. 23: 109–136.

Navaro-Yashin, Yael. 2002. *Faces of the State: Secularism and Public Life in Turkey.* Princeton University Press.

Nietzsche, Friedrich. 1974. *The Gay Science: With a Prelude in Rhymes and an Appendix of Songs.* Trans. Walter Kaufmann. Vintage.

Nordstrom, Carolyn. 1997. *A Different Kind of War Story.* Ethnography of Political Violence. University of Pennsylvania Press.

———. 2000. "Shadows and Sovereigns." *Theory, Culture and Society* 17, no. 4: 35–54.

Nordstrom, Carolyn, and Antonius C. G. M. Robben. 1995. *Fieldwork under Fire: Contemporary Studies of Violence and Culture.* University of California Press.

"Pacto con el diablo." *Semana* (Bogotá). February 16, 2008.

Palacios, Marco. 2006. *Between Legitimacy and Violence: A History of Colombia, 1875–2002.* Latin America in Translation. Duke University Press.

Paley, Julia. 2001. *Marketing Democracy: Power and Social Movements in Post-Dictatorship Chile.* University of California Press.

Pardo, Rafael. 2007. *Fin del paramilitarismo: ¿Es posible su desmonte?* Ediciones B.

Patton, Paul. 2000. *Deleuze and the Political.* Thinking the Political. Routledge.

Pécaut, Daniel. 2001. Orden y violencia: evolución socio-política de Colombia entre 1930 y 1953. Grupo Editorial Norma.

Pezzino, Paolo. 1990. *Una certa reciprocità di favori: Mafia e modernizzazione violenta nella Sicilia postunitaria.* F. Angeli.

———. 1999. *Le mafie.* Giunti Editore.

Radcliff-Brown, Alfred. [1940] 1970. Preface, in M. Fortes and E. E. Evans-Pritchard, eds., *African Political Systems.* Oxford University Press.

Restrepo, Vicente. 1886. *A Study of the Gold & Silver Mines of Colombia.* Colombian Consulate.

Reyes Posada, Alejandro. 2009. *Guerreros y campesinos: el despojo de la tierra en Colombia.* Grupo Editorial Norma.

Robben, Antonius. 2005. *Political Violence and Trauma in Argentina.* University of Pennsylvania Press.

Roffe, Jonathan. 2005. "Capitalism." In Adrian Parr, ed., *The Deleuze Dictionary*, 40–42. Edinburgh University Press.

Roldán, Mary. 2002. *Blood and Fire: La Violencia in Antioquia, Colombia, 1946–1953*. Duke University Press.

———. 2009. *Negotiating Alternatives to Violence in the Oriente Antioqueno*. In Virginia M. Bouvier, ed., *Colombia: Building Peace in a Time of War*, pp. 277–294. U.S. Institute of Peace Press.

Romero, Mauricio. 2000. "Changing Identities and Contested Settings: Regional Elites and the Paramilitaries in Colombia." *International Journal of Politics, Culture, and Society* 14, no. 1: 51–69.

———. 2003. *Paramilitares y autodefensas: 1982–2003*. Temas de Hoy.

Romero, Mauricio, eds. 2011. *La economía de los paramilitares: redes, corrupción, negocios y política*. Random House Mondadori.

Rondero, María Teresa. 2006. "El canciller." *Revista de estudios sociales* 24: 55–59.

———. 2014. *Guerras recicladas: una historia periodística del paramilitarismo en Colombia*. Aguilar.

Rosen, David M. 2005. *Armies of the Young: Child Soldiers in War and Terrorism*. Series in Childhood Studies. Rutgers University Press.

Rozema, Ralph. 2008. "Urban DDR-Processes: Paramilitaries and Criminal Networks in Medellín, Colombia." *Journal of Latin American Studies* 40, no. 3: 423–52.

Safford, Frank, and Marco Palacios. 2001. *Colombia: Fragmented Land, Divided Society*. Oxford University Press.

Salazar, Alonso. 2001. *La parábola de Pablo: Auge y caída de un gran capo del narcotráfico*. Planeta.

Sanford, Victoria. 2004. *Buried Secrets: Truth and Human Rights in Guatemala*. Palgrave Macmillan.

Scheper-Hughes, Nancy. 1992. *Death without Weeping: The Violence of Everyday Life in Brazil*. University of California Press.

Schirmer, Jennifer. 1998. *The Guatemalan Military Project: A Violence Called Democracy*. University of Pennsylvania Press.

Schneider, Peter T., and Jane Schneider. 2003. *Reversible Destiny: Mafia, Antimafia, and the Struggle for Palermo*. University of California Press.

Skidmore, Monique. 2004. *Karaoke Fascism: Burma and the Politics of Fear*. University of Pennsylvania Press.

Sluka, Jeffrey A. 1989. *Hearts and Minds, Water and Fish: Support for the IRA and INLA in a Northern Irish Ghetto*. JAI Press.

———. 1999. *Death Squad: The Anthropology of State Terror*. University of Pennsylvania Press.

Surin, Kenneth. 2005. "State." In Adrian Parr, ed., *The Deleuze Dictionary*, 268–69. Edinburgh University Press.

Tarizzo, Davide. 2007. "La paranoia politica." In Simona Forti and Marco Revelli, eds., *Paranoia e politica*, 288–300. Bollati Boringhieri.

Tate, Winifred. 2007. *Counting the Dead: The Culture and Politics of Human Rights Activism in Colombia*. University of California Press.

Taussig, Michael. 1980. *The Devil and Commodity Fetishism in South America*. University of North Carolina Press.

———. 1987. *Shamanism, Colonialism, and the Wild Man: A Study in Terror and Healing.* University of Chicago Press.

———. 1991. *The Nervous System.* Routledge.

———. 1997. *The Magic of the State.* Routledge

———. 1999. *Defacement: Public Secrecy and the Labor of the Negative.* Stanford University Press.

———. 2004. *My Cocaine Museum.* University of Chicago Press.

———. 2005. *Law in a Lawless Land: Diary of a Limpieza in Colombia.* University of Chicago Press.

———. 2012. *Beauty and the Beast.* University of Chicago Press.

Taylor, Christopher Charles. 1999. *Sacrifice as Terror.* New York University Press.

Theidon, Kimberly. 2003. "Disarming the Subject: Remembering War and Imagining Citizenship in Peru." *Cultural Critique* 54: 67–87.

———. 2009. "Reconstructing Masculinities: The Disarmament, Demobilization, and Reintegration of Former Combatants in Colombia." *Human Rights Quarterly* 31: 1–34.

———. 2012. *Intimate Enemies: Violence and Reconciliation in Peru.* Pennsylvania Studies in Human Rights. University of Pennsylvania Press.

Tilly, Charles. [1974] 1988. "Foreword." In Anton Blok, ed., *The Mafia of a Sicilian Village, 1860–1960: A Study of Violent Peasant Entrepreneurs,* xiii–xiv. Waveland Press.

Trawick, Margaret. 2007. *Enemy Lines: Warfare, Childhood, and Play in Batticaloa.* University of California Press.

Trouillot, Michel-Rolph. 2001. "The Anthropology of the State in the Age of Globalization: Close Encounters of the Deceptive Kind." *Current Anthropology* 42, no. 1: 125–38.

Uribe, María Victoria. 2004. *Antropología de la inhumanidad: Un ensayo interpretativo del terror en Colombia.* Grupo Editorial Norma.

Verdad Abierta. 2009. *Fiscalía inició investigación contra ex generales Mario Montoya y Leonardo Gallego.* http://www.verdadabierta.com/la-historia/1433-fiscalia-inicio-investigacion-contra-ex-generales-mario-montoya-y-leonardo-gallego- (Last checked: July 11, 2015).

Warren, Kay. 1993. *The Violence Within: Cultural and Political Opposition in Divided Nations.* Westview Press.

Whitehead, Neil L. 2004. *Violence.* School of American Research Press.

Wolf, Eric R. 1982. *Europe and the People without History.* University of California Press.

Žižek, Slavoj. 2008. *Violence: Six Sideways Reflections.* Big Ideas/Small Books. Picador.

Zulaika, Joseba. 1988. *Basque Violence: Metaphor and Sacrament.* University of Nevada Press.

INDEX

Acevedo, Fabio (pseud.), 167–71
Agamben, Giorgio, 118, 165
Águilas Negras, 52
Alejandro (pseud.), 161–64
Andrés, Jorge (pseud.), 56–68, 187–88
anthropology: intersubjectivity between
  ethnographer and Other, xxiii, 10, 11,
  17; need to balance study of violence
  between victims and perpetrators in,
  212n5; role in comprehending and
  interpreting violence of, 2–3, 9–11
Arias, Enrique Desmond, 209
Autodefensas Campesinas de Cordoba y
  Urabá (ACCU), 38–39, 87, 90
Autodefensas Unidas de Colombia
  (AUC): demobilization of, 40–41;
  establishment of, 39–40; formation
  and growth of, 94–95; intertwinement
  with state of, 165–66, 170; lobbies
  Congress to pass laws favorable to
  itself, 178–79; narcotization of, 87–88,
  93; negotiation for ceasefire by, 177–78;
  offensive against Bloque Metro of, xxi,
  78; political aims of, 153, 177;
  prosecution of leaders of, 40–41;
  protests peace talks with FARC, 177;
  as sixth division of armed forces, 151;
  terror sown by, 95, 98, 154

Bacrim, 52
Bajo Cauca region: author's visit to, 119–
  21, 126–28, 133–34, 137, 139–40; drug
  trafficking in, 131–38, 140–42;

paramilitary groups in, 126, 131, 139;
  penetration of guerrillas in, 125–26. *See
  also* Antioquia
Barrera, Hugo, 126
Bataille, Georges, 116, 117
Belalcázar, Sebastián de, 122
Benjamin, Walter, 8, 35, 118
Betancur, Belisario, 48–49, 82
Blanco, Griselda, 157
Blok, Anton, 146, 147, 148
Bloque Cárdenas, 61–65
Bloque Central Bolivar, xxi
Bloque Metro: fighting with other
  paramilitary groups and destruction
  of, xx–xxi, 67, 75, 78, 163–64; in
  Oriente, 163; origin of, 220n4; terror
  sown by, xvi–xvii, 98, 105. *See also*
  Doble Cero
Bloque Mineros, 126
Borda, Fals, 36–37
Borsellino, Paolo, 13, 214n6
Burroughs, William, 109

Cacique Nutibara, 215n2; Corporación
  Democracia formed by former members
  of, 219n16; demobilization of, 179–80,
  183–84; demobilized members join
  Héroes de Granada, 75, 180–81;
  domination over Medellín of, 179–80;
  interaction with community of, 164;
  internal war for domination of Medellín
  of, xvii, 20–21, 67, 78, 163–64; as
  network of criminal nodes in and

police *(continued)*
150–51, 166, 171–72, 196, 200; seen as
enemy in slums of Medellín, 162
Poole, Deborah, 21
public secret, xvii

Restrepo, Vicente, 124–25
Río, Rito Alejo del, 151
Roldán, Mary, 36, 96–97, 156
Romero, Mauricio, 38

Salazar, Alonso, 130, 157
San Carlos, 97, 98–100
Sanford, Victoria, xxii
Schneider, Jane and Peter, 145
state, the: as category of analysis, 21; encounter with, at the margins, 21–22;
hybrid, 22–23; intertwinement with
illegals at margins of, 23; the power of
law to be suspended as the foundation
of, 108. *See also* Colombia; intertwinement; *intreccio*

Taussig, Michael, xvii, 12: on commodity
fetishism, 138–39; on numbers and
statistics, 220n3; on paramilitaries and
the state, 151, 201; on protest of
Argentine mothers, 176–77; on "space
of death," 213–14n5; on terror and the
state, 47
Texas Petroleum Co., 41–42

Unión Patriótica (UP), 49, 153, 218–19n6
Upegui López, Gustavo Adolfo, 198
Urabá, 6, 211–12n4; killings by
paramilitaries in, 117, 151; self-defense

groups in, 70, 71, 92, 95, 109. *See also*
Autodefensas Campesinas de Cordoba
y Urabá (ACCU)
Urabeños, 17, 198, 205–6
Uribe, María Victoria, 10, 48
Uribe, Rafael Uribe, 79, 127, 171
Uribe Uribe, Rafael, 79
Uribe Vélez, Álvaro, xxi, 6, 40, 171, 174,
177, 178, 211n2–3

Valencia Cossio, Fabio, 211n3
Valle cartel, 87
Vallejo, Fernando, 158
Vanoy, Cuco, 113, 126
Veloza, Hérbert, 90, 92, 151–52, 156
Villegas, Gustavo, 185–86
violence: as cultural expression and
performance, 213n5; as demonstration
of power, 115; difficulties in research-
ing, 10–11; examples of studies of perpetrators of, 212–14n5; as immanent to
the notion of modernity and the state,
118; as immanent to the state's function,
10, 108; importance of studying victims
and perpetrators of, 11–12, 212n5; landscape of, 95; legitimized, called *limpieza*,
108–11; production of, related to weakness of the state, 45; as purification, 108;
as result of antagonism between guerrillas and state, 106–7

war machines, paramilitaries as, 23, 40, 45,
154, 171, 210
Whitehead, Neil L., 212n5

Žižek, Slavoj, 10